Books of the Dead

Books of the Dead

Reading the Zombie in Contemporary Literature

Tim Lanzendörfer

University Press of Mississippi / Jackson

www.upress.state.ms.us

The University Press of Mississippi is a member of
the Association of American University Presses.

Copyright © 2018 by University Press of Mississippi
All rights reserved

First printing 2018

∞

Library of Congress Cataloging-in-Publication Data

Names: Lanzendörfer, Tim, author.
Title: Books of the dead: reading the zombie in contemporary literature/
   Tim Lanzendörfer.
Description: Jackson: University Press of Mississippi, [2018] | Includes
   bibliographical references and index. |
Identifiers: LCCN 2018011385 (print) | LCCN 2018018618 (ebook) | ISBN
   9781496819079 (epub single) | ISBN 9781496819086 (epub institutional) |
   ISBN 9781496819093 (pdf single) | ISBN 9781496819109 (pdf institutional)
   | ISBN 9781496819062 (cloth)
Subjects: LCSH: Zombies in literature—History and criticism. | American
   fiction—20th century—History and criticism. | American fiction—21st
   century—History and criticism. | Apocalyptic literature—History and
   criticism. | LCGFT: Literary criticism.
Classification: LCC PS374.Z66 (ebook) | LCC PS374.Z66 L36 2018 (print) | DDC
   809.3/9375—dc23
LC record available at https://lccn.loc.gov/2018011385

British Library Cataloging-in-Publication Data available

For Anselma and Anton

Contents

Acknowledgments..IX

Introduction
Zombie Fiction...3

1 Max Brooks's *World War Z:*
  An Oral History of the Zombie War
  Conservative Armageddon and Liberal Postapocalypse 25

2 Pariah and Dying to Live
  Imagining Community after the Apocalypse........................41

3 *The Walking Dead* and the
  Never-Ending Zombie Story
  The Everyday, Community, and the Need for an Ending...............67

4 "So Many Unmentionables About"
  Parody, *Pride and Prejudice and Zombies,*
  and the Politics of Mash-up Fiction 92

5 Sadie and Allison in the Apocalypse
  Zombies and Gender 126

6 The Postracial, Postcapitalist Zombie
  Colson Whitehead's *Zone One* and Junot Díaz's "Monstro" 161

Coda
Literature and the Contemporary Zombie |
The Appropriate Monster 183

Notes 193

Bibliography 199

Index 213

Acknowledgments

I never thought I would type the word "zombie" half as much as I needed to in this book. To be able to do so has been a great privilege, one which brings to the fore the debts incurred. Thanks are due a number of people who, in various ways, cheerfully supported my interest in the zombie. The most important note of thanks must go to Greg Kelley of the fabled, but not outright mythical, Nordost Research Archives. His enthusiasm for the shuffling undead and ready willingness to go out of his way to obtain so many of the materials which I have used for this book (and many more which, sadly, I have not been able to use, yet) are what have made it possible. I'm indebted for books, films, T-shirts, and anti-zombie stickers: if I survive the zombie apocalypse, I owe it to him. He also kindly read a version of this for language, and vastly helped improve it. In a similar vein, thanks are also due to Sabina Vogel for continuously reminding me of the deep relevance of the zombie as a cultural trope, manifested in the various and multifarious news articles on things from zombie walks to zombie volcanoes, at least some of which made it into the book proper—and all of which reinforced my belief that this book was a project that was possible. I would also like to acknowledge Melanie Spahr, who felt this book was a worthwhile idea, and Clemens Spahr, who did not.

My most important debts as always are to my wife Anselma, who has coped with zombie books (and paraphernalia) littering our work and living spaces. Her unflagging support in difficult times and her love I can hardly repay with any words, and so this must remain a bare hint at what debt I know I'm in. Without his knowing, our son enabled some of the work on this book, written while I was on parental leave for eight months after his birth. Thanks a bunch, Anton: you and mom get to share the dedication.

Finally, the professional thanks that are due: this book was finished during a stay at the Department of English, UC Davis, for which I thank its chair, John Marx. Thanks go to George Thomas and the students in my two seminars there for going through several chapters of the book, as well as to Alessa Johns and Chris Reynolds and Elizabeth Miller and Matthew Stratton for their kind hospitality. As always, I would like to acknowledge Anette Vollrath in my home department at Mainz, who keeps everything administrative away from all of us. Versions of chapters in this book have appeared in different venues before: parts of Chapter 1 appeared as "Max Brooks's *World War Z: An Oral History of the Zombie War*: Conservative Armageddon and Liberal Post-Apocalypse" in *Literature in Northern Queensland Journal* 41, in the special issue "Apocalypse." Parts of Chapter 6 and the Coda appeared as "The Politics of Genre Fiction: Colson Whitehead's *Zone One*" in *C21 Literature: Journal of 21st-Century Writing* 3 (1), in summer 2014. I am grateful to the editors of both journals for permission to reprint these passages here.

Books of the Dead

Introduction
Zombie Fiction

"The only modern myth," Félix Guattari and Gilles Deleuze famously note in *Anti-Oedipus*, "is the myth of zombies" (1983, 335). To Deleuze and Guattari, zombies signify the particular relation between death and capital that modern life has produced: they are "a work myth," and their mutilated status is a "necessary condition" (1987, 425) for the contemporary state. But on the roughly 1000 pages of their *Capitalism and Schizophrenia* the zombie is a minor figure: it signifies nothing that is not already otherwise signified, and inhabits no privileged position. It is illustrative, and its unique status—"the only *modern* myth," with emphasis laid on the idea of modernity—is never fully explored. This is surprising only to a very limited extent: when *Anti-Oedipus* was first published in France in 1972, the zombie was a figure still largely confined to the traditions of Caribbean Vodou. Whether Deleuze or Guattari had seen George Romero's pathbreaking 1968 film *Night of the Living Dead* remains at least doubtful. That explains why their zombie, "good for work," was also "brought back to reason" (1983, 335), a description both of whose parts are ill-fitting the ghoulish flesh-eaters which are most familiar to us today: theirs was the zombie of the cane fields of Haiti, where he resembled the ideal worker under capital. Yet the forty years since the first publication of *Anti-Oedipus* have only borne out their initial diagnosis, however little they could have foreseen the expansion which their "only modern myth" would take: today, more than ever, the zombie is the only truly modern myth.

This goes a long way to explain the creature's apparently sudden predominance in popular culture and elsewhere over the last decade and a half. Indeed, it has become a critical commonplace to note the ubiquity of the zombie in contemporary popular culture, its presence in all kinds of cultural artifacts. From its early beginnings as a filmic monster has grown an entire cottage industry of zombie films, capable of attracting both legitimate movie stars and Hollywood money (as in the 2013 version of Max Brooks's *World War Z*, starring Brad Pitt) as well as its own satirical commentaries (such as Ed White and Simon Pegg's *Shaun of the Dead* [2004]). Always a film monster, the zombie has more recently also branched out into television. Robert Kirkman's highly successful comic series *The Walking Dead* has found a devoted audience as a TV show, as well as a spin-off, *Fear the Walking Dead*. It has moved into video games, from high-end first-person shooters to the smartphone-based *Plants vs. Zombies*; and into all manner of cultural activities, including the famous zombie walks (Flint 2009 provides an overview of most of these strands of zombie lore).

Much of this interest is, at least, broadly, literary. There are books instructing you "how to kick ass like the walking dead" (Kenemore 2010), plenty of survival guides (Brooks 2003, Ma 2010, Muir 2010), political science (Drezner 2011), neuroscience (Verstynen and Voytek 2014), and mathematics primers featuring zombies (Adams 2014, Smith? 2014), as well as *actual* zombie primers (albeit for adults; Castro 2011). There are fake zombie histories (Brookside 2009, Miller 2011), zombie haiku (Mecum 2008), zombie cook books (Wilson and Bauthaus 2014), zombie first readers (Bolger 2010), nursery rhymes (Spradlin 2011), love songs (Spradlin 2010), and Christmas Carols (Spradlin 2009). There is *the* Christmas Carol, zombified (Roberts 2009), and very, very short short fiction (Gouvea 2008). Last, but not least—probably, in fact, not even last—the zombie has become such a respectable trope that biologists are willing to publically proclaim the existence of "zombie ants" and "zombie bees" (Gill 2014, Harman 2012).

This interest in the zombie has, unsurprisingly, spawned critical investigations into its role as metaphor, trope, and myth—most of which begin with a litany similar to the one I just offered. Laura Hubner and her coeditors speak of a "global explosion of zombie mania" (2015, 3); Murali Balaji notes that "zombies have seemingly overrun public discourse in North America" (2013, ix); Vincent Paris pithily summarizes, "[t]here's no Business [today] as Zombie Business" (2013, 11); Markus Metz and Georg Seeßlen diagnose an "upturn in the currency" of the term "undead"—the zombie and others (2012, 7); Deborah Christie and Sarah Juliet Lauro suggest "[t]hat the zombie is ubiquitous in popular culture cannot be disputed" (2011, 1); David Flint argues that "zombies are taking over through sheer weight of numbers" (2009, 7); and so on and so forth, all the way back at least to 2008, when Christopher Moreman and Corey Rushton could already diagnose the exponential proliferation of zombie narratives (6).

The zombie trope, critics agree, has penetrated deep into cultural consciousness, permitting the zombie to become a readily readable metaphor, one so ubiquitous that it has become available even far outside the entertainment industry. The global economic crisis of 2008 and the consequent increasing critical engagement with the problems of late capitalism have, not coincidentally, been read through the zombie. Chris Harmon's *Zombie Capitalism: Global Crisis and the Relevance of Marx* (2009) suggests that "21st century capitalism as a whole is a zombie system, seemingly dead when it comes to achieving human goals, and responding to human feelings" (12); David McNally's *Monsters of the Market: Zombies, Vampires and Global Capitalism* (2011) reads the zombie as one manifestation of the "monstrous forms of everyday-life in a capitalist world-system" (2) in line with Luddite Frankenstein's monster and the vampire that populated much of the late nineteenth century's critique of capitalism; and Henry Giroux's *Zombie Politics and Culture in the Age of Casino Capitalism* (2011) compares the "ravenous appetite" (2) of today's capitalism with that of the eponymous monster.[1] In these readings, of course, critics find themselves re-establishing the links which Deleuze and Guattari already saw in 1973: between forms of life, forms of resistance, forms of sociality, and the totalizing economic system of capitalism. But we note the difference between these readings and Deleuze and Guattari's: where the zombie was merely apropos in Deleuze and Guattari, and served them as one illustrative example among many (some of those other examples perhaps more amenable for their purpose), in Harmon, McNally, and Giroux, it has become the central metaphor, whose power rests on its ease of recognition. Zombies have managed to be accepted as adequate metaphors beyond a purely fictional, literary, or filmic engagement.

This is a fact whose valence needs to be understood from two mutually informing perspectives. First, there is the "global explosion of zombie mania" which Laura Hubner et al. identify, and which produces the kind of (to use a poststructuralist term) texts I have listed above: TV series, comics, films, games, public spectacles, emergency preparedness campaigns, and, yes, written, narrative fiction, in which the zombie features prominently, indeed usually centrally. This mania, however, is conditioned on the fact that the zombie can represent something today that it could not, or did not, or perhaps did not need to, represent at a different time. Yes, the zombie is a "twentieth-century monster." Although we can trace zombie-like figures further into the depths of time, as I will do later in this introduction, the zombie as we know it is related to "mass phenomena: mass production, mass consumption, mass death" (Larsen 2011), whether as a voodoo victim on the sugar plantations of Haiti or as a contemporary metaphor. Yet if the zombie originates in the twentieth century and is deeply connected to its political struggles, it has lost little of its potency as a metaphor for the twenty-first century—in fact, the twenty-first century seems to have provided it with a new lease, as it were, on life. Kyle Bishop implies the coincidence between George Romero's resumption of his "Living Dead" series in 2005, twenty years after his last zombie movie, and a greater incipient interest in the zombie: it "clearly had its legs again" (2010, 197). As I will argue in more detail, the zombie does not step out of his grave idly. Rather, it is being resurrected by the very conditions under which it becomes readable again as a means of thinking about the problems of the contemporary. As Jennifer Rutherford points out, "political and social critique whether overt or covert, is as integral to the [zombie] genre as is its splatterfest" (2014, 10). What the particular aims of this critique are in the zombie fictions of the contemporary moment is one of the themes that this book will cover.

The cause for this study is comparatively simple: while zombies have proliferated in all media, not to mention in the zombie walks and zombie role playing games of real life, comparatively little attention has been paid to the zombie in fiction, very much unlike its fellow monster, the vampire, whose popular cultural origins have become elided. Bram Stoker's *Dracula* has successfully made the difficult journey from the pulps to the classics. Few literary scholars would today deny the literary qualities of Stoker's novel, or its engagement, through the vampire, with contemporary Victorian social problems and anxieties. By contrast, the zombie novel is not as widely appreciated. This is all the more surprising given the large number of novels, short stories, and comics which deal with the zombie phenomenon. It is this perceived gap in critical coverage which this book is meant to close, or at least make smaller.

But are those zombie stories not pulp fiction of the worst sort, the kind of writing that no self-respecting scholar should be spending valuable time on? It is, of course, my contention that that is not so; or rather, even where the novels and short stories that I will be discussing in this book cannot and do not aspire to something like stylistic literariness, they engage with the contemporary in a myriad of different ways and frequently reveal fresh perspectives on society. This is surely the function of literature no matter its provenance. Since the appearance, at least, of Max Brooks's surprise bestseller *The Zombie Survival Guide* in 2003, zombies have become part and parcel of both the horror and fantasy sections of bookstores as well as a motif increasingly used by authors of so-called literary fiction. Colson Whitehead and Junot Díaz (see Ch. 6), to name just two writers of critical renown, have written stories heavily indebted to the tradition of the zombie.

Zombie fictions proliferate, and this is the point of departure for this book. It seeks to discover what work zombie fiction does in the contemporary. In doing so, it also shifts the focus of the study of the zombie, which often emphasizes the figure's symbolic or metaphoric meaning. This is a fraught business in the best of times; given the range of permutations these symbolisms have taken, it has led to some critics giving up the quest for meaning permanently. Evan Williams has suggested that the zombie has finally come to "mean nothing" (2011, 144), and Dorothea Fischer-Hornung and Monika Müller, adopting Ernesto Laclau's terminology if slightly unorthodoxly, suggest that the zombie is "an empty signifier to be filled with meaning at will" (2016, 7). These points suggest the problem faced when tracing the zombie as a metaphor across texts. Accordingly, what I propose is to decenter, though certainly not to ignore, the zombie as a metaphor. Indeed, the zombie's metaphorical role, as I will contend throughout this book, is less important than the worlds it enables; rather than stressing its emptiness, we need to foreground that the zombie itself is rarely the most crucial element of zombie fictions' meaning.

In the following, I will not offer a unified reading of the zombie as a trope in contemporary fiction, because such a thing is neither helpful nor, indeed, possible. This is not, however, because, as Williams has it, it has become, through ceaseless repetition, "the vacant and incessant sign of a breakdown both of historical thought and of history's prospects of going differently" (2011, 146). Instead, I will suggest that it has become so prominent because it offers a formal way of imagining radically different futures atop the sediments of the zombie's various and irreducible histories. What I will be arguing is that we must read the zombie as a figure of possibility, one that enables, certainly thematically but especially formally, the exploration of contemporary concerns from capitalism through community to gender and race. Such a reading takes stock of the zombie's history of meanings, and it is this stock of meanings I propose to examine next through a short detour through its literary prehistory, before returning to the question of how to read the zombie today.

Zombies: A Short Literary History

Most, though not all, of contemporary zombie fictions use a version of the zombie that is frequently called the "Romero zombie." To unearth the particular literary genealogy of the zombie almost necessarily must take the detour through Romero's "Living Dead" films. In this parsing, the modern zombie first appeared in George R. Romero's groundbreaking *Night of the Living Dead* (1968), a cheaply shot and in many ways derivative film which Jeffrey Cohen nonetheless calls appropriately, and with appropriate gravity, the zombie's "urtext" (2012, 399). It also is already the point of origin for the critical engagement with the zombie's symbolic functions. A "cunning allegorical criticism of 1960s American society" (Bishop 2010, 95), Romero's film highlighted many of the problems of the Vietnam-era United States. Its depiction of its black protagonist at the height of the civil rights movement revealed many of the fears and tensions which the United States, especially its white majority, was suffering from (120). Romero's film, and the monster which it developed, becomes the starting point of any investigation of the zombie in fiction, and indeed, the "Romero zombie" will be the monster whose impact on contemporary zombie fictions is by far the greatest.

While the importance of Romero's vision of the zombie for contemporary literary representations of the creature cannot be doubted, it pays to go further back. The zombie is a filmic monster and a contemporary one, certainly in the form it today has. The first voodoo zombie story is probably *Le Zombi du Grand Pérou* (1697, see Rath 2014b), but, as Kyle Bishop points out, "no short fiction, novels, or films featuring hordes of flesh-eating zombies predate 1968" (2010, 94). Yet they have important literary forebears nonetheless; not itself an unknown story, but one which bears repeating in light of its potential significance for my later discussion.[2] Its oldest literary progenitor is in the folkloric ghoul, a monster that consumes human flesh, and which appears among the tales in the *Arabian Nights* (1706). The ghoul is a sentient, shape-shifting demon, rather than a reanimated corpse, and only in some tales does it actively prey on living humans, rather than merely consuming the flesh of corpses interred in graveyards (cf. Connors 2007). It is thus only part of the possible progenitors of today's zombies. If the consumption of human flesh is one of the modern zombie's chief characteristics, the second is their status as the reanimated dead. Reanimation became a major trope of fictional writing during the Romantic era: the motif certainly has its echoes in Mary Shelley's *Frankenstein* (1818) and later in several Edgar Allan Poe short stories (cf. Vuckovic 2011, 29–30). And, in the 1920s, H. P. Lovecraft's pulp fiction offered "Herbert West, Re-Animator," who at least does actually reanimate dead bodies. These precursors were individually less influential, however, than the creatures from which the zombie obtained its name: Haiti's Vodou-made walking "dead" (see Bishop 2007, 37–63, Luckhurst 2015, and especially Charlier 2017).[3]

William Seabrook's 1929 book *The Magic Island*, a travelogue narrating Seabrook's experiences in Haiti, is generally acknowledged to be the origin of Western interest in the zombie (Pulliam 2007, 725). As Roger Luckhurst has shown, Seabrook really is "merely one voice in the cacophony that unleashed the zombies that poured into American popular culture" (2015, 41), but his role remains important, even if it is simply because he remains the touchstone for subsequent studies of the zombie phenomenon. Seabrook, a journalist, went to Haiti with the explicit purpose of investigating the nature of Vodou, and was there introduced to the zombie. The process he described in his somewhat sensational (and remarkably brief) account involved digging up a freshly buried corpse and, by some art, returning it to something resembling life, henceforth to work for the person who resurrected him. Seabrook even met zombies himself, but refused to commit himself to a supernatural explanation for them. Ten years later, Zora Neal Hurston's ethnographic account of Haiti, *Tell My Horse*, added further details about the practice, including her own encounter with an alleged zombie woman (cf. Bishop 2007, 48–50).

The image of the mindless, drone-like slave worker resurrected from among the dead, whatever its validity as a description of the actual practices of Vodou in Haiti (cf. Davis 1985 for an admittedly disputed hypothesis on the physiology of zombification), proved a fertile ground for fictional explorations, if not at first in literature. Victor and Edward Halperin's 1932 film *White Zombie* was the first to adapt the Vodou zombie; the success of the Halperin brothers' film ensured that the zombie would remain current in films of the 1930s. In all of these films, the zombies followed the apparent real-world formula of mindless, but not hostile, reanimated corpses, representing to those who raised them in the first place as the chief antagonists and dangers to the systemic (racial) order. In the majority of these films, the exotic Caribbean locale and the mainly black zombies revealed the latent—and often overt—racism of the times.

Zombies and their close relatives also took to the pages of the rising tide of comic books, most notably perhaps in the *Tales from the Crypt* series, from EC Comics. Many rising dead bodies populated this and other series (Round 2011, 211–13; see also Hand 2016), bent on revenge, seeking to return to their homes without realizing they are dead. Among them, too, is the voodoo zombie. In *Tales from the Crypt* no. 23, for example, a story of a car-crash victim returning to life (zombie-esque, if not exactly prime material) is followed by a story in which two travelers in Haiti encounter a voodoo ritual; one of them gets caught, and upon returning, apparently unharmed, to his friend, mumbles " . . . voodoo doll . . . zombie . . ." (1951, 3). While the two journey home, the other man, Bill, is haunted by a voodoo doll. As the doll finally catches up with him and poisons him, Jay reveals that he himself has been turned into a zombie. This zombification story played fully on the Haitian voodoo myths. In a different take on the modern zombie's origins, in *Tales from the Crypt* no. 38, a benevolent association, the Grateful Hoboes, Outcasts and Unwanteds' Layaway Society, turns out to be a group of barely concealed "g.h.o.u.l.s." eating the flesh of dead hoboes laid to rest in their cemetery. Even as the *Tales from the Crypt* adopted many of the various creatures that had populated horror fiction before, it remained derivative both in its storylines, going for the cheap thrills necessary to keep its readers entertained week by week, and in its conception of its monster. It would be left to a different popular medium to bring something new to the table.

George Romero's *Night of the Living Dead* pulled together the ghoulish eating of human flesh and the Vodou-inspired reanimation of dead bodies.

But the film did not merely combine these features: it also added new ones. Romero's zombies are not creatures "made" by human agency; rather, their origin remains mysterious, the modus of their reanimation unclear, and their purposes wholly their own. Instead of willing slaves, Romero's zombies are monomaniacal, seeking only to kill and eat humans. They are still capable, in contrast to some later and indeed most literary emanations, of using tools, but they are not motivated by any purpose beyond the killing and consuming of the living. They congregate largely by instinct around the farmhouse in which the protagonists have holed up. As the undead assail the increasingly doubtful safety of the farmhouse, it is the internal frictions which slowly break down the human defenders: bad decisions, poor judgments, and an inability to communicate. When *Night*'s black protagonist Ben, alone having survived the night, gets killed in the morning by a trigger-happy posse of zombie-killers, *Night*'s central point is underlined: even in a world of rising dead, it is the living that pose the greatest threat.

Romero's film transformed the idea of the zombie. The surprising success of this new form of zombie found many filmic imitators in the 1970s, both in the US and especially abroad. The vast majority of these films fell short of Romero's comparatively complex narrative, focusing on the graphic gore and violence (and often, too, sexual exploitation) that promised quick and cheap profit. Romero's own next film was in part a beneficiary of these successes—with funding coming from Italian producer Dario Argento, who had released several zombie movies of the exploitative kind before (on the Italian zombie film, see O'Brien 2008)—but once more connected its graphic violence with a story that offered societal critique. *Dawn of the Dead* was very much a sequel to *Night*, set in the same situation of a beginning apocalyptic rising of the dead. Also like its predecessor, it certainly did not lack for gore: its infamous shot of an exploding head set standards. But it is chiefly remarkable for its principal setting, a shopping mall in which the protagonists find temporary safety. The cultural significance of the shopping mall, and the consumerist society which has chosen it as a temple, lies at the heart of the film's social commentary; and, like *Night*, *Dawn* proved adept at making the threat of the undead become subsumed under the threats posed by the living to each other.

Dawn of the Dead's success came just before a time when the zombie type which Romero had created had slowly started staging an entrance into written fiction as well. The 1970s had already seen a number of zombie-like creatures in fiction. Robert Silverberg's novella-short story *Born With the Dead* (1974) features walking, talking, thinking reanimated dead people capable of spiritual time-travel; Curt Selby's *I, Zombie* (1981) goes back to the voodoo zombie trope of reanimated undead forced to undertake slave labor, here on a far-future off-world colony of Earth's. Perhaps closest to a Romero zombie are the creatures in Joe R. Lansdale's *Dead in the West* (1986). An itinerant preacher is caught up in a massive rising of the dead: the townspeople have lynched an Indian medicine man, who makes a pact with a demon to give him the power to avenge himself on the town. He kills the travelers in a stagecoach and raises them from the dead. Together, they attack the town, killing—and eating—everyone they encounter. In the end, it is only the preacher who survives, having held off the zombies until the dawn, which serves to weaken the demon's power and thus puts an end to the threat. Lansdale's story has many of the features of Romero's films: the undead survive everything short of a brain injury; they rise in whatever condition they were when they were killed; and they function as a monomaniacal mass. They are controlled by a demonic power—a ploy which some later zombie fictions will return to—but are not capable of thought, emotion, or independent decisions. If much of what Lansdale is doing echoes the modern zombie, Lansdale himself notes that the novella was inspired by an older generation of horror fiction—pulp fictions, EC Comics, and B-movie horror films which did not include Romero's.

Despite its omnipresence in film, the Western, Romero-type zombie by the end of the 1980s had not come close to being a major feature in horror fiction. Given this state of affairs, John Skipp and Craig Spector may be excused for the exuberant tone of their introduction to *Book of the Dead*, the first anthology of "Romero" zombie short fiction to appear. Published in 1989, the book no doubt profited from the growing popularity of Romero's films. As Skipp and Spector acknowledge, their volume is explicitly supposed to "pay homage to the films of George A. Romero" and his "vibrant archetypal landscape" (6). The editors' introduction highlights what they believe is Romero's greatest achievement, the inauguration of the "age of splatter" (8), the graphic depiction of the kind of violence that they argue has "permeated every aspect of our lives" (11) and so, critics to the contrary, deserves a place on screen as well. Skipp and Spector see Romero's achievement not merely in this, however, but rather in his capacity to marry violence to more complex levels of emotional meaning, in which it is precisely not desensitization but empathy which is evoked in the viewer.

Short fictions in which zombies played major though variable roles became more prominent after Skipp and Spector's initial foray. In 1993, the first collection of zombie fictions that sought to trace a historical genealogy of sorts appeared, Stephen Jones's *The Mammoth Book of Zombies*. Including Poe's short story "The Case of M. Valdemar," Lovecraft's "Herbert West, Re-Animator," and Manly Wade Wellman's "The Song of the Slaves," from the 1940s pulp magazine *Weird Tales*, Jones's anthology offered "a unique gamut of zombies, from the traditional to the *outré*" (2). A small but steady stream of similar anthologies appeared throughout the 1990s (see the Bibliography for a short list), but it was not until the mid-2000s that a major rise in the publication of zombie fictions started, one which has lasted until today (and is, in no small part, the major impetus for this study).

The origins of this perhaps surprising development lie in a group of films, comics, and books that appeared around 2002 and 2003: Danny Boyle's quasi-zombie movie *28 Days Later* (2002), Robert Kirkman's comic series *The Walking Dead* (2003–), Brian Keene's *The Rising* (2003), and Max Brooks's *The Zombie Survival Guide: Complete Protection from the Living Dead* (2003). Of the four, Boyle's film is somewhat marginal to the discussion here, but was a tremendous box-office and critical success. While it did not feature the undead, its virus-enraged monstrous humans both helped justify the fast zombies of the 2004 remake of *Dawn of the Dead* as well as to repopularize the apocalyptic monster movie.

Of much greater importance in the recent development of zombie fiction, Robert Kirkman's *Walking Dead* series has run for fourteen years and nearly 160 issues. Kirkman's initial conception of the series as "the zombie movie that never ends" (2007, n.p.) has produced what Jonathan Maberry has called "one of the bleakest, most downbeat and nihilistic stories ever told" (2011, 22). In Kirkman's world, notably, the rules of the Romero-derived zombies still apply: mysteriously awakening after death (any death), the undead seek to kill and eat the living. We follow the fate of a group of survivors led by rural policeman Rick Grimes, whose awakening amidst the ongoing apocalypse indicates already the comic's main interest. Rather than seeking to elaborate on the causes and genesis of the zombie outbreak, it is the interaction between the humans that live and die through it that is in the foreground of Kirkman's series: "this is not a horror book." Instead, Kirkman avers, the series echoes Romero's concern with depicting iterations of human communities and his films' "undercurrent of social commentary and thoughtfulness" (Kirkman 2007, n.p.).

It is this conception of the zombie (and not Keene's dimension-jumping demons possessing dead humans and animals, featuring in *The Rising* and its sequels) as more than a mere vehicle of cheap thrills that has engaged much of the recent spate of written zombie fictions. Max Brooks's satirical, mock self-help book *The Zombie Survival Guide: Complete Protection from the Living Dead* (2003) is both the progenitor of a number of similar endeavors (Ma 2010, Muir 2010) and, despite its farcical content, already looks forward to the concerns of Brooks's later *World War Z*. In the *Guide*, Brooks pokes fun at the genre (and fans') obsessions, but at the same time shows glimpses of how zombie fictions address protopolitical concerns. Brooks's guide offered readers guidelines on how to survive the oncoming inevitable zombie apocalypse, including helpful chapters on weapons, shelter, and an episodic history of previous zombie outbreaks. Having outlined the utility of various weapons for defense and attack, the origins of his version of the zombie (a virus), and a host of other issues related to surviving a zombie apocalypse, Brooks notes: "collective response is always preferable to an individual attempt" (2003, 159). In this, Brooks sets the tone for much contemporary zombie fiction.

Brooks followed this volume in 2006 with an even greater popular hit: *World War Z: An Oral History of the Zombie War*. Written in the style of Studs Terkel's oral reportage, *World War Z* is an interview novel in which a multitude of voices combines to render a multifaceted account of the long history of the war between zombies and humans. I will discuss this novel in greater detail in Chapter 1, but in the context of a history of zombie fictions, it bears pointing out *World War Z*'s tremendous commercial success: it germinated a field, propelled especially by small presses specializing in the horror genres. Permuted Press, one of the most notable of these, was founded in 2004 with the express purpose of publishing an anthology of zombie fiction, *The Undead*. Several zombie novels started as online ventures, among them David Wellington's *Monster Island* (2006) series and Madeleine Roux's *Allison Hewitt Is Trapped* (2010: see Ch. 5). Indeed, these adaptions of online phenomena into print bespeak the resurgent market for zombie fictions. By the mid-2000s, it had become increasingly impossible to list new publications of zombie fiction. From new anthologies of zombie short stories such as John Skipp's *Zombies: Encounters with the Living Dead* (2006) to anthologies of zombie comics such as *The Mammoth Book of Zombie Comics* (2008) to a steadily increasing number of standalone novels or novel series, the zombie had firmly arrived in fiction.

Remarkable among these new zombie fictions are novels that adopt either a preexisting narrative universe for their purposes (such as Joe Schreiber's two volumes set in the Star Wars universe), or a preexisting, out-of-copyright text for their playground. The first of these mash-ups, and still the most successful by far, is Seth Graham-Smith's *Pride and Prejudice and Zombies* (2009), which, as the title with no subtlety implies, pastes Jane Austen's Regency romance onto a background of a zombie-infested Great Britain. It has been followed by such forays as Bill Czolgosz's *The Adventures of Huckleberry Finn and Zombie Jim* (2011) or Eric S. Brown's *The War of the Worlds: H. G. Wells's Classic Plus Blood, Guts and Zombies* (2009). It has also spread to the regional literatures, as *Zombies of Lake Woebegotten* (2010) shows, a novel linking together the writings of Minnesotan Garrison Keillor on Lake Wobegon with the menace of the shuffling undead. There has been at least some debate about the meaning of these exercises in literary mash-up. Potentially, at least, the introduction of zombies into these classic texts breaks up well-known narratives and reshapes them for contemporary purposes, giving them a new lease on relevance (see Ch. 4).

The zombie, like his undead compatriot the vampire, but rather more unlikely, has escaped the horror genre, too. On the movie screen, Edgar Wright's *Shaun of the Dead* (2005) spearheaded the genre's overdue move from straight horror frequently veering into involuntary farce towards the determinedly humorous. Advertised as a "romzomcom"—a romantic comedy with zombies—*Shaun of the Dead* has also found successors not only in film (*Wasting Away* [2007] and *Dance of the Dead* [2008] are notable examples) but also in literature. S. G. Browne's *Breathers* (2009), Isaac Marion's *Warm Bodies* (2010), Jesse Petersen's *Married with Zombies* (2010) and *Flip This Zombie* (2011), and a host of short stories, such as those collected in Lori Perkins's *Hungry for Your Love: An Anthology of Zombie Romance* (2011), have explored the zombie in (comedic) romances. While the vampire's move from supernatural terror to supernatural love interest has antecedents in literary history, the zombie's similar move is more puzzling. The erotic nimbus surrounding the vampire is grounded in classical ideals of beauty (bodily strength, smooth features, alabaster skin, to name a few) as far back as John Polidori's Lord Ruthven of 1819, the ur-type of the romantic vampire, who seduces women erotically as often as he drains them of blood. The zombie, by contrast, is traditionally repulsive, decaying, shuffling, and, but for his monotonous moaning, mute. But if in Wright's *Shaun of the Dead*, the undead were still merely foils, obstacles to overcome in the quest for the living's romantic love, in *Wasting Away*, they have made their way to being the protagonists; in *Breathers*, it is they who live the love story.

The 2000s have thus marked a high point in the publication of zombie-related literature, both in terms of sheer quantity as well as in terms of quality. The contemporary return of the zombie can also be read in conjunction with a decline of more individual horrors—Freddy Kruger, Jason Vorhees—which proliferated in the 1980s and 1990s and thus appears as a movement which emphasizes the systemic over the solipsistic (cf. Williams 2011, 140–41). Nor has this phenomenon gone unnoticed, as the corresponding increase in the output of academic studies of the zombie makes clear. How to read the zombie, how to interpret it both in its individual manifestations as well as its cultural resurgence in general, is the question which the next section of this introduction will tackle.

Reading the Zombie, Reading Zombie Fictions

Zombies, as we have already seen, are the ultimate "modern monsters." Very much in line with modernity's shifting and fluid regimes of representation, zombies are capable of carrying an impressive number, perhaps any number, of metaphorical and symbolic connotations. The question of how to read the zombie—that is, how to interpret the zombie as symptom, symbol, or metaphor, and what to make of narratives in which it plays a (usually major) role—is a vexed one, as I have noted above. It has become a cliché, and bears only the most minimal of additional signposting. Kyle Bishop frames this point most positively, suggesting that "zombies are *the* great metaphorical monsters because they can be tailored and applied to almost any discipline or situation, and people see in zombies what they *need* to see" (2014, 17, original emphases). Most other commentators have been more studiously neutral, and sometimes critical, of this metaphorical malleability. Steven Shaviro notes that zombies can "be regarded both as monstrous symptoms of a violent, manipulative, exploitative society and as potential remedies for its ills" (1993, 87). Mathias Clasen suggests that the "zombie figure represents the gradual, by all means incomplete dissolution of us-versus-them morality in monochrome, a population-level schizophrenia or ambivalence toward war and the enemy" (2010, 19). Kelly Baker argues that "[z]ombies become metaphors for anything from consumerism to terrorism to mindless politics/politicians to banking to epidemics to smart phone users" (2013, loc. 75). Slavoj Žižek has noted that while the vampire is an insider, an aristocrat, zombies are "clumsy, inert and dirty, and attack from the outside, like a primitive revolt of the excluded" (2014, 64); and most recently, Camilla Fojas has called it "a loaded cultural figure that symbolizes a number of social fears about disaster, ruin, and dehumanization" (2017, 80).

Some of these readings pose obvious problems. For example, while Žižek seems to ascribe the zombie a revolutionary potential, he neglects the fact that most narratives of the zombie apocalypse exclude the zombie from the subsequent re-establishment of the world. Agents of the old world's destruction, they are not participants in the (hopefully) more equitable future communities they enable: zombification, the process by which a healthy human being is transformed into a shuffling member of the undead, reduces its victims to bare existence. Or, for a different example of the interpretative problems posed by the zombie, the fact that zombies are usually a monomaniacal mass does not mean that they are necessarily "democratic," as Hans Baumann has it (in Koch 2008, 13), which images of totalitarian rallies from 1920s Rome to 1930s Berlin to contemporary North Korea may attest to.[4]

If these interpretations read too much in to the zombie figure, it is also possible to read it too little. The problem with some other readings is that they are barely readings at all; or, perhaps more to the point, the zombie itself, as a trope, is barely in need of explication. Focusing too strongly on the zombie as a metaphor runs the risk of deep critical disappointment when it turns out—as it often does—that the zombie itself often requires little interpretation. As Evan Williams points out,

> To say that the ending of *Night of the Living Dead,* with the "accidental" murder of an African-American man by the white redneck zombie hunting mob, is largely about race relations is just to say that you've watched the movie all the way through. (2012, 78)

Similarly, as Williams suggests, the consumerist critique of Romero's *Dawn of the Dead* is not actually a matter of interpretation: it is right there on the surface for everybody to see. So, I would argue, are class relations in *Land of the Dead* (cf. Lutz 2010): does anybody require a second look to read the zombie assault, led by a black gas-station attendant, against the privileged upper classes residing in a luxurious apartment complex, as a proletarian uprising against the ruling class? This list may be nearly endlessly prolonged. Such "analyses," then, are ultimately little more than descriptions of what happens, and in and of themselves neither debatable nor particular interesting. (With apologies to Monty Python, we might call these "Zombie Elk Theories.") And even in this, they often seem to miss the mark of critical engagement. As David McNally has pointed out, there is "something lacking [. . .] in the zombie-revolts that emerge in popular culture today. [. . .] By repositioning zombies as crazed consumers, rather than producers, recent Hollywood horror-films tend to offer biting criticism of the hyper-consumptionist ethos of an American capitalism characterized by excess" (2011, 260). They "tend to offer a critique of consumerism, not capitalism—one that fails to probe the life-destroying, zombifying processes of work in bourgeois society" (261). In other words, while a film like *Dawn of the Dead* is remarkable for offering social critique through what in other versions are often simply exploitative splatter movies (as in the Italian sequels to *Night*), it is not remarkable for the difficulty of parsing its critique, nor particularly perceptive in the targets of its critique.

All of these readings, whether too broad or too narrow, highlight the zombie's symbolic power. But it needs to be pointed out that the major shift in the zombie's symbolic potential only came with the films of George Romero: when the undead became both really undead and consumed by a monomania for human flesh, they ushered themselves into a realm where they could, more or less suddenly, come to symbolize a variety of societal issues. The zombie could now "stand for" the excluded and victimized sides under capitalism, of classism, racism, and homo- and xenophobia, to name just a few.

Night of the Living Dead itself, in fact, did not make much of the zombie's new potential itself: for the film, the zombie presents merely the necessary threat that allows it to bring together its characters in a single locale, and to explore the resultant tensions. In *Dawn of the Dead*, however, the zombie takes on a new, and critical, role. Rather than being a mere plot device, *Dawn*'s zombies become objects for critical reflection to the characters. Its famous line that the mall in which the protagonists hide was an "important place in their lives" remains central to *Dawn* being read as a critique of the consumerism prevalent in its particular moment, as what Stephen Harper has called a "radical (i.e., oppositional) anti-consumerist text" (2002, n.p.). This is certainly the widely accepted standard reading of the political thrust of *Dawn*; what is more meaningful than whether or not this is deeply insightful insight is the shifting role of the zombie. As David McNally points out, to the extent that the Romero version of the zombie abandoned the Haitian model of the zombie-laborer, it at least in part redirected its critique away from capitalism as an exploitative system towards our own culpability as zombie-consumers. These modern versions "represent our haunted self-image, warning us that we might already be lifeless, disempowered agents of alien powers" (2011, 253). This is in contrast to the original zombie-laborer both as an anthropological phenomenon and as a subject of such films as *White Zombie*, which presented "the hidden secret of capitalism, its dependence on the bondage and exploitation of human labourers" and, in the famous Hegelian dialectic, the innate dependence of the master-capitalists themselves on the very labor which these zombie slaves provided (cf. 254, 264). As passive victims of an exploitative class, the original zombie-laborers of *White Zombie* might be said to have had little symbolic content, given that they were merely exaggerated versions of the actually existing laborers on plantations (and, by extension, in all kinds of capitalist enterprises). The question of the importance of its Haitian history for the contemporary figure of the zombie is, in fact, rather hotly debated. Some critics, such as Stephen Shaviro, would like to see the zombie as "without an origin or a referent" (1993, 83). Others, like Roger Luckhurst, insist that it "remains connected to the meaning of Haiti and the islands of the Antilles to the modern world, and the systematic violence, expropriated labour, rebellion and revolution in those areas, however far it travels" (2015, 15). Between these radical positions subsist many others; perhaps the most useful is Maxime Coulombe's notion, derived from Aby Warburg, of reading the zombie as the "result of a sedimentation, of a history which has seen it take meaning and then transform in the contexts and cultures which have appropriated it" (2013, 14). It is on this latter view that I will build this book. Coulombe's notion usefully delimits the zombie's metaphoric potential:

it can stand for a lot, but hardly for anything, and the confluence of possible meanings is emphatically historical and context-specific.

If reading the zombie as such seems in danger of becoming an exhausted critical procedure, the alternative to such symbolic readings as I have sketched above needs to shift its critical attention away from the zombie and to focus instead on the worlds into which fictions inscribe them. It is to suggest their capacity as catalysts of postapocalyptic visions of alternative society, in which their own particularity as monsters figures, but in which they become merely a necessary canvas against which to draw human struggles. To concentrate too closely on the particulars of the zombie's metaphorical constitution as Other, or Consumer, or Worker, obscures one of the most important things about the zombie as a modern monster: the fact that, in almost all instances, the zombie is a monster of the apocalypse. The term, derived from the Greek word for "uncovering," has come to mean an end time, and especially in popular culture, the end of civilization. But importantly, as in its biblical origins in the apocalypse of John, it also projects a continuity of sorts, an after in which radical changes have occurred but which is nonetheless related to the previous moment. As Chase Pielak and Alexander Cohen have argued, "apocalypse represents a shift in the world, ideological or otherwise, toward a new relationship between its inhabitants and each other, and the inhabitants and the world at large" (2017, 5). This shift is what is diagnostic, and central to the zombie as a contemporary monster. With rare exceptions, the zombie ushers in a postapocalyptical scenario of a world overrun by the undead, in which new forms of existence are in the foreground. In the contemporary menagerie of monsters, the zombie stands out: no other monster so thoroughly embodies the end of the existing world. No zombie novel fails to make understood that the rise of the zombie is the descent of civilization into desolation: indeed, the zombie appears to require this descent, apparently leaving no room for any other consequence than this complete collapse of existing structures.

It is important to note that this is a formal, rather than a topical, thematic, or narrative matter: the apocalypse is not a choice, but rather, its existence appears as a formal consequence of the zombie's presence, which constrains and demands certain generic moves of the fictions it inhabits. The zombie, then, is a form, one that requires the destruction of the world that is and the imagination of a world to come. Throughout this book, however, my refrain about this will be cautious: if this is what the zombie formally requires, what comes of this requirement is open. The zombie is a figure of possibilities, not of necessary outcomes, and zombie fictions thus run the gamut from the radically utopian to the hopelessly resigned, from modest interventions into the contemporary status quo to absolute disavowal of it. What permits us to talk about possible utopian visions, new conceptions of community and collectivity, and other social issues is the raising of these issues in the texts themselves. At the same time, what we need to talk about are those issues, rather than the zombie catalysts which produce (but not in all cases meaningfully inform) these new situations, and which are now as it were "merely" a formal issue.

The symptomatic valence and symbolic value of the zombie, that thoroughly cinematic monster, comes out best in literary texts, whose very form enables them to offer longer, stronger meditations on the possible consequences and the multifarious phenotypes of the postapocalypse than any game, film, or indeed TV series. Yet because most zombie fiction falls into the broad rubric of "genre fiction," it has not yet been accorded the attention it deserves. Horror films have long ceased to be regarded solely as cheap thrills, as morally reprehensible and, at best, capable of mirroring a general decline of culture. Instead, they have come to be recognized as capable of articulating, in an often highly original way, societal concerns, and to offer cultural criticism in Adorno's sense. Popular fiction, despite an upswing in critical interest in it in recent years, still struggles with the problem of perceived inferiority, and a resistance to critical reflection on its times—an affirmation of the status quo through insipidity. But times are changing—and have been changing, in the eyes of some critics, for quite some time. I take recourse here to the argument Fredric Jameson has sketched—namely, that "the works of mass culture cannot be ideological without at one and the same time being implicitly or explicitly Utopian as well" (1979, 144), and they generally undertake "a transformational work on social and political anxieties and fantasies" (141). For some of the novels which I discuss below, the first part of Jameson's comment is fully accurate, in that they are ideological first (which in this case means reaffirming the preponderant ideologies of their moment) and utopian merely "as well." Utopia, as Ruth Levitas has noted, is at its core the "desire for being otherwise," and its expressions—zombie fictions included—"explore and bring to debate the potential contents and contexts of human flourishing" (2013, ix); utopian fictions are "the expression of the desire for a better way of living" (xii). In this sense, utopia, too, affirms possibility, rather than certainty. Max Brooks's *World War Z*, for example, is largely supportive of prevailing capitalist ideologies even as it produces a utopian vision for the future. In *World War Z*, corporate scams and the uselessness of white-collar workers serve as substitutes for a more engaged concern with the structures of capitalist enterprise, enabling *World War Z* to finally reaffirm the need to have a stable dollar, an enterprising (capitalist) economy, and a liberal democratic conclusion to its apocalyptic events (see Ch. 1). Apocalypse here, as Phillip Wegner has phrased it, is merely a "pseudo-event," with the "world that is figured in the text simply a continuation or repetition of the reigning status quo" (2011, 94). Many more texts, however, need to be read primarily for their genuinely "transformational work."

As Darren Reed and Ruth Penfold-Mounce have pointed out, it is possible to read zombie fictions as what they call "social-science fiction" (2015, 126): "Premised on a number of public issues, such as the disintegration of government and institutional power, and questions about the place of collectivism beyond issues of gender, race and class, it pursues answers through the personal troubles of the protagonists" (2015, 126). My own reading of the zombie in contemporary fiction will very much focus on this connection to the contemporary social situation. At its best (though not always), the "zombie apocalypse [. . .] is the sudden and total unearthing of the savage heart of capitalism's antagonisms" (Williams 2011, 137), and an extrapolation of utopian possibilities, so much so that even more traditional readings of the zombie as an embodied metaphor may be usefully subsumed by it. To give just one example: Jameson has recently discussed the utopian problematic of the temporal life of the body, reading the "theme of resurrection itself" as an expression of the "euphoria of a secular salvation otherwise inexpressible in material or social terms" (Jameson 2013, 196–97). The zombie complicates this reading in that its resurrection is not a benign process, not an overcoming of the limitations of the individual or a transcendence of death. Indeed, the kind of resurrection undergone by humans into zombies becomes a process to be feared, rather than to be hoped for, and the euthanizing of the infected an act of mercy. This theme is picked up in the innumerable scenes of characters begging those close to them not to let them become "one of them," which William Larkin has also noted was the central aspect of the zombie's capacity for horror: "our fear of becoming a zombie" (2010, 20). As Jonah Caine, the protagonist of Kim Paffenroth's *Dying to Live* puts it, most zombie fictions see the need to have "someone to put a bullet in your brain when you went to get back up as a zombie" (2009, 10).

Inadvertently, perhaps, the zombie thus highlights the worrisome belief that a return into the contemporary world is in all cases desirable—it highlights the damning consequence of the implicit eternalization of the status quo. The world of the zombie is a world unchanging except for the workings of entropy, in which the slow decay of the undead body signals the inevitable end of an otherwise static situation. In this way, the zombie, who cannot learn or change or do anything but consume when consumption is possible, becomes a more generalized version of something like Francis Fukuyama's end-of-history thesis, or the sense of inevitability frequently ascribed to the contemporary social situation. To become a zombie in this version is to succumb to the inevitable order of the world; to fight against the zombie is already a utopian move, no matter its consequences. To overcome the zombie thus frequently becomes a fulfillment of the promise already present in the struggle.

There is a different version of this: the one where the zombie comes to stand precisely as the power that sets itself against the status quo. For *World War Z*, given its construction of an at best specifically *liberal* utopia at its conclusion, this is a possible reading. It becomes clearer in Colson Whitehead's 2011 novel *Zone One*, in which the postapocalyptic reconstruction of society overtly tacks towards a corporate-government interaction that exceeds even the contemporary moment's, and in which a second rising of the zombies seems to sweep this away for good. Here, in repeating the event of civilization's Armageddon, the zombie comes to stand for a progressive force, of which even the novel's protagonist finally symbolically becomes a part (see Ch. 6). We might read this with Slavoj Žižek's exploration of the Lacanian notion of a "second death": "the radical annihilation of the symbolic texture through which so-called reality is constituted" (1989, 147). To be sure, this is an awkwardly literal reading of a complex concept, and yet still, I think, relatable. It suggests why the first "death" of the zombies generally fails to succeed in ushering in a stable utopian future, why in Whitehead's *Zone One*, for example, there seems no constitutive difference between the world before the death of everybody and the world thereafter, until (in this case) the second death of the reconstituted system. And it is why no sense of lasting hope gets established in the entire course of Robert Kirkman's *The Walking Dead*, mired as it is in its effort to remain endless. Or why, in a slightly different parsing of the concept, so many zombie narratives require the destruction-as-second death of the *zombie*, which often becomes a prerequisite for the final establishment of a hopeful new future, as in *Dying to Live* or *World War Z*. Or, in yet another variant: why Bob Fingerman's *Pariah* cannot conclude on a note of hope until the main (human, in this case) obstacle to a peaceful communal life dies. The most obvious and fundamental "actual death" in all these cases—the ends of the lives of untold millions, often including some of the characters we have come to hold dear—is not accompanied by "symbolic death." The cessation of biological functions (more or less, in the case of the zombie) is not followed by the "total 'wipe-out' of historical tradition" (Žižek 1989, 150) which only the symbolic death enacts. The zombie comes to be readable as an allegorical representation of this process, in which its living death is, whatever else it is, also a reminder that a second death awaits.

Given this, it is no surprise, I think, that the zombie has recently proliferated, why its formal connection to the imagination of open possibilities now resonates so strongly. We live, after all, in a world in which it is "easier to imagine the end of the world than it is to imagine the end of capitalism" (Jameson 2003, 76). This book, to put it bluntly, will thus read the zombie symptomatically:

as the formal expression of cultural anxieties and problems and the symbolic resolution of the contradictions of contemporary life (cf. Jameson 2002, 65). In its own way, this book is no more than a case study—a series of selective encounters with specific texts to illuminate a larger argument about the nature of all similar fictions. Because it excludes a number of texts that a less strict or differently motivated study of zombie fictions might include, it may easily fall prey to accusations of capricious selectivity, but I hope to make clear that these books really are significant examples of contemporary zombie fiction. Nor should readers mistake the general stance towards a symptomatic reading of the zombie as a unifying critical perspective on the zombie. When, for example, I discuss the zombie's intrusion into *Pride and Prejudice* in Chapter 4, my argument about the zombie's symptomatic valence will be combined with an argument about readerships and mash-up production that is not fully covered by a literary reading of the book. But while I remain within the confines of a reading of the zombie as a figure, rather than a product, I will read it symptomatically. I relate the zombie to the world system in Chapter 1, to contemporary conceptions of community in Chapter 2, and to the question of gender-writing in Chapter 5; but none of these relations exhaust what I am doing in any of those chapters. The interrelations, which the shared figure of the zombie produces, are part and parcel of my discussions in these chapters, and these interrelations are best analyzed through a symptomatic reading.

The Structure of This Book

This introduction has already outlined the major theoretical fault lines of the book proper, and the following chapters will exemplarily discuss their expression in a number of what I take to be central zombie novels—certainly novels which showcase both the reach and limits of the zombie in contemporary fiction.

Chapter 1 briefly discusses what I take to be the point of origin for much of the recent slate of zombie fictions, Max Brooks's 2003 surprise hit *A Zombie Survival Guide*, and then segues into a longer analysis of his 2005 document novel, *World War Z*. While the *Survival Guide* is essentially a humorous, mock-serious takeoff on self-help books, *World War Z*, I will suggest, by contrast is capable of sustaining a closer interpretive reading. Brooks's novel examines a variety of political and societal topics and ultimately mounts a sustained critique of its historical moment, offering the vision of what I will suggest is a "liberal utopia." In lieu of imagining the outcome of a collapse of contemporary society as a chance for a complete systemic remaking of social and economic relations, *World War Z* goes to the limits of a specifically liberal utopian imagination. The novel's solutions, ultimately, waver uneasily between systemic restitution in its reaffirmation of the power—indeed, the necessity—of capitalist enterprise, and political progressivism, in the way it affirmatively insists on collective, transnational action and international cooperation.

Chapter 2 offers a contrastive reading of Kim Paffenroth's *Dying to Live* and Bob Fingerman's *Pariah*, based on their shared premises and ultimate arguments. Both novels feature characters with the ability to move safely among the undead; more importantly, both novels analyze the constitution of different forms of community in the face of apocalypse. As the chapter will show, their different explorations of postapocalyptic group dynamics offer alternative visions of what constitutes the possible futures of community, a concept that has lately come into greater literary-critical focus. Drawing on and adapting the theories of Jean-Luc Nancy and Zygmunt Bauman, I will suggest that the zombie figures here as the perfect symbolization of an extracommunal Other capable of uniting even the most disparate humans against a common enemy. As both novels show, even this Other is no guarantee of social cohesion among survivors, but its emphatic highlighting of the need for unity permits the radical action that makes genuine human community possible.

Chapter 3 will explore what is perhaps the most successful of recent literary expressions of interest in the zombie, Robert Kirkman's ongoing comic series *The Walking Dead* (2003–). Conceived as the "zombie movie that never ends," *The Walking Dead* comics have received less critical attention than the subsequent television series on AMC. Chapter 3 aims to rectify this imbalance. It takes its cue from Kirkman's explicit positioning and evaluates the consequences of such an open-ended narrative. I draw on Frank Kermode's discussion of endings and apocalypse and Eran Dorfman's recent understanding of shock, deferral, and repetition as key to the constitution of the "everyday" to read Kirkman's attempt at never-ending storytelling as symptomatic of a contemporary post-postmodern ambivalence about the desirability of the everyday.

The questions which Chapter 4 is interested in involve the phenomenon of so-called mash-up fiction, whose prime exponent is certainly Seth Grahame-Smith's *Pride and Prejudice and Zombies* (2009). In this chapter, I argue for the need to read this novel together with its prequel and sequel, as parodies acting simultaneously on Austen's original novel and its times, on the contemporary moment, and on Austen's contemporary readers. I argue that despite some critical disdain, the 2009 mash-up and its follow-ups deserve to be read closely, with an explicit attention to their parodic voice, to tease out their critical stances on both the original novel's depiction of class, gender, and race, as well as their critique of a contemporary readership of Austen which foregoes all critical distance in favor of reading *Pride and Prejudice* as an exemplary romance with a happy ending.

If the first four chapters engage their topics from the vantage points provided by individual works, the final two chapters expand their readings more broadly. Chapter 5 tackles the issue of the representation of gender in zombie fiction. It begins with short readings of three texts notable for their gender narratives, and then offers close readings of two novels by Madeleine Roux, *Allison Hewitt Is Trapped* and *Sadie Walker Is Stranded*. As I will argue, despite some overboarding claims to the contrary, there is nothing particularly progressive about zombie narratives when it comes to gender. Following my general argument about the opening of avenues of narrative possibility, the chapter will argue that zombie fictions often forego the opportunity offered them by their own central narrative conceit to return to traditional versions of gender roles. I draw upon postfeminist theories and criticism of postfeminism to develop a sense of where zombie fiction goes with the conception of gender.

Where Chapter 5 engages the greater question of gender on the basis of two novels, Chapter 6 will engage the similarly framed question of race and the zombie by offering readings of two texts by writers of avowedly "literary" persuasion, Colson Whitehead and Junot Díaz, and their use of the zombie motif in conjunction with what Ramon Saldívar has called "postrace aesthetic." I argue that race is an issue which Whitehead's *Zone One* reads only against the backdrop of its greater interest in the capitalist resurgence after the first zombie assaults, and that readings in which it is foregrounded in effect bring their own predetermined assumptions into a text that challenges precisely those very assumptions. In its insistence on seeing race as an effect of economic logics, Whitehead's novel foregrounds concerns similar to Díaz's, whose short story "Monstro" expands on the multiple layers of racial antagonism and the history of racial oppression by returning the zombie, briefly, to Haiti. Ultimately, I suggest, a look at both of these texts throws up questions about the role of the zombie in contemporary literary fiction, and of genre more generally.

Taken together, I believe the six chapters offered by this study give a convincing reading of the zombie as a crucially relevant figure in contemporary literature, providing readings of a contemporary moment that needs to be reminded of the possibility of change. In the Coda, I discuss what all this means for the status of fiction more generally and argue that the zombie represents a general trend which seeks the increasing elimination of difference between so-called literary and genre fiction—a representative position for which I see it as being especially well-suited.

Max Brooks's *World War Z: An Oral History of the Zombie War*
Conservative Armageddon and Liberal Postapocalypse

Few zombie novels provide readers with as panoramic an overview of the global dimensions of a zombie apocalypse as Max Brooks's 2006 novel *World War Z: An Oral History of the Zombie War*. Brooks's interview novel presents a series of individual accounts of survival in a decade-long war against zombies. A "book of memories" (3) as Brooks's unnamed narrator-interviewer calls it, *World War Z* claims to be the residue of the data collected by the narrator for the United Nations' Postwar Commission Report; while that report contained all the "clear facts and figures" and the "cold, hard data" (1), the novel recounts instead the personal stories behind that data. But the personal is, quite frequently, the political in this book. Individual survivors' tales are tied back to a greater narrative of (initial) political and military ineptitude, slowly overcome by a reorganization of society to combat the zombie hordes, ultimately culminating in both victory over the undead as well as a changed—but not decisively altered—political and economic system. *World War Z* holds up simultaneously the importance of collective action and the validity and importance of individual experience, identity, and choice, offering a vision of a nearly ideal twenty-first-century liberal world, based on a strong, if more regulated, capitalism and a system of national and international politics of cooperation.

Mark McGurl, in a perceptive review of *World War Z* and its predecessor *The Zombie Survival Guide*, has argued that the novel "is [...] an allegory of the contemporary world system and its many risks, and characters exist in it to mark representative points on a much larger map" ("Zombie Renaissance"). Certainly, *World War Z* registers like other zombie fictions some of the "extant social anxieties" (Platts 2013, 547) of its contemporary moment. It offers a representational cognitive map, a "way of linking the most intimately local [. . .] and the most global," and produces a viable "political and economical analysis" of its contemporary moment as well as the imaginable alternatives, by the overlapping "limited" but "nonetheless sufficient" data points which its interviews constitute (MacCabe 1995, xvi–xv). As I will argue below, *World War Z* clearly establishes a set of cultural, political, and economical anxieties of the early part of the first decade of the twenty-first century and uses the zombie apocalypse to reveal them. It narrates a neoconservative Armageddon in which the zombies overrun a world in which profit, greed, militarism, partisan politics (in the derogatory sense), and sheer governmental incapacity are swept aside to be replaced, in the postapocalypse, with an idealized liberal, social-democratic, internationalist system where the common danger to all mankind has succeeded in uniting a significant part of it.[1] In so doing, *World War Z* illustrates what Slavoj Žižek notes in *Living in the End Times* is the "basic paradox of liberalism": the liberal imagination is restricted to believing its maximal goal the construction of a "'least worst society possible,' thus preventing a greater evil" (38). In its particular imagination of the postapocalypse, *World War Z* reflects a liberal vision of society as only marginally improved—and with all the failures of the imagination that this implies.

Mark McGurl is certainly right to point to the globalized narrative of *World War Z* as its most distinguishing feature; his invocation of the idea of the world system is a useful pointer allowing us to see both the critiques undertaken in *World War Z*, as well as those it leaves aside. As Fredric Jameson points out,

> all thinking today is *also*, whatever else it is, an attempt to think the world system as such. All the more true will this be for narrative figurations, whose very structure encourages a soaking up of whatever ideas in the air are left and a fantasy-solution to all the anxieties that rush to fill our current vacuum. (Jameson 1995, 4, original emphasis).

Beyond this figurative impossibility of thinking of the world today as anything but a world system, however, *World War Z* becomes difficult to read as a world-systems novel. For one thing, it does not really reflect upon the constitutive characteristics of the world-system (as theoretically conceived), which are finally economically determined and bound to the division of labor between geographically distinct parts of the globe, and require capitalism as the underlying system (cf. Wallerstein 2004, 23–24). And, indeed, we might question whether *World War Z* is truly allegorical, too, if by allegorical we mean saying one thing but meaning another (cf. Fletcher 2002, 2), since it clearly and unambiguously represents the connections drawn in an increasingly globalized world and the consequences that develop from these connections in the face of an apocalyptic epidemic. Significantly, in the novel globalization as a fact of human existence becomes both the source of the gravest dangers as well as, in the liberal utopia which *World War Z* constructs out of the ashes of the old world, the solution to the problem. On the other hand, however, *World War Z* clearly does soak up all the anxieties that filled up its contemporaneous vacuum of political alternatives. If *World War Z* is allegorical, it allegorizes the deficiencies of neoconservative politics as they were prominent in the mid-2000s, but also inadvertently the deficiencies of a liberal response to them.

The World Before: *World War Z* 's Contemporary Dystopia

Much of the groundwork for *World War Z* was laid in an earlier book. Brooks's novel is the follow-up to his 2003 *The Zombie Survival Guide*, a vastly different offering but a very necessary precursor. A "fiction without fictional characters," as Mark McGurl has it ("Zombie Renaissance"), the *Survival Guide*'s major conceit is that "[t]he dead walk among us" (xiii) already—indeed, have always done so. It provides the zombie with a natural explanation: Solanum, a virus that kills the host, infects the brain, and renders it independent of oxygen, allowing it to function without the support of a body (or so, at any rate, the *Guide*'s logic goes). The virus is transmitted by fluidic contact, zombifies its victims within twenty-four hours, and produces unreasoning and unthinking undead whose sole aim is to attack living humans in order to perpetuate the virus. Having established its zombification mechanism, the *Guide* takes some time to set its "real" version of the zombie off from both the voodoo and the Hollywood zombie ("Hollywood zombie films stray, in some cases wildly, from the reality on which they are based," it rather archly notes; 23). It then proceeds to instruct readers in a choice of weapons and their use (from the humble stick to the flamethrower), tactics for home defense and for the attack, as well as more basic survival skills in a world overrun by the undead. The *Survival Guide* advises its readers that they should not "discount any section of this book as hypothetical drama," because "every lesson in this book is rooted in historical fact" (xiv). Indeed, the final section of the book is a recounting of human history suggesting that outbreaks of zombie-ism were responsible for, among other things, Egyptians removing the brains of their mummified dead (184), the demise of Viking settlements in

Greenland (193), the disappearance of the Roanoke colony in Virginia (197–78), the Donner-Party-like annihilation of the "Knudhansen Party" on the trail to California (206), and were part of the medical experiments undertaken by the Japanese Imperial Army in Manchuria in 1942–45 (220–22).

The *Guide* is a parody of self-help books and a satire of the zombie film genre's cherished plots and devices, from chainsaws to abandoned malls. It is also, however, a necessary precursor to *World War Z*, laying in the mechanisms by which the novel's undead function and highlighting the historical dimension of their existence. It ends with what amounts to the preview of *World War Z*'s backstory and a nod towards the zombie as a particularly contemporary danger in a globalized age:

> The world's population is growing. Its center has shifted from rural to urban zones. Transportation has linked the planet with increasing speed. All these factors have led to a renaissance of infectious diseases, most of which were thought to be eradicated centuries ago. Logic dictates that Solanum can flourish in such a ripe environment. Even though information is being recorded, shared, and stored as never before, it cannot hide the fact that zombie attacks are on the rise, their frequency mirroring the "development" of this planet. At this rate, attacks will only increase, culminating in one of two possibilities. The first is that world governments will have to acknowledge, both privately and publicly, the existence of the living dead, creating special organizations to deal with the threat. In this scenario, zombies will become an accepted part of daily life—marginalized, easily contained, perhaps even vaccinated against. A second, more ominous scenario would result in an all-out war between the living and the dead: a war you are now ready for. (247)

It is exactly this war that *World War Z* narrates, and whose global perspective makes the novel stand out. The novel takes us all around the globe: from China's backcountry to heavily urbanized Western Europe, Israel, South Africa, Japan, and, of course, the United States, where most of the narrative is set. The novel's first interviewee is a Chinese doctor who recounts his encounter with what may have been Patient Zero, the point of origin of the entire, Solanum-driven epidemic. The "contagion narrative of world zombification" (McGurl, "Zombie Renaissance") which the *Survival Guide* establishes and *World War Z* enacts here nods towards the 2002–2003 SARS epidemic as a danger to the globalized world, but soon develops away from this simple and natural risk towards a political critique that sidelines the medical component of the plague. *World War Z* highlights early on that the world that is swept away by the zombie apocalypse is suffering from more problems than the undead and their viral infection. The doctor who diagnoses the first patient is "incarcerated without formal charges" (11); despite the disease, smuggling people between China and the outside booms due to bribery (13); there are illegal transplantations in Argentina using Chinese organs created by "political expediency" (i.e., executed prisoners; 23, 27), and helped along by the police (25), and systematic intelligence failures at the CIA (45–50). Each of these issues marks one of those "representative points" which demarcate together the reality of the political and economic system critiqued by *World War Z*, and to which the zombies are an immediate fantastic solution—or, at least, a means of breaking up the system.

Despite its global reach and the universality of the problems which it identifies, the heart of the novel's political criticism is not global: it lies in its narrative of the US reaction to the crisis, politically, socially, and militarily. Faced with the crisis, the US administration (a thinly veiled George W. Bush is president) finds itself unable to do more than surgical strikes using commando units, because the necessary "massive national undertaking [. . .]" is no longer thinkable. "That kind of effort [which] requires Herculean amounts of national treasure and national support" (52) has become impossible to marshal in the face of American apathy towards military solutions and disenchantment with the treatment of military veterans. The pointless and futile Iraq War, the narrative suggests, has grave consequences now, leaving the US both unwilling and unable to defend itself on the necessary scale. And even when it does act militarily, on the scale it is capable of, it fails to understand the nature of the threat, basing its tactics on the successful shock-and-awe of the Iraq War against an enemy that "can't be shocked and awed. [. . .] Not just won't, but biologically *can't!*" (104, original emphasis). Mismatched tactics, a misapprehension of the threat: *World War Z* sees its contemporary military forces as more of a hindrance than a help, and the very choice of traditional, high-tech military force as a fundamental mistake of politics.

At the same time, the business-friendliness of Bush's administration comes under fire because it permits the release of a worthless drug claimed to be a vaccine against the zombie disease: the novel's vociferous critique here becomes systemic, representing "big time, prewar, global capitalism" as a cynical game of playing with peoples' fears, and one which implicates an entire politico-industrial complex. Asked by the interviewer what would have happened if someone had discovered the uselessness of the drug, Breckinridge Scott, the drug's salesman, replies:

> Who was going to blow the whistle? The medical profession? We made sure it was a prescription drug so doctors stood just as much to lose as us. Who else? The FDA who let it pass? The congressmen who all voted for its acceptance? The surgeon general? The White House? It was a win-win situation! (57)

Politics, another interviewee informs the narrator, does not solve poverty, or crime, or disease, or unemployment, or war, but only makes it so that these problems do not impinge on one's power base (61). Pre-apocalyptic society in *World War Z* is deeply cynical, self-involved, racist, and unconcerned with the world outside each individual's own narrow concerns. As another interviewee notes of her prewar situation

> Oh yeah, I was worried, I was worried about my car payments and Tim's business loan. [. . .] I was worried about our portfolio, even though my e-broker assured me this was just first-time investor jitters and that it was much more profitable than a standard 401(k). (64)

At the same time that it identifies the pervasiveness of financial worry, the novel takes at least some glee in presenting the leveling effect of the plague: "very wealthy investment bankers" in "rumpled and torn" Armani suits (17), the vaccine producer's exile in Antarctica (54), the transplantation doctor's existence as "guest, mascot, or prisoner" somewhere in the Amazon rainforest (21). What the zombie apocalypse takes away, then, is certainly a set of concerns intimately tied to life under contemporary capitalism, from which the novel itself sees no other escape. Ultimately, however, it is not the systemic problem of capitalism that *World War Z* implicitly identifies as its central issue (even if it punishes the individuals complicit in the system). Rather, it is a whole host of smaller issues, each (because of the economic system's totalizing potential) certainly connected with capitalism, but, crucially, independently resolvable: militarism, an insufficient control of political power, clientele politics, reactionary neoconservativism. The major step towards the symbolic enactment of this smaller scale political change is the establishment of an American coalition government. Without explicitly naming names, the novel here envisages George W. Bush replaced by his vice president (Colin Powell)—Bush is apparently removed for disability—who nominates Howard Dean as his own vice president in turn (it even gestures, just perhaps, towards the possibility that Dean's Democratic Party might actually have wanted Barack Obama).

With that (and the successes which this coalition government achieves), the zombie apocalypse has swept away both a broken political system as well as what it conceives as a broken political ideology. To take up Evan Williams's words (though not his point), the zombies in *World War Z* "are the crisis which allows for powers that be to declare a 'state of emergency' [in which it is okay to sedate and remove the sitting president], to suspend normal channels of legislation and to bring about drastic changes" (2011, 105). This process becomes part of a liberal utopian solution to society's problems precisely because of the dysfunctionality of the existing normal channels; when change cannot happen within the system, it must come from the outside.

Perhaps it is more than merely suggestive to return here to the conclusion of *The Zombie Survival Guide* and its juxtaposition of two options: the future in which the zombie is easily contained, "an accepted part of daily life," and "all-out war" (247). *World War Z* at least initially suggests that the first solution to the problem of the zombie—whatever it may stand for—will not be simple acceptance. Such a peaceful resolution, the integration of the zombie, would also appear to be a conservative solution, one which changes nothing, and so the violence of the narrated "all-out war" suggests the novel's investment in a solution that is not conservative. *World War Z* insists on representing the underlying political and social problems of the contemporary as insolvable and indeed even unperceivable within the current political setup. The zombie apocalypse thus becomes both literally a revelation of these problems as well as a means of changing the world's politics. Yet, as we shall see, what it envisions as a future, its utopian visions, is an improved version of American liberal capitalism, rather than a genuine systemic change.

In each of its episodes of criticism, economical or political, *World War Z* highlights a problematic aspect of late capitalism and its neoconservative, neoliberal political manifestations. It does not, however, identify these individual points of data as symptoms of a larger problematic beyond reading it as a problem of the political (rather than the economic) system. Early on, Breckinridge Scott's question to the interviewer highlights the limited critique made in *World War Z*: "Do you understand economics? I mean big-time, pre-war, global capitalism? Do you get how it worked? I don't, and anyone who says they do is full of shit. There are no rules, no scientific absolutes. You win, you lose, it's a total crapshoot" (54–55). Scott's cynical and self-serving analysis is, on the one hand, clearly meant to offer a general appraisal of late capitalism circa 2006, a stepping stone in *World War Z*'s critique. Yet notice that the novel's insistence is on "pre-war, global" capitalism and not capitalism per se. Indeed, as the next section will show, it ends up seeing the re-establishment of the capitalist system as the final point in its imagination of the postapocalypse.

"Scarier than the Living Dead": The Liberal Utopian Postapocalypse

To be sure, very little of my initial reading of *World War Z*'s imagination of its contemporary situation requires literary interpretation: the novel wears its politics on its sleeve, and draws its characters and its analysis of the political and economic system in fairly broad strokes. Yet it bears mentioning these elements of the novel because they set the stage for its initially radical, finally negligent imagination of the *post*–apocalyptic world. One of the features that sets Brooks's novel apart from its peers (and indeed, from almost literally all zombie *films*) is that it is avowedly postapocalyptic, a counterexample to Evan Williams's claim that "the vision of the zombie apocalypse is never a postapocalyptic vision, not a single event and revelation out of which we regroup and attempt to rebuild" (2011, 85). In fact, its apocalyptic, revelatory moment already lies in its narrative past: while zombies persist, and, as far as we can tell, zombification remains the fate of all those who die with their brains intact, they have after all been seamlessly integrated into the evolved but still-existing system. The novel is in fact just as interested in what the zombies reveal about its contemporary moment—that is, in the apocalyptic potential of the zombie—as in what they may fantastically enable in the zombie's postapocalyptic appeal.

World War Z's postwar situation cannot be reduced to people "cooperatively providing for their own food, shelter, and defense" (Collins and Bond 2011, 193), though an intensified communitarianism is certainly one of the features of its postapocalyptic vision. Rather than seeing a society barely past the threshold of a primitive social contract, the aftermath of war in *World War Z* shows a resurgent humanity that has established a coherent system of international cooperation, a restructured but resilient capitalist economic system, and a clearer appreciation of private, communal cooperation.[2] Technological advances have lessened the world's reliance on fossil fuels, locally based economies have (at least in part) substituted for the global, and international, transnational cooperation has replaced national competition. Each of these points of data reveal *World War Z*'s underlying belief in the efficacy, the necessity, of positions broadly to be conceived as "liberal" (in the American political sense) and social-democratic or indeed Green elsewhere.

It is in bits and pieces that *World War Z* reveals its advocacy of liberal politics through the description of a world in which the values of liberal democracy have already succeeded. The headnote for the second interview is perhaps the first instance highlighting this belief in progressive politics after the apocalypse. In Lhasa, now the most populous city on Earth, and the capital of the People's Republic of Tibet, free elections bring the Social Democratic Party to power (12). In at once imagining a free Tibet, the possibility of free and fair elections in what would conventionally be thought to be a Communist dictatorship (as in the People's Republics of China and North Korea), and in the outcome of this election (a win by a Social Democrat party), *World War Z* manages to put a number of pointers towards its belief in liberal politics together. Numerous other instances, most of them in headnotes and hardly ever emphasized narratively, combine to fill out this picture. In Barbados, the interviewer describes the future of nautical commerce, trimaran-hulled sleek, fuel-celled "infinity ships" (28). Control of the ongoing anti-zombie operations at the arctic circle rest with a UN-led—rather than a national—force (50). In Amarillo, Texas, oil has given way to biofuel plants using cow dung (59), serviced by a former member of the Bush administration. In America's "New Community" housing model, solar panels and small gardens render inhabitants independent of greater economic structures (63–64). "Radio Free Earth," broadcasting globally without regard for nationality, is described as "the first real international venture" (194–95); and finally, newly constructed buildings are "energy-independent" (228). Each of these issues figures as a data point in a larger picture of the results of the zombie war, and each of them implicitly redounds to the victory of liberal ideals.

Frequently, these victories take the form of overcoming the kinds of stereotypical enmities which, *World War Z* implies, must necessarily take a backseat when faced with a newer, common enemy. Perhaps the clearest example of this underlying belief in the power of external threats is *World War Z*'s treatment of the Palestine-Israeli conflict. The Israeli response to the zombie apocalypse is narrated by a Palestinian refugee living with his family in Kuwait. Israel decides to impose upon itself a voluntary quarantine, one that extends its welcome to "any foreign-born Jew, any foreigner of Israeli-born parents" and, most notably, "any Palestinian living in the formerly occupied territories, and any Palestinian whose family had once lived within the borders of Israel" (37). As the choice of words indicates, the Israelis have already left Gaza, and a "Unified Palestine" is slated to come into existence. Despite this apparent two-state solution to the Palestine-Israeli conflict, then, Israel has decided to also protect what are now, for all intents and purposes, foreigners. The Palestinian interviewee sees through what he believes is a ruse:

> Here's what I thought: The Zionists have just been driven out of the occupied territories, they say they left voluntarily, just like Lebanon, and most recently the Gaza Strip, but really, just like before, we knew we'd driven them out. They know that the next and final blow would destroy that illegal atrocity they call a country, and to prepare for that final blow, they're attempting to recruit both foreign Jews as cannon fodder and . . . *and*—I thought I was so clever for figuring this part out—kidnapping as many Palestinians as they could to act as human shields! I had all the answers. Who doesn't at seventeen? (38, original emphasis)

Instead of seeking shelter under Israel's protection, the interviewee is prepared to join a terrorist youth organization. Dragged by his father against his will to Israel, he finds himself surprised and eventually brought around to seeing the justice of Israel's actions. Israel, under a coalition government, finally sees its way to opposing its own religious right (still strongly against Palestine and against the abandonment of settlements) to the extent of accepting a civil war in which the Israeli Army defends both Israelis and Palestinians. The zombie apocalypse here paves the way to the rational appreciation of an ostensibly unsolvable conflict. While we never discover the reason for Israel's decision to also shelter Palestinians, the decision permits the novel to suggest the validity of both the two-state and the one-state solutions to the problem: both are, effectively, enacted in *World War Z*. What ultimately solves the Palestine-Israeli conflict is not, indeed, either of these solutions, but rather the decision to abandon conflict. This overcomes even the deeply ingrained hostility of the would-be terrorist and now-supporter of Israel who, by the time of his interview, has become a town-planning professor at a university in Bethlehem.

A similar emphasis on the symbolic, personal, emotional solutions to inter- and intrasocietal conflict underlies the novel's discussion of South Africa. The plan which ultimately proves successful in installing safe zones in most countries has been developed here for a vastly different purpose. Its origins lie in the apartheid government's longstanding "Plan Orange," which "was the doomsday scenario for the country's white minority, the plan to deal with an all-out uprising of its indigenous African population" (106). Developed by a white Afrikaner, Paul Redeker, it becomes the blueprint by which South Africa is able to fight its war against the zombies. It also becomes the point where South Africa most demonstrably finds its peace with apartheid. Redeker, living in disgrace in a lonely cabin, is found and brought away by an intelligence agency team composed of agents of "all colors: black, Asian, colored, and even a white man" (108). In a similarly ostentatious, and maudlin, moment, Redeker finds that his presence and his plan have been personally requested by (the unnamed but recognizable) Nelson Mandela: "And then came that moment, the one that historians will probably debate until the subject fades from memory. He embraced the white Afrikaner" (110). The embrace shatters Redeker into the discovery of his own black African side, so that, when the interviewer encounters him in the psychiatric clinic to which he has been remanded, he lives there under an adopted indigenous African name (105). The South African episode is remarkable both for its implicit and problematical call back to the equation between a black uprising and a zombie apocalypse that engaged, especially, the zombie films of the 1930s. It is also interesting for its overt suggestion that the lasting conflict between black and white is not at heart a consequence of the problematical heritage of apartheid—especially economic inequality—but rather an easily transcended emotional boundary. In other words, if only people had simply accepted and embraced one another as being equal "persons of my region," as Mandela has it (110), there would be an escaping of the racial divide.

Paul Redeker himself puts what amounts to *World War Z*'s view of racism best: "racism is a regrettable by-product of irrational emotion" (106), rather than a structural problem. As Margo Collins and Elson Bond note, in Brooks's narrative, there is almost "no racial component" (2011, 191). Brooks's somewhat blithe solution to the problems of apartheid is even more surprising given that one of the first outbreak narratives we get is set in a Cape Town township, in which the residue of apartheid oppression still lingers measurably, and in which the old instincts to run when "'they' were ever coming" (30) are still ingrained. *World War Z* is, at times, fully aware that racism cannot be so easily overcome. In narrating the political developments in the United States, the replacement of Bush by Colin Powell, and his own elevation to the vice presidency, Howard Dean notes in his interview: "I knew I wasn't the first choice. I know who my party secretly wanted. But America wasn't ready to go that far, as stupid, ignorant, and infuriatingly Neolithic as it sounds. They'd rather have a screaming radical for a VP than another one of 'those people' [this may be veiled reference to Barack Obama]" (147). We should not miss that Dean's reference to how "Neolithic" this sounds makes clear that the kinds of sentiments he is referring to have also passed, certainly for him and his interlocutor, but more likely more broadly. The passing of race as a point of contention appears to span most of the globe: it is an issue of the past.

There are clear limits, then, to the possibility of envisaging a postracial society even in the aftermath of apocalypse; and, if *World War Z* offers "challenges to racism" (131), it does so within the limits of its own realist liberal worldview. Not only does *World War Z* suggest that in the face of the zombie plague, "racial, political, and religious divides [. . .] are forgotten" (Collins and Bond 2011, 190): more importantly, they are never remembered afterwards. In practical terms, then, *World War Z* considers divides such as the Israeli-Palestinian conflict and the South African legacies of apartheid as largely the products not of systematic political and economic oppression (which, of course, the largely unreconstructed systems restituted in the novel would also reproduce), but of something like a lack of imagination. If it is the immediate danger of the zombie apocalypse that brings people to surmount their differences, there is nothing that would have necessarily prevented any similar rapprochement before that apocalypse. *World War Z*, in other words, expects the solution to these problems to lie in simple human acts, in not merely asking if we cannot all live together, but rather in deciding that yes, we can all simply live together. If this is clearly a utopian vision of the postapocalyptic world, it is also a simplistic one.

Most notable and crucial in identifying the limits of *World War Z*'s utopian vision, however (and this brings us back at least somewhat to the world-system), is the way the novel treats old-fashioned labor. Labor becomes symptomatic of its reading of the possibilities of the postapocalypse, an apparently systematic critique that is never fully realized. Establishing a so-called safe zone behind the Rocky Mountains, the remaining United States embarks on a program that fundamentally restructures the nature of work in the US. As Arthur Sinclair, director of the department of strategic resources, notes in his interview, "[o]urs was a postindustrial or service-based economy, so complex and highly specialized that each individual could only function within the confines of its narrow, compartmentalized structure [...] We needed carpenters, masons, machinists, gunsmiths" not the financial analysts, day traders, executives, consultants, and others, who under the new conditions now are labeled as "possessing no valued vocation" (138–39). As with the various developments of localizing energy and food production, the general tendency of the novel here is to emphasize use-value over exchange-value, manual labor over the kinds of work which merely perpetuate the infinite creation of capital, and to explicitly denounce these latter occupations as valueless. The novel explicitly recognizes the potential of such a development as shattering, and puts it into an easily recognizable version of Marx's general formula of capital, MCM, the system in which money makes more money through the production of commodities:

> The more work you do, the more money you make, the more peons you hire to free you up to make more money. That's the way the world works. But one day it doesn't. No one needs a contract reviewed or a deal brokered. What it does need is toilets fixed. And suddenly that peon is your teacher, maybe even your boss. For some, this was scarier than the living dead. (140)

World War Z's take on labor, in other words, seems deeply critical of the contemporary economic system's priorities, and, at least tentatively, to be on the verge of systemic critique, suggesting that its postapocalyptic society recognizes the value of unalienated labor and has already produced major shifts in the perception of survivors. It is here, however, that the novel's imagination runs into difficulties related to the by-now almost stereotypical insight that it is "easier to imagine the end of the world than it is to imagine the end of capitalism" (Jameson 2003, 76). Indeed, it is in part the unexpected resilience of capitalism that, in *World War Z*'s narrative, marks yet another aspect of its specifically liberal utopia. "Cuba won the zombie war," as one interviewee says: as Brooks's novel narrates it, through a combination of military preparedness and communist ruthlessness, Cuba successfully manages both to keep itself safe as well as to integrate a large number of US refugees. Yet this integration leads to a great change in Cuba: the island, once the last existing socialist country in the western hemisphere, becomes, almost naturally, a liberal Western capitalist democracy. As the novel describes it:

> Over the next several years what occurred was not so much a revolution as an evolution, an economic reform here, a legalized, privately owned newspaper there. People began to think more boldly, talk more boldly. Slowly, quietly, the seeds began to take root. [. . .] We had money, lots of it, money that created an overnight middle class, and a thriving, capitalist economy that needed the refined skills and practical experience of the Nortecubanos [as the US immigrants are called]. (232)

Cuba becomes a democracy, a capitalist "superpower," in what is a suitably ironical reversal of roles. The Cuban interviewee sums up the Cuban experience with a quote from Churchill: democracy is the worst form of government, except for all the others. As Slavoj Žižek notes so perceptively: the Churchill quote "holds even better for liberalism," which, seeing little prospect for any radical betterment of the human condition giving human nature, "presents itself as the best of all possible worlds; its modest rejection of utopias ends with the imposition of its own market-liberal utopia" (2011, 38). If Cuba cannot but become a liberal, capitalist democracy, it is small surprise that the US, too, ultimately finds its creation of a use-value based economy merely a measure of expediency for the immediate state of emergency. By the time the interviews are conducted, this emergency has passed and the postapocalyptic society gets back onto its economic tracks. As Sinclair states in his final interview: "Getting people away from barter, and to trust the American dollar again . . . not easy. [. . .] Confidence, it's the fuel that drives the capitalist machine" (337). Then, having established that his new primary goal will be to get Americans away from using Cuban pesos and back to dollars again, he hands the interviewer a bottle of root beer, the same drink that had earlier figured as a symbol for the problematic global connections that had made the establishment of the local manufacturing that saved human civilization such a hassle. Both capitalism and globalization are here to stay; whatever critique the novel had lavished at these systems become lost in the impossibility to imagine an "after" to capitalism in this world.

In the way it initially appears to revalidate labor, *World War Z* seems to be prepared for a more radical critique of its contemporary moment than it is ultimately able to sustain. Not only is *World War Z*'s vision for the postapocalypse based on the return to the economic status quo ante, including the kinds of currency wars and globalized economies that the novel had both implicitly condemned and then explicitly shown to be dangerous, but it also offers barely any rationale for this return. Within the economy of use-values that Sinclair's department has set up, it is not clear that there is any room or indeed any need for getting away from barter, as Sinclair insists needs to be done. The capitalist system is simply ingrained: it imposes itself on the new world order as readily as it had on the old not on the strength of what it can do, but due to the failure to imagine alternatives even when those alternatives have been proven to work. It is here that *World War Z*'s imagination fails most signally: it is not that it cannot imagine an end to capitalism, but that having imagined it, having explored its failures and its limits, and having replaced it with the beginnings of a system in which use-value dominates in localized and nationalized economies both, it foregoes it without comment.

Conclusion: If Only We Chucked the Politics

I begin this book with *World War Z* for several reasons. As the first widely successful zombie novel, it deserves pride of place: without its success, it certainly is debatable whether zombie fiction would have taken off as it did. But more importantly, *World War Z* lets us see the main points I want to make about zombie fiction. It is apocalyptic, and it uses its apocalyptic moment to imagine a postapocalypse. It opens to view possibilities contingent on the radical destruction offered by a zombie apocalypse; and it fails to fully realize the potentials it itself sees. It signals that there is a difference between the enabling of narratives capable of thinking of different societies and the actual realization of a radically progressive vision for the future.

World War Z's ethics is best exemplified in its own words: "Who knows what we could have accomplished if we had only chucked the politics and come together as human bloody beings" (262). It is this celebration of voluntary collectivity that the novel produces both in its content as well as in its form. The greater vision of the postapocalypse is assembled through the kaleidoscope of individual narratives of survivors; and, as noted, these individual narratives are perceptively selected to highlight some of the most notable problems of *World War Z*'s contemporary moment, performing as points on a larger cognitive map that plots the anxieties of its day. Apocalypse figures into it as a means of revealing these anxieties, and as a means to imagine change. In *World War Z* (and elsewhere), "zombies," as Evan Williams suggests, are the fantasy form of the real necessity of "creative destruction" (2011, 104) that precedes radical systemic change. They permit the kinds of interventions into the (political) system that enable the novel to conceive of alternatives to the existing: a world focused to a much greater extent on international cooperation, on small-scale societal cohesion, on advanced and progressive technologies capable of supporting human civilization in the long term. Indeed, contrary to critics' readings, "highly advanced technology" does not "occup[y] an ambivalent place" (Collins and Bond 2011, 193) in *World War Z*. It is resoundingly celebrated, unless it is military technology, because most of the technology we see is green technology: solar panels, solar-energy plate glass, fuel-cell engines for ships, biofuel power plants. *World War Z* emphasizes that these technologies are game-changers. They will permit humanity's lasting survival, and thus counteract the dangers of neoconservative industrial politics of the early 2000s with their disregard for ecological damage. Significantly, however, these technologies serve as mere signposts in *World War Z*'s larger progressive narrative. To become better "bloody human beings" is the novel's chief answer to the problems it identifies: "racial, political, and religious divides that had separated the nation[s'] peoples are forgotten"; and its postapocalyptic scenario depicts a "regeneration following the plague's scouring" (Collins and Bond 2011, 190).

Apocalypse in *World War Z* thus functions as the place for the revelation of the particular anxieties of the novel's historic moment and its belief that these anxieties are largely the product of a particular brand of politics within a largely workable, indeed necessary, economic system; postapocalypse functions as the place where an alternative society may be envisaged and explained. The novel's agenda thus is necessarily both apocalyptic and postapocalyptic, simultaneously requiring the exposition and dismantling of the old as well as the creation of the new; it is not, as is the case in so many other texts in its genre, merely interested in survival after the end of contemporary social system. Rather, it is avowedly utopian, emphasizing throughout its suggestions for post–collapse alternative, better ways of living.

These better ways are, to be sure, not all-encompassing. *World War Z* enacts a liberal democratic triumph that is nearly—but, significantly, not entirely—global: Russian recidivism into religious extremism is a notable exception to the rule that in the aftermath of apocalypse, progress has been achieved. Yet even in its resistance to totalizing the liberal democratic victory, it is possible to see its insistence on the ideal liberal order. To imagine—indeed, to narrate with some sympathy—another system, no matter how different and no matter how apparently incommensurable with the ideals of the liberal rest of the world, is to affirm also the historical necessity of pluralism. If, as Russell Jacoby has it, liberalism's ascendancy in the wake of the collapse of the Soviet Union killed the utopian imagination (leaving it with nowhere to go, and no sense of real alternatives), it is perhaps necessary for *World War Z* to disavow liberalism's global triumph. Only in positing it as a genuine systemic alternative, only in contrasting it with other, clearly worse systems, can it also function as a utopian vision of the future.

But the way it does so is disappointing on its own terms. It is precisely because of its belief in the possibility of (mere) regeneration, as Collins and Bond have it, that Mark McGurl is vastly too optimistic about the "utopian dimension" of Brooks's novel. When "the starkly depopulated post-WWZ world turns to Cuba as the engine of the renewal of global commerce," this Cuba can hardly stand for a "'phase shift' in the ecological and social systems we inhabit" ("Zombie Renaissance"); after all, it is explicitly a *capitalist* Cuba that emerges stronger from the destruction of the pre-apocalyptic society. It is also difficult to subscribe to Aalya Ahmad's suggestion that *World War Z* offers a genuine "vision" of survivors setting out to "rebuild their world along radically different lines" (2011, 139; see also Ahmad 2010). Brooks's novel is utopian only in the narrow sense that it envisages a liberal utopia of international cooperation, of bipartisan politics (its politics being either international or American), of collective, social-democratic resurgence. The world dismantled in Brooks's novel is neoliberal and neoconservative and capitalist; the world rising from the ashes is (in its better parts) social-democratic and communal—and capitalist, too. Given the acuity with which Brooks's narrative had highlighted the necessity of envisaging new conceptions for labor, for community, and for the economy at large, *World War Z*'s hesitant economic progressivism reflects the limits of its utopian imagination.

Pariah and Dying to Live
Imagining Community after the Apocalypse

Bram Stoker's *Dracula* (1890), perhaps the epitome of literary horror fiction, ends with the victory of good over evil, with the destruction of the vampire and the safe return of most of the protagonists. Yet strikingly, in doing so it does not avow the status quo, as Gregory Waller has pointed out. The group of protagonists that succeeds in eradicating the individualistic evil which Dracula represents are "a moral community that is both fully opposed to the egotism and evil of the undead and completely divorced from and at times even antipathetic to the institutions, laws, and modern beliefs of late Victorian society" (2010, 42). The small group of women and men struggling against Dracula manage their survival only as a group, but a group that is not society at large: instead, it is a community of common interest and shared ideals at odds with larger society. Even if "this community is not formed expressly as a utopian social experiment or as a self-conscious political and cultural alternative to the status quo" (43), *Dracula* suggests both the need for such a community in the face of modernity's unraveling of alternative social structures as well as the quasi-apocalyptic belief that "such a community will only arise when man is forced to confront and do battle with a threat the magnitude of the King-Vampire, when life, in other words, becomes quite literally a struggle for survival" (44).

Community, then, "the most ancient myth of the Western world" (Nancy 1991, 10), lies at the heart of Stoker's implicit imagination of a utopian alternative to the existing—and the impending—social conditions of his age. I begin this chapter with a reference to Stoker's novel because it highlights the ways in which, historically, horror fiction has been used to discuss the possibility of imagining community, and because it emphasizes the preconditions by which horror fiction is capable of such an imagination. *Dracula* stresses the necessity of existential terror, of the fear of death, and of the collapse of existing society, as a precondition for *imagining* community; while to imagine *community* requires something different yet. As Gerard Delanty notes, the contemporary resurgence of the "idea of community is related to the search for belonging in the insecure conditions of modern society" (2009, x). Now as then, these fragile conditions are being explored by authors of horror fiction: zombie fiction, as I will argue below, takes up this challenge to be a vehicle for the contestation of forms of human communal living as alternatives to existing society. As explicitly apocalyptic horror fiction—narrating life after "the end" of the world—it asks questions about the possibility of imagining forms of social life different from those which the apocalypse has expunged.

If the example of *World War Z* showed zombie fiction's capacity to imagine large scale changes in society's make-up—even with the limits noted in Chapter 1—zombie fiction is also capable of representing the more intimate question of the contemporary meaning and possibility of community. I will discuss the contestation of forms of community in Kim Paffenroth's *Dying to Live* and Bob Fingerman's *Pariah*. Both novels hew to the time-honored premises of a zombie apocalypse, in which complete societal collapse is followed by individual struggles for survival; in the case of Paffenroth's and Fingerman's novels, however, this struggle for survival becomes the struggle to survive in and as community. In the sheer imagination of their versions of community—difficult though they are—both *Pariah* and *Dying to Live* already also imagine a form of utopia. Community, Zygmunt Bauman notes, "stands for the kind of world which is not, regrettably, available to us—but which we would dearly wish to inhabit and which we hope to repossess" (2001, 3). Community always implies a resistance to the state's (and the capitalist system's) insistence on a solitary identity: utopia in these novels thus resides in the possibility of imagining a radical and apocalyptic break with the statist present in order to envisage better forms of living (Agamben 1993, 85–86; Bauman 2001, 15–17; Bloch 1980, 70). From their similar generic premise, *Dying to Live* and *Pariah* produce different visions of communal existence as utopian visions of life after the end of the contemporary world. They enact literarily what Chris Wright sees as the "search for 'community'" at the heart of a quest to "reclaim the future" (2000, 93).

In what follows, then, I will juxtapose the two versions of apocalypse and resurgent community that the novels envisage. In *Dying to Live*, we follow Jonah Caine, the somewhat heavy-handedly named narrator, in his journey into an unnamed town in which he hopes to find supplies. Noticed by zombies and increasingly in danger of being caught, he receives help from a well-organized group of other survivors holed up in the city's brick-walled museum. Jonah is taken in by this group, discovering for the first time a workable community of fellow survivors, led by the half-zombie, half-human Milton, who can move without danger among the undead. The dangers in *Dying to Live* lie outside the museum, in another group of survivors holed up in a nearby prison. In narrating the defeat of this outside threat, *Dying to Live* envisages the final victory of the museum community, which even transcends the need for Milton's ability to move among the zombies. *Dying to Live* narrates the success of a community bound by rules and responsibilities and motivated by a quasi-religious figure whose moral guidance and physical support secures the community's existence, but whom the community must ultimately transcend.

By contrast, the vision of community in *Pariah* is much more narrow, indeed more ambivalent about the possibility of community. The novel focuses on the survivors living in a single apartment building in New York, cut off by the masses of undead outside their windows and struggling with their internal differences. Like *Dying to Live*, *Pariah* features a character who can survive outside because the zombies will not attack her: Mona, who arrives at the apartment house by chance. Through Mona's help, the steadily dwindling group of survivors escapes starvation but needs to combat their internal troubles. Ultimately, in *Pariah* it is the elimination of the internal threat which permits something like a community to come into existence, a community into which Mona integrates herself instead of continuing her solitary life outside. *Pariah*'s vision remains tentative and uneasy, however: where *Dying to Live* establishes a vision of a lasting future for the museum community, *Pariah* only hints at the possibility of long-term survival, suggesting the fragility of any kind of communal life.

Despite their different conclusions, *Dying to Live* and *Pariah* both speak to the contemporary resurgence of an interest in community, as well as to the apparent impossibility of envisaging it outside the complete collapse of existing society. Between them, then, the two novels employ the possibilities of zombie fiction to negotiate visions of communal living as utopian alternatives to contemporary life. Milton and Mona are the key figures in both books precisely because their lives within the communities of survivors are voluntary: either could leave at any time. Mona, especially, perhaps should leave, given the dangers of remaining inside. Their services to the community indicates the importance which the two novels ascribe to the sense of communal living. Perhaps counterintuitively, both Milton's ultimate move outside the community and Mona's move inside validate their respective communities and, more importantly, the importance of the concept of community to contemporary fiction. Milton can leave because he has established a successful, prospering community of survivors which can last without him; Mona can stay because the community of survivors has finally become safe. In either case, a stable community becomes the benchmark by which postapocalyptic survival can be called successful: rather than the re-establishment of civilization at large, both novels rest content at having created a small-scale, successful form of human social life.

The Community of Others: *Dying to Live*

I begin with what may initially seem like a detour. Jean-Luc Nancy is perhaps the most prominent, if ambivalent, critic of the idea of community. For Nancy, community as it is usually understood is an inherently nostalgic concept, an idealistic but flawed call-back to a past that never really existed in the first place. Its mythos nevertheless inspires attempts at its reconstitution, which, almost inevitably, aligns the ostensible members of the community against some Other, usually racial, ethnic, or cultural; community, in this sense, serves as a way of keeping outsiders out as much as a way of keeping insiders together. This is a "politically inspired mythological vision of community" (Hutchens 2005, 15). Against this, Nancy proposes to understand community as an open, insubstantial linkage of what he calls the "community of being": "something very much like a 'feeling' at the moments of sharing in contact between irreducibly singular beings who do not even share the property of 'belonging together' in a cohesive group" (104–5).

Nancy, then, is clearly suspicious of all tendencies that seek a return to the mythical community in the contemporary; and to that extent, the communities constituted in *Pariah* and *Dying to Live* run counter to his analysis. Nonetheless, I would suggest that much of his argument can be fruitfully, if at times only suggestively, connected to the discussion of community which these two novels offer. Most importantly, perhaps, Nancy has connected the experience of death with the experience of community, and highlighted the importance of understanding community precisely not as the sublation of death—as when masses of soldiers go their deaths in the service of the nation—or a transcendent essence lasting beyond the individual's death (cf. Nancy 1994, 12–15). As Nancy puts it, "[c]ommunity is revealed in the death of others; hence it is always revealed to others" (15). The connection drawn by Nancy between the witnessing of death and the way in which this experience of death as a loss of the shared connection constituting community is suggestive for novels in which the experience of death is literally omnipresent. One might contend that the facts on the ground of the zombie apocalypse reveal fundamentally what Nancy suggests about the nature of death and the nature of community. If a "community is the presentation to its members of their mortal truth" (15), the conditions of a world in which the dead being remains bodily speaks more eloquently of the truth of mortality than any ever so extensive burial rite. Nancy speaks of the need for "identification with the living body of the community" (9); such formulations seem oddly apropos in novels in which most bodies are mobile but dead.[1] If it is impossible to draw any political practice from Nancy's sense of what community is, we are nevertheless pointed to the need to think about community and to regard such thinking as in and of itself a challenge to ideologies denying community's possibility in whatever form. In a simple—admittedly, probably too simple—parsing for my purposes here, death and reanimation in zombie fiction reveal to survivors their potential for community by juxtaposing overtly their own "living bodies" with the dead bodies that are a group but clearly not a community—forces them to recognize, in fact, the fundamentally communal nature of their status as the living. What is usually hidden by burial practice, religious tradition, and patriotic fervor is that death does not sublate the individual into a "community, yet to come" (13) but is instead a mere "cessation." Zombie fictions present the spectacle of the cessation of life in the permanent presence of the dead.

It is helpful, I would contend, to take in Nancy's philosophy of community even if it is at this stage no more than suggestive of a conceptualization of the interplay between the specific conditions of a zombie apocalypse and the search for a human way of living in and with that apocalypse, of living in and with the presence of the living dead. Though lacking in subtlety, Kim Paffenroth's novel juxtaposes three ways of dealing with life after the societal collapse. Jonah Caine's initial existence is solitary, as his double-outcast name suggests. He moves from place to place, scavenging for food, medical supplies, and safe harbors. It is a life filled with extreme danger and little payoff. Mere collective life, however, is not the answer, either: the prison group he and others encounter later epitomizes perhaps the worst possible existence, one in which strength and violence rule and which does not build but destroys—it is a society red in tooth and claw, as it were. Against these modes of existence after the collapse of society, the novel sets the idealized community which grows up in and around the museum complex which serves as the main setting of the book. Indeed, Paffenroth's community within the museum's walls seems at times almost too good to be true, and this makes it all the more surprising that *Dying to Live* foregoes the obvious gambit of making it collapse from internal strife: instead, it affirmatively builds up the museum community as a successful utopian venture.

Dying to Live sets out its own theory of community very early: Jonah Caine has been braving the dangers of the zombie apocalypse alone for some time but notes that there was a natural tendency to band together. As Caine describes it,

Groups of survivors quickly came together into little groups, little communities with a pecking order and rules and authority, but also some of the little perks of being around other people—companionship, conversation, sex, someone to hold your hand when you die, someone to put a bullet in your brain when you went to get back up as a zombie. [. . .] You didn't have to be a damned philosopher to know that we're social animals, and would be till the last zombie bit the last human and dragged us all down to hell, which, judging by the zombies, looked like it was going to be the most unsociable place imaginable.

Yes, humans always build their little communities in order to survive, and in order to make surviving a little more bearable. Except me. I was alone. And it sucked. (8)

On the one hand, the impetus towards community here is both emotional as well as practical, involving both rules and companionship, and it contrasts with the "life" led by the zombies; yet on the other, it remains somewhat vague and unspecific: how precisely are those "little communities" constituted? This is the question that lies at the heart of the novel. Caine's wanderings take him into an unnamed city, where, still alone, he is cornered by a horde of zombies. He survives because he is rescued by a group of survivors living in the town's high-walled museum complex. The group takes Caine safely inside the museum. Under the guidance of Jack, who leads the sally that brings Caine in, he is introduced to some of the protocols that make the museum work: he surrenders his weapons and bag, and is given a brief tour of the complex. Caine shares in the communal meal and then splits a bottle of bourbon with a smaller number of the survivors. Awakening the next day, Caine, for the first time since the beginning of the apocalypse, has "an overall feeling of well-being, of safety, and belonging" (51). Belonging is a central concern for all conceptions of community (cf. Delanty 2009, xiii): here, it becomes especially poignant in its opposition to Caine's prior existence. At the same time, such a feeling of belonging is not a sufficient condition for the existence of community. Caine has been introduced to the workings of the museum community, but in order to become a member, he must integrate himself more firmly within its rules and customs.

Paffenroth's novel is clearly concerned with the question of what it takes to be communal, and the difficult but necessary transition entailed in becoming a member of a community. Caine is asked to take part in a training exercise in which he would have to exhibit his fighting prowess:

I realized then the difficulties of joining this new community. Like Popcorn [a young boy who lives in the museum community], I'd picked up killing on my own, it was a private, emotional, and most of all, shameful ordeal each time.

Now I'd have to do it in front of others, and play at it, and joke about it. It would definitely take some getting used to. (59)

Caine recognizes that entering successfully into the museum community will entail making the private public, and opening up to the group. Yet this abandonment of the private is not negatively connoted: indeed, as Bauman notes, there is a necessary connection between insecurity (such as Caine experienced while moving alone through the country) and privacy (cf. 2001, 144). Notably, Caine evinces no doubt about the necessity and correctness of abandoning privacy for the security of community: it "would definitely take some getting used to," to be sure, but will clearly be worth it. This belief is reaffirmed later as well: having saved other survivors, Frank and his infant daughter Zoey, from a flat near the city's hospital, the group probes the depths of his experiences. Finding that Frank is keeping something from them, Caine notes: "It was an uplifting, almost inspirational story, but we all knew we couldn't leave it at that. It was another Pandora's box, only this one was now a part of our community, so he had to open up" (135). Private anguish cannot be allowed to fester, lest it break free and endanger the community; sharing one's troubles is the answer, even if it does not occur out of one's own free will. Indeed, Frank finally submits successfully to the repeated proddings of the group to open up. His pregnant wife, bitten by a zombie, died in their barricaded apartment; returning as a zombie, she did not go for Frank, but rather tore open her own uterus to get at her unborn, living baby (this may be allusion to *Dawn of the Dead* [2004]), forcing Frank to kill her (140). Making Frank tell this story is both cathartic for him as well as necessary for the community; it gives him the option of being a full, willing, and active member, who eventually sacrifices himself for the community which has rescued him.

This notion that life in a community depends on the acceptance of a set of rules, all of which are designed to foster the existence of the community, is echoed repeatedly in Paffenroth's novel. There cannot be "the joy of belonging without the discomfort of being bound" (Bauman 2001, 69). Rules and responsibilities naturally—and inseparably—structure life in the museum community:

> Some were straightforward [. . .]: no weapons, no hoarding food, no stealing, hands off anybody else's man or woman. The usual Ten Commandments stuff. Rules for sanitation and for dealing with infected people. Rules of settling disputes. But once we had those, Milton still thought there had to be something more, something other than prohibitions. Responsibilities, something that made us a community and not just a bunch of people who still had a pulse and had ended up at the same place. So we started having two levels of citizenship.

> First, if you're part of the community, then you work. You do whatever you're good at, and we all take turns with the jobs nobody wants. If you don't work, you don't eat. We'd already pretty much been doing that, but we made sure it was a rule, and everybody agreed to it. [. . .] Then we had the trickier one, the one that would involve an initiation rite. We decided that anybody could stay here and be protected, so long as they did some kind of work, but they couldn't be full citizens and participate in making the group's decisions unless they fought. If you don't fight, you don't vote. (61)

Dying to Live offers community in a two-tiered system. Becoming a citizen in this community requires public service: a journey outside the walls to secure supplies, luxury items in particular, such as toys, books, and other non-essentials. *Dying to Live* echoes Robert Heinlein's much-derided *Starship Troopers* (1959) here in its insistence on a demonstration of a will to community prior to the full adoption in the citizenry of the museum. And like Heinlein's novel, it also distinguishes between mere membership in the community—a path chosen by several of the people in the museum—and full citizenship. The community of survivors does not abandon anyone to their fate (unlike the collective housed in the prison, of which more in a minute), and it does not measure individual worth, but honors individual engagement with a greater role. And, most notably, and in a significant departure from the system of *Starship Troopers*, the sort of service required of prospective members of community are not merely utilitarian: they are explicitly geared towards securing for the community the "beautiful and uplifting." It is going out to face the undead in an effort to secure such items that "made people ready to enter the community" (81), as the community's "not exactly" (35) leader, Milton, has it.

Milton is the most enigmatic of the characters in the novel. He shares something like a leadership role with Jack, but, as Jack notes, he is "more like the pope or the dalai lama" (35) to Jack's businesslike practical guidance of everyday matters. Milton, as we find out a little while later, is indeed special: a survivor from a research facility that investigates the biological aspects of the zombie outbreak, he and a colleague are bitten by what they take to be zombified dogs. Despite their wounds, they survive, and discover that something has changed in them: they are in constant pain, they smell like they are decaying, but in return, they repel the zombies around them. Milton eventually finds his way to the museum, where his gift comes in remarkably handy. Able to go wherever he pleases, Milton is able to gather supplies of all kinds without any danger. More than a mere tool, however, Milton becomes a spiritual focus for the community, behind whom the community can come together. The community's rules, to be sure, have to a large extent been created by Milton. His condition made the incipient museum community initially see him as a "messiah sent to save them" (65), yet Milton's role eventually developed out of his study of "books on history, literature, politics, philosophy, mythology, religion" (66) to create a working model of community. By the time the novel meets him, Milton has become less of a savior than someone who can "motivate people to organize politically, to have an agenda and make sacrifices to accomplish something and become something greater than themselves" (82). He serves the community gladly—"[m]y pain is a little price to pay to help build up this community" (79), he notes—but recognizes the ambivalence of his leadership. He refuses to consider his ability as anything but a "wild, unforeseeable side effect of a mutant virus" (78), even as the others are ready to accept him as a miracle, as somebody sent by God, even as a savior figure. But, as Milton notes, "[n]o one is really a savior, I don't think. I think we just help each other. Or, we're supposed to" (79). He embodies the spirit of community that has kept the museum's people alive—but, as he himself notes, he is not the cause of their survival. Rather, it is the work undertaken by the community itself, its rules and its actions, that keeps people alive and prosperous.

Such a reading is only superficially complicated by the major action of the novel. Following signs of human habitation, Jonah and Jack, on reconnaissance with Frank, Tanya, and Popcorn, discover that the local prison is apparently occupied by living people. As befits the somewhat heavy-handed symbology of museum community versus prison group, Jonah and the rest of his group (save Jack, who is left behind wounded) are captured by the violent group of prisoners that has made the penitentiary their lasting home. The discrepancy between this collectivity in the prison and the community in the museum could not be more stark: not merely in the unconditional readiness to resort to violence and murder that initially introduces them, but also in the structures by which the prison works. The prison group is obviously capable of survival: when they capture the museum expedition, they are out on the hunt for deer; inside the prison, they have planted rows of corn; but their system of governance, such as it is, is evidently fragile.

Copperhead, their ostensible leader, can hardly draw on the respect of his fellow former inmates (147). The inside of the prison is a "smashed-up mess," which the prisoners have not cleared up despite the months of time they have had; and the museum group, as it is dragged to a cell, is greeted by catcalls and leers rather than by the careful welcome extended to newcomers in the museum. In lieu of the careful husbanding and intimate sharing of alcohol that was a major part of Jonah Caine's introduction to the museum, here gallon cans of fruit are fermenting into spirits; in lieu of a communal decision-making process on what is shared and how, Copperhead keeps tight control over these supplies (149). And whereas the museum community's excursions into the city that surrounds them is both a source of valuable supplies, an opportunity to exercise communal action, and a chance to become a voting member of the community, the prison group refuses to engage more than necessary with its surroundings. This is at least in part a problem of a lack of mutual trust: as Copperhead notes, to go out on a large scavenging expedition, the prison group would have "to have somebody guard the gate when they go out, and open it up when they come back, and fight all those dead assholes, and find gas" (189). It is a matter of finding someone capable of taking on these roles as well as a matter of organization. The contrast between the proactive and well-organized museum community and the people in the prison is illustrated through this different relation to shared work. Community, the novel argues, is not merely an effect of collectivity, but is established through shared labor, organization, and other forms of action—and not least, as we have seen Milton argue, in restituting not just bare survival but the various markers of civilized behavior whose securing is part of the citizenship ritual of the museum group.

To be sure, in contrasting the museum group to the prison group, these issues pale beside the much more mundane ways in which the two are set off from each other: in their casual and dehumanizing violence towards women, their willingness to sacrifice their prisoners for their own amusement, their fundamental laziness, the men (it is exclusively male) in the prison are evidently far removed from any but the most savage order. Indeed, the novel lays this contrast in explicitly. "[L]ike animals in the wild," the prison group eats (and, presumably, does everything else) "in descending rank" (155): a hierarchical structure that not only recalls again pre-societal structures, but at the same time suggests in no uncertain terms the fundamental difference to the cooperative venture that is the museum group.

The members of the museum group now trapped with the prison group prepare themselves for the worst; but even as they do, they find the necessary humanity in themselves to fight back. Popcorn, the young boy, bites a man trying to rape him; a fight breaks out, and Frank, whose introduction into the museum group has given us the greatest insight into how the group works, sacrifices himself in trying to defend the boy. Jonah avers that "being safe with us had made him less able to carry on in the face of absurd and dehumanizing cruelty" (160), and realizing that his daughter, Zoey, is now safe in the museum, Frank marshals all his strength and courage to defend Popcorn—successfully for the boy, but with Frank dying in the process. Paffenroth's narrative symbolism, again, is not precisely subtle. Frank's sacrifice for Popcorn involves him being pierced in the side by a spear, Jesus-like. To his friends, forced to bury him hastily, his wounds take on the guise of "stigmata" (163). And, if this were not enough, Jonah and Tanya trade Bible verses: "They led him like a lamb to the slaughter," Jonah says, half remembering the line's reference to Jesus Christ; and Tanya adds, "O Lord of hosts, that judgest righteously, let me see thy vengeance on them" (164). Instead of saving grace, Frank's sacrifice earns the museum captives a day's grace; and the next evening, once more under threat of murder and rape, they again set themselves against their tormentors.

In the fight, it once more becomes clear how different the two groups function: while Jonah, Tanya, and Popcorn attempt to help one another, and seek to set themselves together against the prisoners, the prison group looks on as Tanya takes on Copperhead, seeking the thrill of watching a fight over a cooperative attempt to win a shared battle. In the end, the museum captives manage to overcome and kill Copperhead, with Jonah noting that he "would've been much more inclined to show mercy to one of the undead" (173). And then, just as the tide promises to turn and the prisoners are on the verge of taking Tanya, Jonah, and Popcorn's lives after all, in a late assault, a mass of zombies smashes into the prison and starts to kill the prisoners. The museum group retreats to the safety of a cell; and there, suddenly, they find themselves witnessing the parting of the zombie crowd and the appearance of Milton. As the zombies devour the prison group, the rest of the museum group comes to the aid of their fellows inside the prison, blowing a gap into the prison wall and extracting Milton, Tanya, Popcorn, and Jonah.

Finally safe outside the prison, a surprise awaits the group, however. Milton, securing the zombies inside the prison, where they can finish what they have started, comes to conclude that this might be a good way of approaching the entire problem of the zombies: to use his ability to herd zombies into corrals and thus secure vast swaths of land for humanity again. As he ventures out alone, the rest of the group returns to the museum, safe from both human and non-human predators. As a short epilogue informs readers, things are looking up: the museum is expanding its crops, taking in farm animals, with expectant mothers and increasingly bright prospects ahead. As Jonah summarizes it, the members of the museum group now have "our little community" (190); and on this supremely hopeful note, the novel ends.

We cannot fail to recognize that *Dying to Live* is couched in the metaphors of Christian religiosity, in the notion of Milton as a possible messiah, in Frank's sacrifice, or in the name of Jonah Caine—which, as Milton helpfully parses after the rescue from prison, can be read differently at the end, given that Cain is also a city-builder, and that Jonah Caine seems to have come through the belly of the beast (the prison) unscathed (186). These references culminate in the reading given to Milton: on the final page, Tanya, observing him work the grounds around the museum like a shepherd of the undead, notes that he looks "'like a damn zombie Jesus'" (239). As she notes, Milton, half-zombie, half-man, seems ideally suited to save the undead; and if nothing comes of this notion of Christian salvation for the hordes of the dead, the religious imagery suffusing the novel at least suggests tentatively something of the fundamental values that unite the museum's inhabitants.

Perhaps more importantly for the praxis which the novel enacts, however, *Dying to Live* is also concerned with linking its vision of a possible community to politics. If it is a throwaway line, it is no coincidence that it is Copperhead, the prison group's leader, who spouts the inane rhetoric of capitalist enterprise: "Let's not forget, boys, the business of America—is business!" (152). The Calvin Coolidge-derived quote means nothing in the context of the prison's—or anybody else's—economy in the aftermath of the zombie apocalypse, of course, but it suggests the ways in which the novel would like to see the group's behavior understood, and to which ideologies it sees them as connected. In a comparably overt moment, after Milton reveals to Jonah his insistence on the need for more than just food and safety, but also the better things of life, which are part of the citizenship ritual at the museum, Jonah reflects: "I could see a glimpse of how he could motivate people to organize politically, to have an agenda and make sacrifices to accomplish something and become part of something greater than ourselves." If, as Jonah also notes, Milton's speech is not up to the standards of Martin Luther King or John F. Kennedy, it "was miles ahead of the 'No child left behind,' or 'I feel your pain' kind of rhetoric to which we'd become so debased and accustomed" (82). The novel's insistence is on the importance of a hopeful vision for the future that would exceed bare survival: bare life, in Giorgio Agamben's terms. If bare life is "a zone of indistinction and continuous transition between man and beast—nature and culture," neither the biological *zoe* of "natural reproductive life" nor the "qualified" (Agamben 1998, 109) life of *bios*—little represents this problematic better than the form of life chosen by the prison collective. In its refusal to engage with the world outside except for the minimal function of hunting, and especially in the contrast between this and the museum community's quest for the "qualified life proper to men" (66), the prison group signals the abandonment of the political. Bare life does not figure as something exercised upon groups of people by sovereign power in *Dying to Live*: it becomes a state of affairs confronting those who are not willing to actively pursue alternative ways of living, to struggle against the imposition of a minimal, boundary state of being. This is, perhaps, a problematical insight, in the way it ultimately suggests that those upon whom bare life is imposed are at least partially to be blamed for this imposition, and in the implicit impugning of the characters of those who are brought under a bare life regime. But in its decided emphasis on the need to remain hopeful, active, and willing to confront opposition, at least it gives a sense of possibility. The community created in the museum in the face of a regime (if we may call it that) of the undead that seems to threaten the general imposition of a state of bare life on humanity (such as the life led, too, by Jonah Caine before his arrival at the museum) signals the possibility of overcoming such an imposition through communal action.

Perhaps paradoxically, Milton's decision to leave the community of the museum in fact validates that community: it will thrive, now, even without his guidance, thus becoming more closely a community of equals. But it is actually more significant than that: by removing the zombies from the immediate vicinity of the museum, Milton's departure even more clearly highlights the isolation in which the survivors find themselves here. It is not merely the danger of the zombies that has kept the museum community out of touch with other survivors (save those in the prison); rather, it is the great distances, and the possible nonexistence, of other groups, that is the problem. This is, strangely enough, the final affirmation of the lastingness of the museum's community. If it is the limitation of external communications that helps define community (cf. Bauman 15–16), thrown back on itself, reduced to internal communication because there is literally nothing outside anymore, not even zombies, then the museum community finds, through Milton's departure, community indeed.

Dying to Live, then, offers a genuinely utopian vision of life after the zombie apocalypse. The museum community indeed looks like many utopian communities of both the mythical past and of real, if failed, utopian ventures, from Brook Farm to Upton Sinclair's Helicon Home Colony. Self-sufficient and self-organized, it suggests the need to come together in a genuinely cooperative venture, based on mutual trust and shared engagement. Dangers to this community reside outside: those who have not found a way of establishing a genuinely communal venture, and of course the forces that seem to require the forming of community in the first place. If Paffenroth's novel ultimately affirms the possibility—indeed, the necessity—of community, Bob Fingerman's *Pariah* offers a more ambivalent image of collective life after the end of the world, one focused on the internal structures of the haphazardly thrown-together lives we lead, and offers a highly illustrative comparison to *Dying to Live*.

Pariah: Dangers Inside and Outside Hope

In *Pariah*, the outbreak of a zombie apocalypse and its aftermath are depicted from the perspective of a group of people trapped in an apartment building. For some of them, it is their own home: the place in which they lived even before the outbreak. For others, it is a refuge where they ended up by coincidence, in lieu of returning to their own homes. *Pariah* seems almost painfully interested in offering its cohort of survivors as something like a miniature of US society at large. The group that eventually ends up locked away safely in the building includes an elderly Jewish couple, Abraham and Ruth; a married pair, Ellen and Mike; a single, middle-aged painter, Alan; two twenty-something college guys, Eddie and Dave (who is gay); and Dabney, a black man who has made his home on the house's roof. For the first five, the apartment house at 1620 York Avenue has always been home; Eddie, Dave, and Dabney, by contrast, are exiles, brought to the building by happenstance, stranded refugees from elsewhere. *Pariah*'s setting is very narrow indeed. The ground floor entrance solidly barricaded, with access to just a similarly barricaded neighboring house via the rooftop, the action remains strongly confined. Inside the house, the survivors eke out a slow-moving, drab life of bare survival; outside, the streets are crowded with zombies, gathered in a huge mass that blankets all routes of movement.

Despite their omnipresence, however, *Pariah*'s zombies are remarkably unthreatening. Indeed, only three people fall victim to them, all of them largely by accident. Mike early on falls from his window and, unable to get back in, is overwhelmed; Karl is severely injured much later in breaking through a floor on a trip and, unable to move quickly, is also killed; and Eddie is killed by zombies a while later, the only character who suffers the same fate despite being in full health. While this is an appreciable quota of the characters we encounter, the zombies pose no threat at all unless encountered on their own territory—they never seek entrance to the buildings in which the survivors live. Both Ruth and Abe die, of natural causes, in the course of the novel, and are resurrected as zombies; yet while threatening, they do not pose a real danger. Indeed, encountered individually and as former individuals, they are objects of pity. The zombies mill about, but they do not threaten; they prevent movement, but do not force action; and with no characters outside the building, they are, at worst, a distant, vague threat.

Setting these two camps—zombies outside, humans inside—so firmly apart, the novel initially produces a surprisingly uneventful narrative. For much of the early part of the novel, there is an almost eerie sense of a lack of a difference between being inside the apartment building and outside on the street. With no plans of action, and nothing to do but wait, nothing to strive for, the people locked inside the building live a life little different from the meaningless death which the constantly present zombies outside their doors have—here, again, are shades of bare life. The shred of humanity which fills the beginning of *Pariah*'s pages is, as it were, in a persistent vegetative state, alive but not *alive*—not quite undead, but certainly not far from it. Squarely in the middle of what appears to be a largely abandoned city, *Pariah*'s setting thus introduces a number of things which condition its narrative: the barely living survivors holed up in their apartments; the undead masses populating the city; and the city's own presence as an abandoned remnant of civilization. This last point, as Antonio Sanna has noted of the *Resident Evil* franchise's similar interest in abandoned cities, leaves a looming question: "what is the remaining function of the city in the absence of consumerism and the human being" (2015, 67; see also Bishop 2014 on the city in *Zone One*)? *Pariah* tackles this question only implicitly, but in its later focus on the supermarket across the street as a goal for the group at 1620 York, it will offer something of a commentary on the question of what the useful extent of consumerism and its critiques are.

As with *Dying to Live*, at the heart of *Pariah*'s narrative lie not the dangers of the zombie apocalypse itself but the complex interhuman relations produced by the challenges of life in confined spaces and with minimal resources. But while *Dying to Live* makes us privy to no internal dissent among the members of what is even at the beginning of Jonah Caine's encounter with it an almost perfect community, *Pariah* frequently foregrounds the consequences of the chance that brought its community together. It is the conflicts between the residents—especially between most other residents and Eddie, a sex-obsessed, dimwitted jock type—that shapes much of the early narrative, and which suggests the absence of a real community. The inhabitants share a merely "*collective woe*" (43, my emphasis), the fully stocked supermarket across the street that they cannot reach on account of the undead outside. Inside their improvised fort, the tensions of imminent starvation, Eddie's violent behavior and the atomized nature of neighborly relations make a mockery of the silent recognition that "*We're all in the same boat around here*" (53, original italics). It is the process of transforming the collective of people into something like a community that *Pariah* enacts in the ensuing narrative, a narrative that starts off with a significant reorientation of the sense of danger:

> Karl stared at the wall, or at least in the direction of the wall. It was so dark he couldn't see it, but it was there, a thin layer of protection between him and them. And he wasn't even thinking about the big them. The capital T them. He was just thinking about the them that constituted the others in the building. His neighbors. (19)

Karl's concern for Them outside is muted by the more immediate worries he has about the people with whom he shares the comparative safe haven of the apartment building—a notable concern especially since the novel has not at this point given us any sense of danger emanating from the other people in the building. Their living together, this much is clear early on, is not a community, a construct which, as Zygmunt Bauman notes, always already contrasts the safety of the "in here" with the dangers of the "out there" (2001, 1–2). Without a safe "in here," the survivors of *Pariah* struggle to find a closer collective—they constitute, as the novel has it, at best "a tattered kibbutz" (132), fraying at the edges. The novel builds up Eddie as the primary antagonist: despite sharing in homosexual dalliances with Dave, he is a homophobe. He increasingly reveals himself as an anti-Semite (calling Alan, for example, a "fucking Jew" [335]), a "total racist" (342) in Dabney's words, a man interested solely in his own benefit, virulently antisocial. While the rest of the group proves to be both empathetic, willing to share both in terms of emotional and material support, Eddie's interest is solely in advancing himself. The internal conflict among the survivors is thus largely centered on both the danger posed by Eddie physically and psychologically: a reminder that there is neither shared interest nor a shared sense of purpose at work at 1620 York. Eddie is a constant threat—he blackmails Alan, threatens Ellen, and nearly breaches the integrity of the house's defenses; as the novel ultimately demonstrates, this sense of Eddie's being the gravest danger to the well-being of the people inside the building is not an error, notwithstanding the overtness with which the character is drawn.

Pariah's zombie apocalypse begins early in the year, but most of the novel is set in high summer; the summer heat reinforces the novel's sense of inertia, and the passed time has made the situation inside the building increasingly dire. Short on food and water, the relations between the survivors inside the apartment building grow ever tenser. In this sense at least, the collective of *Pariah*'s early pages is not far removed what Bauman calls the "'really existing community'" (2001, 4), which "will feel like a besieged fortress being continuously bombarded by [. . .] enemies outside while time and again being torn apart by discord within" (15). It is from this (poor) "really existing"—haphazard and contingent, driven entirely by circumstance and chance—community that *Pariah* begins to take us towards its own sense of what kind of community is possible.

The engine of the change from a coincidental collective to something different, and better, is Mona, a teenage girl who is immune to the zombies outside. Like Milton, she can move freely; thus, when she arrives at the apartment building, she is immediately recognized as a savior to those inside. This becomes evident as early as her initial appearance, when Abraham, standing by the window, sees this: "From the south a tiny figure cut north through the multitude, parting it as Moses had the Red Sea" (147). If nobody follows Mona as her Israelites at this stage, later on, she leads the survivors stranded in the apartment building to the promised land across the "dead sea," the supermarket which had seemed unreachable before. It is especially remarkable that the task set for Fingerman's characters is in its impossibility so horribly mundane: crossing a street, going to the supermarket, tasks which promise the immediate satiation of the most urgent of desires. The supermarket, for all its allure, is not the mall of *Dawn of the Dead*, the "important place" in zombies' previous lives that they seek out even in death, nor does it echo the strong consumerist metaphor that George Romero's movie placed at the center of its critique of American society. Rather, and perhaps more profoundly, it becomes symbolic of the fragile constitution of contemporary life. If it is merely the width of a street separating the house's inhabitants from the necessary riches of supplies which the supermarket houses, this separation is nonetheless insurmountable until Mona's arrival.

The comparative material plenty which Mona's first trip brings for the survivors transforms, at least for a while, the nature of their internal relations: with the food brought, the survivors gather on the rooftop to "share their first communal meal since they'd been forced into these straits" (157). This notion, in which sharing offers a first meaningful step towards community, is reinforced by an analepsis in which, towards the beginning of the apocalyptic events that eventually trap the inhabitants at 1620 York, Alan, who has stocked up on supplies, suggests that Ellen and her soon-deceased husband Mike share in those supplies. But this is an offer that is exclusive to the two: "I can't feed everyone," Alan notes (188). The rooftop feast thus already signals a step towards a close relationship among the survivors; but given that it is Mona who, almost literally, can feed everybody, the event also signals the lack that still exists in the development of true community. Together, the two images of Mona's arrival and the meal on the rooftop suggest also something about the different framings of the humans inside the apartment building and the zombies outside. As Michael Hardt and Antonio Negri write, the "multitudes that are not peoples or nations or even communities are one more instance of the insecurity and chaos that has resulted from the collapse of the modern social order" (2004, 192). The term "multitude" in the description of Mona's arrival suggests a parallel reading: one in which the zombies through which Mona needs to pass are merely more overtly threatening manifestations of a collapse that effectively long preceded their zombie-being. It is more a taking away of masks than a signal change: the overt clarification that the multitude without a will or means to institute a "shared common wealth" (Hardt and Negri 2010, xiv) is a regressive, not progressive, force. If "multitude" as a term thus opens up a view of the zombies below, the dinner on the rooftop, "communal" in the adjectival form already suggests its own limits. Inasmuch as it is an action aimed at the creation of community, and one which assembles those who might form the community, it is communal: but it is not community that the rooftop diners experience as yet.

Among the issues which preclude it being community is the somewhat striking fact that the dinner excludes Mona. Mona's help has, of course, been entirely crucial in enabling the communal meal in which everyone now shares; her absence from the dinner and the reaction to the realization that the house's inhabitants have not asked her to join them are important for what they suggest about the status of community at this point. Ellen, shocked to realize that Mona has not appeared, wonders whether they are "insane," "ingrates," or "assholes" (158), an issue conditioned by her realization that Mona represents an unlooked-for lifeline. Mona is the precondition for the possible community simply because only she can sustain it over the long-term (though for Ellen, at least for a short while, Mona, young, healthy, and female, represents also a more pointed threat to her own relationship with Alan). Mona, as Ellen discovers, does not mind her exclusion. Perhaps as a consequence, the group keeps working without her on the list of goodies they desire her to bring from the supermarket. The discussion they have as part of drawing up a list highlights (if it were needed) the fault lines in the group, but also the utilitarian considerations which so far undergird the group's engagement with Mona. While Eddie is dismissive of Mona's own personal needs and desires, Ellen realizes that they might be running a risk of running Mona off with too many demands (177). As it turns out, they do not: Mona returns from a longer, larger expedition, and stays with the group.

Like *Dying to Live*, *Pariah* echoes Bauman's belief that any community can only thrive where communications are restricted to the community itself, with no one on the outside to speak with (cf. 2001, 12–14). Mona's affirmation that she has encountered no other survivors on her wanderings through the city (cf. 224), unlikely though it may seem, is a necessary precursor to envisioning the survivors in York Avenue as a community unto themselves. From very early on, *Pariah* lays in this realization. As Alan tells Mike before offering him and Ellen a share in his food supply: "We're sealing ourselves into our crypt. The cavalry isn't coming for us" (187). Without hope for help from outside, the necessity of falling back onto one's own devices here conditions the possibility for realizing social coherence. The novel is clear about the fact that mere isolation is an insufficient condition for community, however; by itself, it merely complicates the already complicated interhuman relationships that can no longer be dissipated among a larger group. This becomes evident, too, in the way the inclusion of Mona into the group of survivors initially plays out: Mona becomes both a potential savior as well as a bone of contention.

As the dynamics shift inside the house (Mona's attractiveness a lure for Eddie, a concern for Ellen, a draw for Alan), the question of what her secret is, why she can survive among the zombies outside, becomes a focal point of the narrative. As it turns out, her distanced behavior is related to her drug use: the group finds her with ample supplies of all kinds of antidepressants. They conclude that this must be the reason for her repelling the zombies, and venture to experiment by stealing Mona's drugs. Karl volunteers to leave the building, with Mona at his side—without letting her know that there is an ulterior motive to his going with her. The attempt is a disastrous failure: Karl falls through the damaged floor of a bookstore and breaks his back; Mona, seeking help, returns to the other survivors. They break the news that they have taken her drugs to experiment with them. Mona, it turns out, had realized this all along, and tells the group that the drugs themselves are unlikely to be the reason for her immunity: rather, she believes the important fact is that she has been born addicted to them, and takes them only to keep her brain chemistry in a kind of precarious balance (328–29). Alan convinces Eddie to save Karl, but the mission turns into what seems like a predictable disaster: Eddie gets bitten after slipping out of Mona's protection, and, in a final fit of rage, rapes Mona and gets killed afterwards, forgetting that he needs her to save him from the zombies. When Mona fails to return, Alan ventures out to retrieve her, protected by an improvised protective suit made from layers of cloth. He manages to find Mona and return her safely to the house. This is notable precisely because Alan uses the tool that promises autarky from Mona's abilities—a chance to move about freely, without being attacked by the zombies—for the purpose of saving Mona. Whatever mercenary considerations had previously governed, or at least inflected, the community's decisions are now replaced by a simple moral calculus.

The novel ends with a rapid jump forward in time, and a glimpse of hope: Alan, watching from the windows of the house, sees the zombies' numbers "perceptibly thinning," for one thing. But more important are the changed dynamics among the few survivors of the novel's events. Dave is "gone from a grief-inspired suicide," so that only Alan and Ellen, Dabney, and Mona, now firmly ensconced at 1620 York, remain. Ellen is pregnant, while Mona is increasingly capable of emotional participation. The scene opens with Ellen, Mona, and Alan playing Monopoly, in the now "cozy" (365) atmosphere of a winter's day.[2] Sheltered, supplied, and safe inside and out, the survivors have achieved a radically different bond from the loose assortment of individuals featured in the start of the novel; surprisingly, this bond almost appears familial—as the shared board game implies in no uncertain terms. Yet the emphasis should lie on the "almost" here. Ellen does not know if the baby she carries is Alan's or Mike's; Dabney, who spent all of the novel living on the roof, rather than in one of the apartments, now finds his way into them as well; and Mona, though almost readable as having been adopted by Alan and Ellen, remains the most crucial person in the small group—and hardly the one in need of the paternal and maternal protection that the family implies. For *Pariah*, then, the tiny community which finally evolves at 1620 York is marked by the deep personal connections of the family. This move resembles the one which Gregory Waller sees at work in Stephen King's vampire novel *'Salem's Lot*, in which the protagonists Ben Mears, a thirtyish writer, and Mark Petrie, an eleven-year-old boy, succeed in destroying vampires in a small New England town and eventually become akin to father and son (even though they are not). Waller points out that even this miniscule, unfinished family functions like community (2010, 249). It also returns us to the opening of this chapter, the way in which *Dracula* itself sees community figured in familial constructs, where Van Helsing now functions as a familiar patriarch, a grandfather figure, and the survivors of the encounter with Dracula have been happily married for some time (cf. 48).

Perhaps the most crucial difference between the way *Dracula* and *Pariah* frame this family-community conclusion is the situation in which each is formed. In *Dracula*, the count's arrival in London goes largely unnoticed by society at large, which continues to function as it always did. The menace that it promises is averted in time: the changes which Dracula himself stands for never come to pass. We may, as Franco Moretti has suggested, read *Dracula* as symbolizing the struggle between a modern, virulent version of capitalism and the "capitalism ashamed of itself" already well established in Britain—a reading in which the successful destruction of Dracula is achieved by "a bunch of fanatics who want to arrest the course of history" (1983, 94). We may also, like Gregory Waller, read the family-community's triumph as a differently reactionary move which pits "'primitive' communal life" against an evil forgotten in modern society (2010, 40). But in either case it is the threat of significantly altering the societal status quo posed by Dracula that forces the creation of a community to set against him, to prevent this alteration of the status quo from ever coming to pass. This, quite obviously, is not what happens in *Pariah*: here, the family-community is established in the wake of a previous event, one which has already signally altered the status quo.

Pariah thus enacts the structure of "two deaths." As Slavoj Žižek has noted with recourse to the psychoanalytical logic of Jacques Lacan, "everybody must die twice" (1989, 148)—which we may read, too, as "everything must die twice"; or perhaps more to the point here, for anything to change lastingly, it is not enough that death occurs, as it does copiously in the form of zombies. What the zombies remind us of is that there is still a second death required. But it is not, in this case, the death of the zombies that permits what Žižek calls "the destruction, the eradication, of the cycle itself, which then liberates nature from its own laws and opens the way for the creation of new forms of life *ex nihilo*"

(149, original emphasis). What is required instead is the death of the significant living obstacle to communal life, Eddie. To read Eddie's death as a figuration of the "second death," as the necessary precondition of breaking with the symbolic order of the past, may seem strained given that this deeply individual death is set against the death and return of millions. Yet in the logic of the novel, such a reading helpfully elucidates what is at stake. Community certainly cannot be created until Eddie dies: his death, which represents also the death of gender and race-based violence, enables the rest of the survivors—as few as remain—to function. Whatever possibilities are open in the new world, none of them are possible until the reactionary remainders of the past are eradicated. Eddie, in the very overdrawn way in which he combines homophobia, anti-Semitism, racism, misogyny, and mindless violence, can stand symbolically for this final demise. The gap between the first and second deaths, as Žižek notes, "can contain either sublime beauty or fearsome monsters" (150); and so the coincidence between the apparent, possible diminishing of the zombies outside and the establishment of community inside 1620 York becomes readable as a symbolic enactment of a necessary closure.

Conclusion: The Limits of Zombie Jesuses

Jean-Luc Nancy notes that "community, far from being what society has crushed or lost, is *what happens to us*—question, waiting, event, imperative—*in the wake of society*" (11, original italics). In both *Pariah* and *Dying to Live*, this sense that community is something that becomes possible *after* society is enacted in the representation of a struggle between alternative forms of life together. Society as such, understood as the form of life we already have—with all its exclusionary and inclusionary practices, its laws, governments, and so on—is, of course, already gone in both. But the death or demise of society does not automatically create community. Rather, it opens the possibility for community, and permits the foregrounding of the underlying struggles on the way to community. This, as this chapter has sought to establish, is something zombie fictions find themselves debating, and something that it may be argued the particular form of postapocalyptic narrative that the zombie engenders excels at. The zombie brings into sharp relief issues of collectivity, multitude, mass society, and the alternatives to them: individuality, community, and family, as it were formally, by necessitating a recovery of some type from the dissolution of preexisting ways of life.

Pariah and *Dying to Live* share an interest in juxtaposing community and individual, wondering about the role of distinguished individuals in holding together communities faced with an outside threat. But their answers are profoundly different. *Dying to Live* explicitly disavows solitary life—ample evidence for this is given, on the one hand, by Jonah Caine's own ready acceptance of the museum community in lieu of his more desperate single life and, on the other, by the example of Frank and his family. Caine looks for the safety of the larger group, and obtains it; Frank's fate, the death of his wife, and his near-starvation clearly suggest the limits of a survival strategy based on the nuclear family. Both the individual as well as the family prove the wrong unit for restructuring life after the collapse of society; but neither does just any form of collective life suffice. The prison group, with the barbarous "bare life," represents the final disavowed form of postapocalyptic life, against all of which the ideal community of the museum is set.

Similar but different processes are at work in *Pariah*. Like *Dying to Live*, Fingerman's novel is interested in setting individual ways of life—Mona's, certainly, but also the ultimately individually lived if spatially constrained lives in 1620 York—against an ideal of community. It offers somewhat different conclusions, however. If Jonah Caine realizes personal safety in joining a functioning community, in *Pariah*, the outsider figure Mona is perfectly able to survive on her own; in fact, she sacrifices her safety in joining with the survivors at 1620 York and only thereby enables the constitution of community in the building. Her arrival functions in this sense as a catalyst, and a necessary catalyst at that, which helpfully brings to a crisis both Mona's own sense of belonging and the survivors' previous structures of living. Where previously the dividing line between Us and Them, between Karl's "others in the building" and the "big them" of zombies outside, had been at best problematical and certainly not a clear-cut boundary that permitted more than the most perfunctory sense of being together in the same place, at the end of the novel, such a clear boundary finally does exist, delineating the family-community of survivors from the (apparently thinning) horde of zombies outside. Both novels, then, see the achievement of a form of community as crucial to figuring survival in the zombie apocalypse, with hope for a better life in the future being at least coincident, as in *Pariah*, on the establishment of community. This is why the thinning of the zombie horde, whether it is actually taking place or merely signifies Alan's own better spirits, is important: it is the first sign of the possibility of (thinking) better times to come. In a similar vein, the end of *Dying to Live* sees the museum community looking forward to a safe and prosperous future, not least because they are thrown back upon themselves, a community on their own. I will return to this point shortly.

A second issue is crucial to both of these novels: the ability of Mona and Milton to repel zombies—to be immune to the danger posed by the undead.

They are not, to be sure, in any way immortal, but perhaps, as Margo Collins and Elson Bond seem to suggest for Milton, they embody the posthuman (2010, 201–203). But while Collins and Bond are essentially correct in suggesting that the worlds which these people inhabit are already posthuman, to read Milton (and by extension Mona) in those terms foregoes seeing that his role is both unique (and thus certainly not a harbinger of future humanity) and explicitly geared towards a separation of humans and zombies in practice. Also, Milton's unique status is not so much a projection of a future as a call back of a decidedly Christian past. Milton certainly lends poignancy to the idea that "humans and zombies have little to distinguish them from one another, and that only a savior that partakes of the nature of both the living and the undead can possibly save post-human humanity" (Collins and Bond 2011, 202). As Christ is half-human, half-god, "Milton's part man and part them—no offense to him, you understand—so he can save them. And us" (Paffenroth 2006, 190), as Caine has it. But in fact, the novel does not answer the question what "saving" zombies should entail; in this lies the problem with Collins and Bond's reading. Milton's exertions make the world safer for humanity—at least for the immediate community of survivors that we are aware of—but it neither changes the nature of the zombies nor ultimately offers a path to a "posthuman" future. Indeed, Milton's relation to the zombies is a negative one: "they just avoid me" (79), as he notes to Caine. Instead of suffering the children to come unto him, he herds and jostles, drives and segregates the zombies; he uses them and removes them from the immediate vicinity of human society. Caine is only half-wrong: Milton cannot save the zombies, but he can, by removing them, keep the rest of humanity safe.

Despite this metaphorical confusion, it is significant that both novels stylize their potentially posthuman figures emphatically through religious metaphors. *Pariah* and *Dying to Live* share the notion of a "savior" at the heart of apocalypse, and they develop this concept in similar ways, offering individuals who are not threatened—indeed, who bodily repulse—the zombie hordes. In using this device to investigate questions of reconstituted communities in the aftermath of apocalypse, however, they come to different conclusions about the possible nature of such communities. Milton's decision to leave the museum community to its own devices is indicative of the growth of the community there: it requires no more help from him, freeing him to do what he can "for" the zombies. The overtness with which the novel draws the parallel with Jesus Christ—its insistence that Milton's status as half-man, half-zombie makes him somebody's savior (whether mankind's or the zombies' remains unclear)—is distinctive, but it is also distinctly haphazard. *Dying to Live*'s religious overtones remain somewhat vague and suggestive: what Milton's possibly saving of the undead might practically entail is as unclear as what the parallel between him and Christ ultimately achieves. What they do suggest, whatever else is the case, is the importance of meaning-making and mythopoesis for the constitution of larger communities. Milton serves this role well: his departure makes him, if not quite a legendary figure, at least a distant founder, upon whose aid the community may still call, but from out of whose moral dependence it has grown.

Mona's role in *Pariah*, by contrast, remains eminently practical. Rather than overburdening her with the position of a spiritual or moral savior, the novel makes her ability to survive among the undead a necessary prerequisite for the further communal-familial life at 1620 York, simply because of her ability to forage for supplies. In fact, the way Karl declines into a Christian believer in the end times suggests the novel's distance from religious readings. Yet although the one is decisively grounded in Christian thought and the other is not, both see their "blessed" characters as deficient when it comes to creating a postapocalyptic way of life. In this way, both novels highlight the limits of their savior figures: Milton can serve as a moral center but neither as a solitary leader nor as a sufficient cause for the community's safety and prosperity. He must, in fact, leave for it to become a community in the first place sufficient unto itself. Mona, for her part, cannot by herself achieve the creation of community either—she can, in the novel's imagery, lead "her" people to the "blessed land" of the supermarket, parting the "dead sea." Yet this journey alone does not end the strife within a too disparate set of survivors.

A third and final point about the way the two novels imagine the constitution of community bears mentioning. For both novels, the constitution of community is logically bound to the dissolution of communications. Both novels imagine the destruction of mass culture precisely because it is a prerequisite to imagine community. As Zygmunt Bauman notes, community can only thrive where communications are restricted to the community itself, with no one from the outside to speak with (2001, 12–14). In fact, both novels insist on the singularity and isolation of their respective communities. Mona, when asked, notes that she has not encountered any other survivors (224); likewise, after the destruction of the prison group, no other survivors are encountered in *Dying to Live*. The novels' geographical limitations stand in contrast to both the broad global sweep of *World War Z* as well as to the constant movement in *The Walking Dead*—and also, though less so, to the narrow focus on New York which *Zone One* exhibits. This narrative choice forecloses the novels' ability to speak to a broader societal resurgence, but this is precisely the point. Instead of erecting on the ruins of the old world a new, better world, as *World War Z* does, *Zone One* suggests is impossible, and *The Walking Dead* is ambivalently meandering around, *Pariah* and *Dying to Live* focus explicitly on a small-scale world, presenting it as an option in the apocalypse and an opportunity. Their version of community is directly opposed to the postmodern version which Gerald Delanty describes as "nomadic, highly mobile, emotional and communicative" (Delanty 2010, 104): the novels' communities are bound (by farming, or by "home") and immensely immobile; based more on resolution and a social contract than by emotion; and explicitly incommunicative, at least when it comes to the outside.

To be sure, in their return to small-scale communities, well-defined and transparent in their workings, which, to borrow from Nancy, play back to themselves by their institutions their own "immanent unity, intimacy and autonomy" (1991, 9), these utopian visions indulge in a form of nostalgia which sits awkwardly besides their hopeful appeals. What saves them from being the very kind of regressive fantasy which Nancy derides—and, indeed, which Hardt and Negri suggest they are—is their setting in a space of possibility. What makes the vision of small-scale community problematical in the real world is its impossibility, the fact that it seeks to establish what cannot be established against the forces of a globalized world. In the worlds of the two novels, by contrast, community can be established against a clearly defined Other, both morally—in bounding off humanity against non-humanity, those who wish to survive against those who wish to kill—but also practically, in the way the usual markers of Otherness come to be supplanted by the extremity of the Other against which the new, all-encompassing human community has to struggle. If "a loss of familiarity, fraternity and conviviality" (Devisch, n.p.) circumscribes the sense of what is lacking to those who strive for narrow communities in the present, if in the absence of a more unifying threat the categories of ethnic, national, racial, or cultural difference can supply a backdrop for the reactionary conceptions of community deplored by Nancy—safeguarding "ours" against "them"—the two novels utilize the zombie figure for its unifying potential. Community is formed against the undead, not against other humans, and it is bound by behavior instead of identity. It is, obviously, not indifferently inclusive, as both the prison collective in *Dying to Live* and Eddie's fate in *Pariah* demonstrate: merely being human is insufficient grounds to guarantee inclusion in this new community. Here lies the most overt utopian potential of the novels: their constitution of a sense of how community can be created on the basis of shared codes of behavior, shared ways of life and being, and need not (indeed, must not) be founded on identitarian categories.

If, as Zygmunt Bauman says, we strive today to seek certainty and safety by investments in ourselves, to seek "biographical solutions to systemic contradictions" because our "body and soul have a longer life expectancy than anything else in that world" (144–45), it becomes perhaps clearer why it becomes easier (if not easy) to imagine community in the face of apocalypse. Genuine community, as *Pariah* and especially *Dying to Live* suggest, offers the opportunity to build something that lasts: something that does, in fact, have a longer life expectation than any individual (especially in a world where life is as precarious as in the zombie apocalypse). The systemic contradictions of the moment have been resolved for good, and biographical solutions—personal fulfillment, private bliss, and so on—need no longer be entertained. *Pariah* and *Dying to Live* thus highlight the way in which community is a possible option for life in a potential future after the systemic contradictions of the contemporary moment, our very own *Dracula* moment, that is. Of course, what can become of those potential futures outside of a zombie apocalypse remains unclear.

The Walking Dead and the Never-Ending Zombie Story
The Everyday, Community, and the Need for an Ending[1]

> In apocalypse there are two orders of time, and the earthly runs to a stop; the cry of woe to the inhabitants of the earth means the end of their time; henceforth "time shall be no more."
> FRANK KERMODE, *The Sense of an Ending*, 90

Much of the history of the zombie in fiction is the zombie in comics, from EC Comics' voodoo zombies to more recent iterations, from *Marvel Zombies* through George Romero's *Empire of the Dead* miniseries, to *iZombie* or the successful adaptation of Archie comics as *Afterlife with Archie*. Indeed, despite the undoubted success of both of Max Brooks's zombie books, the most successful example of zombie fiction in the 2000s is a comic (and TV series). Begun in 2003, Robert Kirkman's *The Walking Dead* is still on-going. As of writing, 170 issues have been published, collected into twenty-seven trade paperbacks and several larger compilations. The comic has also become a remarkably successful TV show, eight seasons of which have been produced by AMC so far. "Kirkman's series has become one of the best meditations on society popular culture has yet produced" (Rushton and Moreman 2008, 5)—an effective cultural mirror that successfully speaks to contemporary concerns: issues of security, both national and personal; of the body, agency, and posthumanity; trauma, psychosis, and objectivism; community, individualism, and the possible futures of society at large (see Keetley 2014, Lowder 2011).[2] To the seasoned zombie critic, this list, while impressive enough, at the same time appears to be par for the course: these are, after all, the issues that the zombie again and again becomes connected with since its appearance in Western popular culture.

My discussion of *The Walking Dead* in this chapter, by contrast, will focus on two issues that are unique to it: its complicated relationships to the issue of endings and to the everyday, two things which, I will argue below, are conflated in a highly complex and revealing manner in the comic. It is not just that *The Walking Dead* "consciously expands the moves, tropes, and themes of a Romero film into a long, unfolding narrative" (Williams 2011, 90):[3] for writer Robert Kirkman, "*The Walking Dead* will be *the zombie movie that never ends*" (Kirkman 2007, n.p., my italics). Of course, we may be almost sure that *The Walking Dead* will, sooner or later, end, somehow or other: sales numbers might wither, Kirkman might retire, or an actual zombie apocalypse might come and end comics publishing as we know it. All narratives end, and more interesting than the impossible reality of Kirkman's aspirations are their narrative consequences.

I aim to take Kirkman at his word: understanding *The Walking Dead* to be intimately concerned with a desire to "never end," I will argue that we can understand this best in connection with two issues, one cultural and one literary. On the one hand, I will frame my discussion of *The Walking Dead* through Eran Dorfman's analysis of the shifting nature of the everyday, suggesting that *The Walking Dead* is symptomatic of and narratively enacts a doubled, postmodern sense of the everyday, one in which a sense of loss and bewilderment combines with a narrative sense of "everydayness." *The Walking Dead*'s protagonists exhibit a desire to find spaces of safety in an increasingly threatening and listless, and more pointedly telos-less, postmodern world. The comic's nostalgia for what was before suggestively represents a contemporary confusion about what must be accepted as everyday life. The series' complicated relationship with the everyday is manifest in the unease between the desire to see its characters re-establish themselves in a simile of the way "things were before," safely ensconced in a "home," and its insistent destruction of their fleeting moments of safety. It is manifest in the shocking violence of this destruction and its equally shocking ultimate meaninglessness, in the way the experiences of the characters appear to meander so horribly between apparent everyday life in restituted safe places and shocks which shatter safety and everyday life, and the way it is this very movement from safety to danger to safety, endlessly repeated, which constitutes something like an everyday in and of itself, especially for the reader. It does so not just by (it is to be hypothesized) reassuring her of the desirability of her own everyday existence, contrasted with the characters', but also by a narrative of repetitions "over and over again, until the new is eventually integrated into the old" (Dorfman 2014, 2). That is to say: with each displacement, shattered hope for a stable place to live, and ostensibly shocking plot twist, *The Walking Dead* reproduces a reassuring version of itself, in which instability itself becomes a stabilizing narrative element—the same-old, same-old of shattered hopes. John Edgar Browning has argued that *The Walking Dead* produces "ambulatory survival spaces" (2016, 24) and reads the comic's "new motif of ambulation" as a journey towards hope. By contrast, I will suggest that it offers very little sense of hope indeed, largely because of its peculiar formal and narrative structure.

In all this, *The Walking Dead* must be read symptomatically of a larger contemporary problematic. If "[t]he modern everyday consists of countless voluntary and involuntary shocks and 'extraordinary' events, but none of these seem to mean much and they only add another link to the repetitive chain of everyday life" (Dorfman 2014, 18), *The Walking Dead* appears to question the very notion of what constitutes the everyday and what the shocks, what counts as extraordinary and what must be made to mean. In so doing, *The Walking Dead* speaks to a time which has seen the state of exception become the state of the norm. If this is at heart a cultural diagnosis, I am also arguing that this reading of the comic necessarily depends, literarily, on its serial, meant-to-be-endless form. Taking a cue from Frank Kermode, I will relate the comic's "sense of no ending" to its narrative form. As Kermode points out, we depend on our expectations of an end for the constitution of narrative logic: only if there is a conventional expectation of an ending can there be a meaningful sense of narrative surprise and progression (2000, 18–19). As we shall see, there is considerable consonance between these points: playing on versions of cyclicality and linearity, shock, surprise, and repetition, they enable us to understand *The Walking Dead* as, among other things, symptomatic of how life is lived in the absence of an anchoring sense of narrative ends. Without knowing what the end of the narrative is meant to be, it becomes impossible to know what the shock is, what the extraordinary event is, and what the everyday, a postmodern life which has largely resigned itself to retiring, along with grand narratives, the possibility of making sense and meaning of existence.

Endlessness and the Everyday: Theories in Practice in *The Walking Dead*

The Walking Dead follows Rick Grimes, a small-town sheriff's deputy, through the aftermath of a zombie apocalypse whose origins remain obscure. Having woken up alone in the hospital where he had been left after a gunshot wound before the apocalyptic events, Rick manages to link up with a group of survivors including his wife Lori and son Carl. His subsequent journey, during which he loses Lori, takes him from the outskirts of Atlanta to Alexandria, Virginia, with a changing cast of fellow survivors. Along the way, the group falls into a striking sort of routine: driven from apparently safe places by zombie or human threats, they end up at a new one, only to start the process over.

First, they abandon their initial campsite as being increasingly unsafe, a fact demonstrated by a growing number of human losses, only to reach the gated community of Wiltshire Estates, an apparently safe haven soon discovered to be already overrun by zombies. Fleeing, the group reaches Hershel Greene's farm not much later. This, too, proves untenable, easily overrun by the increasingly numerous zombies. The survivors then move to a prison near (the real) Woodbury, Georgia, whence they are driven by the psychopathic "Governor" of the inhabitants of Woodbury. Now moving north on a surprise quest to help a fellow survivor reach the seat of government, allegedly with information about the source of the zombie outbreak, they end up at a community in Alexandria. This turns out to be part of a larger network of communities, including the Saviors, led by a man named Negan, who becomes a deadly threat to Alexandria and its two allied settlements, the Hilltop and the Kingdom. Rick and his fellow survivors manage to defeat Negan and build up the network of towns into a thriving cluster, only, in the most recent installments, to find themselves endangered again, this time by the Whisperers, a group of survivors who don the skins of the dead to mingle with them safely outside the walls.

The Walking Dead thus enacts a repetitive series of safety and danger and flight, safety and danger and fight, without a clearly communicated sense of where its narrative is ultimately headed. This is the most crucial aspect of *The Walking Dead*'s narrative structure: the quest to find a suitable place for long-term habitation repeated over and over by new journeys as these places are destroyed, a seemingly endless quest with no apparent end point. Interwoven into this iterative succession of homes found and lost is the desire to establish anew the survivors' sense of pre-apocalyptic everyday life, as best they can, a desire which becomes at once stronger and more complicated as their various safe places turn out not to be safe at all. It is so far, and promises to continue to be, an endless narrative not because it will never end, but because it has no clear end in sight: As Robert Kirkman points out in his introductory note, it is marked by the need to follow a single character, Rick Grimes, and the way he "change[s] and mature[s]"—to "stay with him as long as humanly possible" (2007). In the absence of more than this, *The Walking Dead* may continue as long as it sells, or terminate as simply as it is to kill off Rick Grimes as a character.[4]

As Frank Kermode has argued, we have a "deep need for intelligible Ends" (2000, 8). People, Kermode claims, "make considerable imaginative investment in coherent patterns which, by the provision of an end, make possible a satisfying consonance with the origins and with the middle" (17). In the way *The Walking Dead* not only as of now de facto, but also theoretically and in its ambitions, denies us the "intelligible End" lies a profound stumbling block to making the kind of "satisfying coherence" which, Kermode suggests, drives our appreciation of literary narrative. What may initially appear to be a throwaway line in a rambling introduction to a series whose potential even Kirkman could hardly be expected to envision while writing here becomes key to unraveling much else that is going on in *The Walking Dead*. Kermode, writing in 1967, feels that "we need ends [. . .] even when the history of the world has so terribly and so untidily expanded its endless successiveness [. . .] In the middest, we look for a fullness of time, for beginning, middle, and end in concord" (2000, 58). *The Walking Dead*, a half-century onwards, appears to disagree: its narrative, which begins very affirmatively in the middest, with Rick awakening in the hospital as the apocalypse is already ongoing, refuses a firm, stabilizing connection to either the beginning or to its remote and unplotted end.

Parsed through Kermode's belief in the necessity of an intelligible End (and we should read this to mean both telos and simple end point), the problem of *The Walking Dead* becomes clearer. Providing no such end, it makes it difficult to imbue the events presented with any sort of ulterior meaning—or even to integrate them as parts of a larger narrative. This is nowhere more evident than in the way the comic's characters treat their own pasts. Thus, for example, late in vol. 17, musing on the death of Glenn, one of the very first characters the comic introduced, Andrea (another long-timer) says to Rick: "And now he's gone . . . and we're not. Same old story, right?" (fig. 1). For Andrea, but more particularly for the narrative itself, Glenn's death means nothing: it is a point along an endless succession of deaths and survivals, their momentary shock ultimately easily integrated into an ongoing present. Narratively, the lack of an intelligible end must necessarily make it so: character deaths are almost the sole narrative driving force in *The Walking Dead*, largely because its other events are already marked as fleeting and inconsequential (how to invest emotionally in a new home, which we surely know will not be the end point of the narrative journey). But by driving its narrative largely through character losses, the only non-circular events that the comic has left, these deaths become progressively less shocking and invested. Like Andrea, readers may easily surrender themselves to the conclusion that it's the same old story over again.

Read this way, *The Walking Dead*'s endlessness is a symptom of its times. "[O]urs is the great age of crisis," wrote Kermode in 1967: an assertion "no

Fig. 1. Andrea being callous. The ease with which death can be ignored suggests the problem of emotional investment in the characters. *The Walking Dead* 17: *Something to Fear*. Image Comics. All rights reserved.

more surprising than the opinion that the earth is round" (2000, 94), and perhaps truer now than it was then. What is it a crisis of, though? Kermode's list—"technological, military, cultural"—bespeaks its mid-twentieth-century origins; what *The Walking Dead* instead enacts is a different crisis, one which is perhaps more postmodern than modern. In the great acceleration of events, of production, of communications, in the ever-increasing inflow of things to take care of, to witness, to participate in, or simply to take in, we may with Eran Dorfman identify it as a "crisis of the everyday" (2014, 5), or perhaps what Fredric Jameson has called the "reified numbness of everyday life in the fallen world" (1991, 121). Dorfman's notion of the everyday involves to twofold, circular movement, one of which is the stable, global, everyday, the other the actions and events that transcend this everyday, but which are always reintegrated into the everyday in the end (fig. 2). Dorfman argues that "in late modernity [. . .] the actions and events that transcend the everyday become shocks [. . .] parried from rather than integrated into the everyday." Dorfman's point, of course, is far more mundane than the zombie: for him, a shock might be as minor a disruption of the everyday as a sore tooth. Yet more pertinently, this sense of genuine shock from so minor an issue as a hurting tooth is bound up in the way "the unprecedented number of possible actions and events in modernity makes everything that presents itself as new be considered as a potential threat: an attack or a strike—that is, a shock" (2014, 5–6).[5] The problem which Dorfman identifies is that the traditional mechanisms by which we integrate events, actions, and change into our existing everyday no longer work. While the everyday still "works," as it were, an event occurs within the everyday and changes it, "and eventually [becomes] itself a part of the foundation. However, this movement is never singular; it must repeat itself over and over again, until the new is eventually integrated into the old" (2); repetition, in other words, slowly wears away the resistance of the old everyday to create the new. In the meantime, the everyday is deferred: the routine of the everyday is broken, until a solution to the integration of the event is found. As Dorfman argues, "*late modernity* marks a radical change in the quantity, quality and object of deferral, such that shocks are either hardly deferred or deferred too much" (4, original italics).

As I will argue in greater detail below, we see much of this play out in *The Walking Dead* over and over. At the very highest level, the zombie apocalypse itself becomes symbolic of this "unprecedented number of possible actions and events" which overwhelm life in the present, and literalizes the potential, ever-present threat. The zombie is symptomatic of the way that, as Dorfman argues, in modernity "the extraordinary has become an everyday possibility, yet one which is too shocking to be integrated into the everyday" (2014, 10); it is "a foreign body that the everyday does not manage to integrate" (14). Sitting outside the chain-link fences and concrete walls of the repeated versions of safe places that *The Walking Dead* produces, the zombie becomes the literal foreign body at the same time as the increasingly present specter of death highlights the "vulnerability of the body" (2) that also destabilizes the everyday. Impossible to integrate into the attempts at recreating an everyday inside the walls and yet a part of it, it signals the ambivalent nature of the everyday both in modernity at large and more especially in the series itself. More particularly, the series also enacts the way in which under these conditions (where the zombies represent a radically overwhelming modern life), a feeling of being

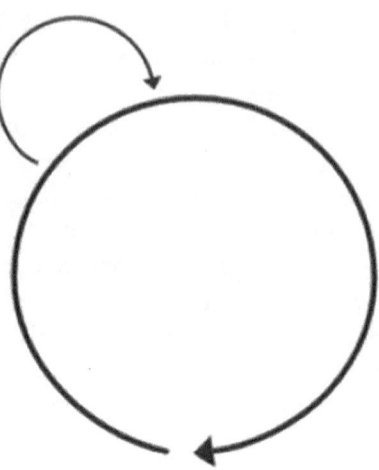

Fig. 2. Eran Dorfman's dual circular movement of the everyday. The large circular is the everyday, itself a cyclical, repetitive movement; the smaller circular is the shock, which springs out of the everyday and needs to be integrated into it for the everyday to resume its course. *Foundations of the Everyday* by Eran Dorfman. Copyright © 2014. Used by permission of Rowman & Littlefield Publishing Group. All rights reserved.

perpetually under threat takes on added significance. Under the conditions of the apocalypse, the survivors react with extreme suspicion to anyone and anything that newly presents itself to them; at the same time, reflecting the conditions of its production, the comic presents ever-new threats, seemingly unable to figure out a way of advancing its narrative that is not a threat. The "new" that the comic needs to produce every couple of issues necessarily is a threat: the Governor, the cannibals, Negan's Saviors, and more recently the Whisperers, whose challenge has not yet been resolved. Thus the comic manifests Dorfman's generalized sense of the new and potentially dangerous: in it, (almost) everything new genuinely is a threat.

The consequence of all this, Dorfman argues, is a loss of mental bearings, in which the plethora of shocks cannot be integrated into a stabilizing sense of the everyday anymore: we lose our sense of what it means to be "at home" (6). It is this latter phrase which will recur often below in my discussion of *The Walking Dead*. As the survivors we follow creep from shock to shock, they keep searching for an everyday "home" at which to stabilize their sense of themselves; but the narrative logic of the never-ending zombie story (which here becomes readable as merely a metaphor of postmodern life) militates against this. It requires the constant repetition of ever-new shocks, destabilizing the sense of homeliness and everyday, making sure that "the restless pursuit goes on *ad infinitum*" (6, original italics). At the same time, some measure of integration does take place, which can be traced through the use of another phrase by the comic: the idea of "how things were before." Taken together, these two concerns—the re-establishment of a stable sense of place, of life, and of everyday pursuits—are relativized by an unreflected but crucial awareness of a shifting sense of what can be achieved and what cannot. *The Walking Dead* thus enacts both an unease with the threatening fluidity of contemporary life as well as the impossibility of fully denying the import of events on one's conception of an everyday life.

As Eran Dorfman notes, "I am [. . .] aware of my own everyday only at its transitional moments" (2014, 33), a point clearly illustrated at the very beginning of *The Walking Dead*'s run. The first encounter between *The Walking Dead*'s protagonist, Rick Grimes, and a fellow survivor ends with his head being hit by a shovel. As he comes to, a deeply domestic scene awaits him (fig. 3). From the horror of the first encounter with the dead, the comic transitions again, revealing the state of Rick's everyday in a moment of transition. This "everyday is life in its most homely, familiar and safe element" (Dorfman 2014, 6), and here, fresh from his hairbreadth escape from the hospital, Rick is presented precisely with this. Dinner is set, a serving bowl is carried to the table, lights burn in the background; the man, Morgan, is even wearing a tucked-in shirt, framed from Rick's perspective as though looking in on undisturbed family life. The juxtaposition here is both one in which the reader participates (this is his dinner as well as Morgan's, set off against the horrors Rick has just witnessed) and one which initially sets out the concept of everyday being for the rest of the series.

The appearance of normality in this first encounter reflects the survivors' aspirations in *The Walking Dead*, a return to "how things were before" that sets "before" as "before the apocalypse," and as chiefly marked by safety and homeliness. The comic perpetually returns to the idea of the lastingly safe haven: the gated community, Hershel's farm, the prison compound, Alexandria, all repetitively assert the possibility of obtaining a "home," understood as a safe, everyday place: a homeliness that extends beyond the mere physical to the nature of the relationships lived in it. As Rick leaves Morgan and his son to go to Atlanta, he is saved right in the middle of the city by Glenn, on a supply run for a group of survivors. Brought to their camp, Rick is greeted, somewhat improbably, by his wife and son, and so returned to the bosom of his family: thus the comic sets out its own ideas of what life in the zombie apocalypse might look like. The nuclear family is reconstituted, life is lived in the repetition of life before the apocalypse, and if the details have shifted, the grand narrative remains intact: this is what the survivors aspire to, and what they will continue to aspire to throughout. The trappings of pre-apocalyptic society remain crucial bearings. In the course of the comic, when Glenn and his partner Maggie adopt a survivor girl, and when Andrea after Lori's death becomes Rick's partner, the bonds they form are explicitly couched in parental terms: Sophia calls Glenn and Maggie "dad" and "mum," and Carl, Rick's son, calls Andrea "mum" as well:

Fig. 3. Domestic tranquility in the apocalypse. Notice the perspective looking in from an apparent outside. *The Walking Dead* 1: *Days Gone Bye*. Image Comics. All rights reserved.

in this way, the comic valorizes a thoroughly normalized model of relationships (it does so too, arguably, in the way it handles Glenn and Maggie's marriage earlier). It recurs to the models of "before": a move which reinforces the sense that this is what constitutes the homely and familiar.

Throughout the series, the question of finding again a "homely, familiar and safe element" is latent in everything the survivors do, always tied, however, to the more conflicted and shifting idea of a return to the way things were that signals their partial adaptation to the shocks they experience. In the course of the first volume of *The Walking Dead*, both Rick and his wife Lori echo this desire in despairing, as Lori does just before the volume's end, "it's never going to be the same again. We're never going to be normal."[6] Much of *The Walking Dead* takes place between these two positions: a desire for the everyday of the past, the normality of domesticity and safety, and the periodic, shocking recognition that the repetitiveness of the "the same again" is unattainable in the postapocalyptic world—except, perhaps, by moving the goal posts of what the same could possibly be. Thus, when Rick, towards the end of *The Heart's Desire* (vol. 4), in the middle of a long speech justifying the shifting moral norms in the fragile prison community, exclaims, "nothing will ever be the way it used to be," it is because he finds himself obliged to remind his fellow survivors that things have changed; but he himself, at the end of vol. 2, had somewhat blithely dubbed the prison "home" (fig. 4), an echo of the way things were in a much larger sense than the mere enumeration of material plenty. But if Rick is correct (at least so far) that many mundane, everyday things—television, grocery shopping, bank visits, school drop-offs—are not going to return, the everyday still creeps back into the life of the prison community.

In vol. 5, still in the temporary safety of the prison, Lori soon thinks about how they will "spread out here—move some more furniture into the cells around us, have a sitting room, Carl's own bedroom, things like that," and Tyreese echoes Rick's earlier belief that the prison will be "home." These moments already suggest what Rick will state right out towards the end of vol. 6. Under assault by the Governor's forces, Rick's group in the prison has nearly been overrun by a horde of zombies. With the grounds finally cleared, Rick takes Carl out to show him the area is safe again. In doing so, he shows how far the group has come in normalizing their everyday lives in the prison: "There's nothing to be scared of, Carl. Everything will be the way it used to be. You'll see" (fig. 5). The choice of words, of course, is telling: "the way it used to be" is not the pre-apocalyptic world of televisions and shopping tours but the relative safety behind the fences and walls of the prison—in other words, the life the group has built for itself in the last months.

The return to a new normal (which, crucially, includes also Glenn's repeated runs outside the fence to scout for supplies, an integration of postapocalyptic behavior that has the feel of the familiar)—that is, the establishment of a life reminiscent of but distinct from the pre-apocalyptic lifestyles that the group had at least in theory clung to before their establishment at the prison compound—signals the way the community has at last managed to integrate at least some of the shocks they have encountered into their lives. Much of vol. 7, appropriately entitled *The Calm Before*, is devoted to establishing a sense of normality that is repeatedly broken by the kind of small-scale shocks that now barely figure as a blip on the everyday lives of the community. Dale, another long-time group member, is bitten but survives. Carol, also with the group from the start, commits suicide. Lori gives birth to a baby daughter. Maggie and Glenn marry. The deaths and damage notwithstanding, the volume appears

Fig. 4. Rick's appraisal of the prison, on the final page of vol. 2. *The Walking Dead* 2: *Miles Behind Us*. Image Comics. All rights reserved.

Fig. 5. The shifting valence of the way it used to be. *The Walking Dead 6: This Sorrowful Life*. Image Comics. All rights reserved.

to insist on something like a return to a new normal. But the comic is not content to let the characters rest there. Regardless of whether a new everyday has been established in the volume, it is challenged on the final pages by a new (returning and repetitive) threat—this time, the Governor's arrival at the prison compound and his beginning of a full-scale assault that results, by the conclusion of the next volume, in the death of Lori and her new daughter, as well as a large number of the community's remaining survivors, and Rick and Carl in a lonesome, headlong flight from the compound. Even the assaulting group, the Governor included, does not survive, however, as the undead stream into the compound.

The conclusion to vol. 8 illustrates the way *The Walking Dead* complicates the construction of meaning through its endlessness. Whatever the prison complex's security, and Rick's conflict with the Governor, were in their ongoing development, the conclusion, which almost fully resets the narrative back to the beginning of vol. 1 (with the exception that this time, Carl is with Rick), wipes the slate clean. Whatever meaning is to be drawn from the previous narrative is, at the very best, nihilistic: there are no victors in the struggle for the prison, and no resolution to any plotline, except those concluded by character death. The prison falls behind entirely, without a sense that its having been means anything anymore—and this sense is only reinforced by the way the story continues.

While Rick and Carl reunite with a number of survivors from their previous group, and then some new ones, the narrative reverts to the quest structure it had before; and when this new group reaches Alexandria, Virginia, a thriving, apparently safe community of survivors, they settle. To be sure, they are now a little more suspicious of their fellow man, a little more willing to use violence even against those who appear friendly (see also Bishop 2014, 73–88). But more to the point, the fact that despite everything that happened in the prison, Rick's group of survivors settles again at Alexandria even though safe places are not safe highlights the way the narrative repetitively returns to a similar sense of home, and indeed a sense of returning to the "way things were before."

Early in vol. 12, as Rick's group slowly settles in with the Alexandria community, Rick is told that "for the most part, we are able to return to the life we remember within these walls"; and indeed, this sense of restored normalcy carries over into Rick's group and himself. Douglas, leader of the Alexandria community at this stage, enlists Rick to be what he calls the "constable," fitting Rick with a policeman's uniform (fig. 6). Rick's missing right hand, barely visible against the background, is the sole reminder that all is not as it was before: with a typical suburban scene in the panel's background, the comic marks the way Alexandria here initially figures as the kind of familiar and homily place that can anchor a renewed sense of everydayness. Indeed, this is laid in throughout the volume. Glenn saying how much he missed washing the dishes, and Rick and Andrea watching in astonishment as a well-dressed lady passes by while walking her dog all, address the way the survivors seek a sense of home, and the way the comic is repeatedly willing to offer this sense, even as it becomes increasingly improbable.

Much of the narrative's thrust in the course of the Alexandria narrative is in a similar direction. At the end of vol. 14, Rick muses on the logic of an Alexandria that he has, in the wake of several deaths and of conflict with Negan, all but taken over to lead (fig. 7). The description of why Alexandria should be a good "home" to the survivors recalls all their previous "homes," of course: the fence, which, it has already turned out, is not much stronger or much safer than those previously shielding the survivors; the houses, which recall the Wiltshire Estate of the second volume. The belief that a home can be made in Alexandria, which simply echoes similar previous beliefs about the suitability of previous habitations, sounds very much like what Rick offered at the end of volume two, seeing for the first time the prison from a hillside above it: "Look at that fence. It could be made to be safe. That place has beds, supplies, clothes, maybe even some food [. . .] we could make a life here. [. . .] We can make this work." It also echoes Lori's comment earlier in that volume when encountering Wiltshire Estates: "This place is perfect. We could start a new life here." Having forgotten that the same things which hold true for Alexandria held true, too, for the previous habitations the group encounter, Rick's estimation of the value of Alexandria sits somewhat uneasily against the knowledge of the group's past. Indeed, Rick's conclusion—"we have been lazy up until now"—works largely as a rationalization, given the work which went into making the prison compound livable.

The Walking Dead and the Never-Ending Zombie Story   81

Fig. 6. Rick back in a policeman's uniform in Alexandria, having come full circle. *The Walking Dead* 12: *Life Among Them*. Image Comics. All rights reserved.

But these points we should not miss in reading *The Walking Dead* through the lens of its complicated relationship with the everyday: Rick ignores the group's shared past, their previous efforts, in his own continual desire to start anew in the endless journey to a safe place. In vol. 16, Rick is taken to an even larger, more impressive settlement, the Hilltop, whose inhabitants Rick describes on the final pages: "Those people in there don't live in fear, they don't worry about what's outside of that wall. Frankly, they are completely incapable of dealing with anything from outside. They just live." He then pitches fighting on the Hilltop's side against Negan, arguing that "this is the place [. . .] We can rebuild civilization now. We're one step closer to getting back to the way things were before." This is a notable retrenchment from the last time the phrase appeared: it marks a lasting, recurring, ambivalent desire to return as far as possible to a pre-apocalyptic life, uneasily interwoven into an awareness that such a return remains foreclosed or that, at the very least, it remains conditional

Fig. 7. Rick's argument for making Alexandria home. *The Walking Dead* 14: *No Way Out*. Image Comics. All rights reserved.

upon the kind of willful ignorance of the real conditions of existence marked by Rick's description of the Hilltop group: "they don't worry about what's outside." Indeed, Rick appears occasionally aware of this. In vol. 21, he notes to Andrea: "We'll take down Negan, and we'll rebuild our community . . . get it back in working order. We'll go back home." If it is not quite "back to how things were before," the baseline of Alexandria and the Hilltop are the sufficient working order. Strikingly, in this volume it is Negan, the sociopathic leader of the momentary enemy faction, who complains to Rick: "I'm trying to restore order . . . get back to where they were before you came along," only to have Rick tell him that "we could fix it all, Negan . . . everything. We may never be able to get things back to the way they were—but we can get damn close." Negan's and Rick's "befores" are, obviously, different, marking their distinct impressions of how things have changed and what can be returned to. Negan's impression is much closer to the one Rick has in mind when, early in vol. 24, he justifies not executing the now-captured Negan by saying "if we ever go back to how it was before . . . kill to survive . . . all that . . . that's when all this starts to fall apart." This is perhaps the most surprising shift in Rick's use of the term: where it had previously always meant something positive, something that should be sought and desired, it now signifies the immediate postapocalyptic past. It does so because of a more fully developed sense that the other "way things were before" has already been achieved, because of Rick's belief that the Alexandria and Hilltop communities will genuinely prove to be home.

This idea of "home" and the shifting concept of "the way things were" are, I believe, at the heart of the comic's narrative. "Home," understood as a fundamentally safe place, never actually appears in the comic, Rick's certainty notwithstanding. No place is safe, either from the zombies or from the human figures who periodically appear to threaten Rick and his fellow survivors. The narrative logic of *The Walking Dead* cannot help but dismantle safety in the name of endless momentum; and thus it can come as no surprise that, in the same vol. 24 in which Rick appears to have fully adopted Alexandria as home, Alpha, the leader of the Whisperers, goes in and kills a dozen people. What is at the heart of "home," the familiar and the safe, remains entirely elusive. The striving for home stays alive regardless of the circumstances: no number of shocks can shake the survivors' insistence on trying to re-establish it or feeling they have managed to achieve it. Yet if this sense of "home" does not shift, the idea of "the way things were" does. From a simple yearning for the pre-apocalypse, it moves to a more complicated effort to restitute previous almost-homes and almost-safe places in the face of new dangers. It continues to an even more complicated sense which realizes the limits to the possibility of ultimately restoring a pre-apocalyptic lifestyle and yet strives to get as close as possible to it, and finally a sense of achievement that allows for the phrase to now reference the postapocalypse itself as past. Even as they appear, therefore, to be hunting for an elusive sense of a past everyday way of life, the survivors also establish a different sense of everydayness, one predicated entirely on a willingness to forget their pre-apocalyptic and postapocalyptic pasts, or at the very least to leave them safely behind, a desire nowhere better expressed than when Maggie, now in charge of the Hilltop, says "we have a chance to start over . . . to relive history, in a sense" at the end of vol. 21. Certainly, in order to relive history, one must be, in the broadest sense, aware of history—and indeed, periodically, characters will reflect on their lives after their losses, wondering about how they can be happy, or indeed even alive. But these moments are fleeting, masked by a sense that any restoration of the way things were before requires forgetting what went on between that quasi-mythical time and the characters' contemporary moment. The uneasy paradox of a simultaneous desire for home, conceived in terms of an irretrievable past and the simultaneous insistence on living life without reference to past sorrows is, however, only one of the paradoxes of endless everydayness in *The Walking Dead*.

The Walking Dead and the Paradox of the Everyday

I have already offered a glimpse at what I take to be the paradoxes of the everyday which *The Walking Dead* enacts. On the one hand, there is the everyday which the characters are trying to return to, the pre-apocalyptic everyday that remains forever elusive. Woven into this is a progressive development of something like a tentative acceptance that this everyday is foreclosed and has been replaced with the kind of next-best version that the various achievements in the prison community and so on represent. They stand for a partial integration of the various shocks that the survivors have gone through into their sense of everydayness. But there is a different level to this action, as I have already intimated above. The characters in *The Walking Dead*, presumably like the readers, understand their lives as a progression of nearly restituted everydays (at their initial campsite, in the gated community, at Hershel's farm, in the prison, at Alexandria, at Hill Top), broken every so often by the kinds of shocks which need to be reintegrated into their lives. These include the conflict between Rick and Shane; the surprising presence of the dead in the gated community; the loss of security at Hershel's farm; the Governor's assault on the prison; and the repeated threats to Alexandria. As these events play out in their (cyclical) certainties, surprising exactly no one in their narrative necessity, they also become difficult to differentiate. To take up the words Dale uses in the last panel of vol. 10, exasperated at Rick's leadership: "I'm anxious to see the next way he's going to endanger all of us." Yet this sense of anxious expectation wears off quickly, as repetitions of the dangers set in. They, in and of themselves, become something like an everyday.

As Dorfman notes in a quote I have already offered, the "modern everyday consists of countless voluntary and involuntary shocks and 'extraordinary' events, but none of these seem to mean much and they only add another link to the repetitive chain of everyday life" (2014, 18). Again, this appears to be fairly descriptive of the way the comic handles even such major storyline breaks as the destruction of the prison compound or the death of Lori and other major characters: they simply do not seem to mean very much as they are added to the chain of events. At the same time, however, in their very meaninglessness and repetitiveness, they form a different kind of everyday life. The survivors of the zombie apocalypse already have an everyday: the very sequence of temporary safety and repeated danger that present themselves as actual, desirable everyday and non-everyday shocks. *The Walking Dead*, here, enacts the complicated postmodern interplay between a nostalgia for a past that cannot ever return and a commensurate refusal to accept the real present. The very act of refusing the everydayness of the endless series of arrivals, dangers, and departures is, however, what makes this series possible: every arrival must, potentially, be an end point to their journey—that is, not just one more everyday moment, but a necessary precursor to the real, if elusive, everyday existence the survivors crave. Otherwise, everyday life for the survivors would be limited to the endless trek through the wastelands of the dead (precisely the solution that, as I will argue, the Whisperers have opted for). Thus, one part of the paradoxical nature of the everyday in *The Walking Dead* lies in the way it is constituted by a refusal of the everyday.

The comic produces another everyday, though, one which is in some ways more problematic but also more closely connected to the endless narrative: the reader's everyday. Forced by its quest for endlessness to produce ever more twists and turns, each perhaps more radical than the last, *The Walking Dead* at the same time becomes everyday in a narrative sense: that is, whatever radical turn the story appears to take as it progresses becomes ever less radical, ever more mundane. The killing of Andrea's sister, Amy, towards the end of the first volume, in an apparently peaceful camp site, may have been shocking, and its uncertain import for the rest of the story a challenge to the reader. But by the time the story proceeds to the killing of Glenn (murdered by Negan with a baseball bat in vol. 17), much of the meaning of such actions has been blunted by the fact that we've seen it so often, lost so many characters we cared for, and more importantly, realized that the plot of *The Walking Dead* is largely powered by such deaths. They have become everyday. And even as the comic ups the ante, as when the Whisperers kill twelve men and women in a stroke, there is perhaps more of a sense that we have no connection with more than half of those people, that we would not have been able to pick them out of a group image, than that something genuinely radically shocking has occurred. *The Walking Dead*, then, makes the shocking everyday to the reader. With no expectation that any safe place will be lastingly safe, with no expectation that anybody but Rick will survive from issue to issue, this readerly everyday finds the kind of homely security in the very narrative cyclicality that the characters experience as a series of shocks to their own sense of everydayness.

The Walking Dead layers uneasily a number of senses of the everyday, none of which fully corresponds with any other or even can be regarded simultaneously. And, indeed, many of these senses appear to necessarily open to criticism the way its narrative endlessness produces a narrative without meaning and without development, one which appears, in more simple terms, to show the nostalgic efforts of a group of people unwilling to come to terms with their new lives in what has become an increasingly boring read. Perhaps this is the case, but is there a more charitable way of reading the comic?

This question brings me to my final point, which is to open up the view of the nature of the survivor's relation to the everyday in light of what has been going on in the last three volumes of the series. In order to do so, let me draw a final theoretical idea from Dorfman's argument, namely, the differentiation between flexibility and plasticity: flexibility, "an ability [. . .] to adapt oneself to the surroundings, to change in a reactive, conciliatory and docile way" is modernity's substitute for plasticity, which dialectically combines creation and destruction. Dorfman's point is that the "crisis of the everyday and experience" (which, as I am arguing here, *The Walking Dead* symptomatically stages) "stems from a crisis in plasticity," defined at least in part as "the inability to admit negativity (absence, lack and loss)" (2014, 20). It is this crisis of plasticity that has heretofore been a central coping mechanism to the characters in the comic—a refusal to look back, a readiness to forget their losses, or at the very least not to dwell on them and mourn too deeply—and it must be read more complexly as an attempt to restitute a sense of the everyday falsely assumed to require such distancing.

Juxtaposed against a radically different version of how to cope with the changes of the apocalypse, the Whisperers, we may give this a different spin: for all their failing to achieve a return of the everyday, at least Rick and his group seek a return to plasticity, a creative/destructive agency against the constraints of their times. That they have hitherto failed, that they have hitherto only reinforced the sense of the impossibility of resuscitating a familiar sense of everyday existence, should then not, maybe, detract from the fact that their quest to return to the everyday is still preferable to its clear alternative, a wholly flexible submissiveness to the conditions of an overwhelming reality. The storyline of the last four volumes has seen Rick's group of survivors challenged by another outside threat: a large group of other survivors whose strategy of survival is to skin the dead and wear their skins, in order to camouflage themselves. Initially led by a woman named Alpha, the Whisperers threaten to kill anyone who enters their territory, and mark their threat by, killing a dozen of Alexandria's inhabitants in the middle of the town and then sticking their heads up on the border. On the one hand, then, the Whisperers figure as a physical threat; on the other, however, they also represent a completely opposite sense of life in the postapocalyptic world from the one which Rick and his group are living. In Rick's long encounter with Alpha at the end of vol. 24, the Whisperers' leader derides precisely the kind of attempts to restitute an everyday that has engaged them for the past two dozen volumes. Describing the Alexandria survivors as "children playing a game of make-believe," Alpha tells Rick he "strive[s] to return to a life as slaves of our petty desires," while she recognizes "the gift that this world has to offer." Her essential argument, as it turns out, is that the Whisperers "don't look at the world the way we used to . . . the way people thought we were supposed to" (fig. 8). In other words, she holds that the Whisperers have discovered, in the new world, the right way of life.

What Alpha takes to be a natural consequence of the way the new postapocalyptic world is, at the same time, using Dorfman's terminology (taken from Catherine Malabou), a fully "flexible" way of approaching life. As Dorfman has it, flexibility is a response to a general state of instability and lack of continuity. In these circumstances, one cannot afford anymore to be plastic; one needs, first and foremost, to adapt and survive. Plasticity may be defined as the ability to link the old to the new, to act and create upon a solid enough background, such that this background is transformed and partly annihilated during the act of creation. (2014, 20)

Acquiescing to what they take to be the changed circumstances, the Whisperers turn out to be anything but radical. In donning the skins of the dead, in walking with them, they rather represent the "reactive, conciliatory and docile way" of reacting to radical shocks and radical social change. The Whisperers, in the words of their leader, regard the lost world of the pre-apocalypse with a derision that allows them not to have to deal with a sense of loss and negativity: in the very way they seek to become zombie-formed themselves, the Whisperers highlight their passivity to the events surrounding them. In this sense, they more fully represent the way contemporary society expects such a reactive adaptation to the shifting conditions of everyday life than the way Rick's survivors struggle. If Rick's survivors cling to a past sense of what everyday life should look like, they, at least, struggle against the mere acceptance of the way things are. In this, they herald a return to plasticity: to an effort to be creative in the way they handle the shocks in their lives. As Dorfman notes, "plastic creation alone allows the creator to become subject to his or her own history" (2014, 20). "*The Walking Dead*," as Darren Reed and Ruth Penfold-Mounce have pointed out, "raises fundamental questions about agency" (2015, 127): it does so, I would argue, by contrasting the kind of fake-agency that leads the Whisperers to become as close as possible to zombies themselves with the plastic efforts of Rick's survivors to struggle against the new everyday of the world. For all the fault it is possible to find with the single-minded repetitiveness of their efforts to restore home and safety in recognizably pre-apocalyptic, if non-modern, surroundings, at least Rick and his fellows do not surrender to the logic imposed on them by their surroundings. Instead, they seek to shape and create their own way of life.

This, then, is the final ambivalence and final paradox of reading *The Walking Dead* through the everyday: in their very efforts to return to a past everyday that appears to fail to integrate the present shocks, we may now see, in the most recent volumes of the series, a glimmer of hope for an actual everyday. This becomes visible, really, only in the contrast between the radically other way of life that the Whisperers have chosen.

Fig. 8. Alpha explains her view of the world. *The Walking Dead 24: Life and Death.* Image Comics. All rights reserved.

Conclusion: The Narrative Logic of the Never-Ending Story

In the way it represents shifting and often paradoxical senses of what constitutes an everyday and in its narrative insistence on endlessness both, *The Walking Dead* is symptomatic of its time. It features characters who strive, in a world without anchors, for a return "home," encoding a large number of different things: safety, certainty, familiarity, but also a quasi-mythic irretrievable past. Such a quest certainly takes on added meaning in the wake of similarly nostalgic right-wing populist successes in recent years. In the characters' pursuit of their nostalgic sense of home lies something like displacement: a refusal to acknowledge the realities of the postapocalyptic world, and by extension an anxiety about the contemporary. If this is what it does narratively, it formally merely reinforces this sense: its endless narrative makes it the very sort of restless succession of events that bewilder the characters in their quest for stability. We may link this again with Frank Kermode's aim in *The Sense of an Ending* to elucidate, philosophically as well as in literary fiction, the "temporal image of the world" (2000, 83) as it changes through the ages. *The Walking Dead* lets us see a contemporary temporal image of the world, too: one which at once conceives of the apocalypse as an end, and an endless, desperate aftermath. We should probably not miss the philosophical import of this: as Kermode notes, apocalypse, the end, is expected by men to "reflect their irreducibly intermediary preoccupations" (6) to be in concord with origins and middles, to mean something in a grander scheme of things. "Apocalypse," says Kermode, "depends on a concord of imaginatively recorded past and imaginatively predicted future . . . [i]ts predictions, though figurative, can be taken literally, and as the future moves in on us we may expect it to conform with the figures" (8). The end figured in *The Walking Dead*, however, is no end: it is endlessness. What it predicts is more of the same, and where Kermode says we "need ends [. . .] even now when the history of the world has so terribly and so untidily expanded its endless successiveness" (58; shades of Dorfman's modern everyday), *The Walking Dead* appears to agree with something akin to capitalist realism: we had better accept the endless successiveness of modernity, not to expect meaning to be possible, and abandon the notion that our lives will cohere, or even our stories. Endlessness in this parsing becomes a philosophical, somewhat radically negative statement, but one which obviously and strikingly connects narrative form and commercial agenda. After all, a narrative that is endless promises endless sales, and what better narrative to be endless than one which has already accepted its own repetitiveness? My point here is not so much to criticize *The Walking Dead* as a commodity but rather to point out the confluence between formal properties, narrative aim, and its own conditions of production, all of which indicate the importance of realizing the limits of its "endless" conception. *The Walking Dead* here emerges as a profoundly conservative work, one which accepts a contemporary logic of life and commerce both: it sees the contemporary's endless series of events and mirrors it in its own narrative logic.

I noted in Chapter 1 how Max Brooks's *World War Z* highlights the limits of the liberal utopian imagination. *The Walking Dead*, as a few glimpses above into its conception of gender relations have already indicated, tends towards a deeply conservative worldview. This does not just include such obvious points as its insistence on unitary, non-democratic leadership as a precondition of survival (in Rick's case, insulated even against the gravest and most frequent errors of judgment) but the very narrative movement itself. Indeed, even where it appears to counteract its own symptomatic representation of the world as in constant inconstancy (in its characters' apparent desire to re-anchor their world outside the eternal flux, in shutting themselves off from the sweep of zombies behind the fences of prisons and towns, in restituting a different sense of everydayness from the hectic, overwhelming postmodern everyday) it appears profoundly conservative. Home and the everyday are peculiarly backwards in *The Walking Dead*, not so much because they are functionally unattainable in the postapocalypse but because of the particular way they are conceived. They correspond more to the "stifling Eisenhower realities of the happy family in the small town, of normalcy a nondeviant everyday life" (Jameson 1991, 280) than to any actual, twenty-first-century version. What's more, in *The Walking Dead*, the big cities—Atlanta and Washington, DC—are hostile ground, not just practically but also metaphorically. They are, as Antonio Sanna has written of the *Resident Evil* films, "pictured as deserted places, haunted by the monstrous and ghostly remains of humanity" (2015, 56), and the safe places which the survivors establish for themselves, especially at Hershel's farm and later at the Alexandria complex, refract a sense of loss that is very postmodern in its absence of historicity.

To couch the city in these terms suggests a sense of home that actively promotes the small-town coziness of a mythical American past, one the comic had already laid in in the very beginning of the narrative, of course. Rick's and Lori's origins in the small town of Cynthia, Kentucky, condition his sense of how home should look;, the assumption that cities will be dead, or deadly, and settlements small, rural, and far-flung is a common postapocalyptic move (from David Brin's *The Postman* to Emily St. John Mandel's *Station Eleven*). But as the examples of both *Pariah* and *Dying to Live* have demonstrated, it is not a necessary move at all. To make it suggests something about the way *The Walking Dead* conceives of the world at large, and what in it is worth saving. The narrow confines of the small-town, near-communities finally endorsed by the comic represent its argument for conceiving "home" narrowly, personally, and slightly regressively as something lost even today, not available since a mythical golden age: "the way things were before," in other words, with "before" neatly eliding any concrete historicity, and "things" neatly avoiding any concrete sociality. *The Walking Dead*'s vision of the contemporary is a nostalgic, imprecise yearning for the past, a past whose historical existence is immaterial to it.

In their struggle against zombies who may be read as symbolic of early twenty-first-century life, with its endless array of shocks to the everyday, the survivors of *The Walking Dead* may at times suggest (and not just because of their rural southern background) the Trump voter feeling an urgent desire for the return of the coal mines, of strictly delimited male and female bathrooms, of the nuclear family, manufacturing, and the time when men could be men. These echoes also persist in the way the comic imagines the communities at the Hilltop and Alexandria, notably perhaps in these communities' return to pre-capitalist modes of production. Much of vol. 22, for example, is devoted to images of the new communities' small-time farming and manual, pre-industrial labor (inclusive of master-apprentice relationships). This culminates in vol. 24 in what amounts to a medieval trade-fair; and while the narrative logic of the comic certainly permits this to develop organically, nonetheless it is striking that it figures resurgence of human civilization through these nostalgic images of self-sufficient, pre-modern life. This particular form of the comic's nostalgia in fact goes beyond the contemporary right-wing populist belief in a better life under an earlier capitalism, one that is merely less culturally diverse and less global.

A final point is still in order. What I have characterized above as a paradox, the formal reinforcement of this sense of aimless ever-onwards produces a sense of everydayness during the act of reading: the returning anxieties and dangers, the repeated retrievals and losses of some form of home, become in their own way homely, safe, comfortable—they become an everyday reading experience. With Jameson, perhaps we may say that the comic's explicit choice of narrative endlessness is a "symbolic act, whereby real social contradictions, insurmountable in their own terms, find a purely formal resolution in the aesthetic realm" (2002, 64). That is, the awkward contradiction between the desire for a secure and stable sense of home in the midst of a present that has no place for such security and stability becomes formally resolved in making stability out of the very narrative of this impossibility. *The Walking Dead*'s concern for endlessness and the everyday thereby becomes key to unraveling what work it does on the contemporary—and, not to put too fine a point on it, what work zombie fiction can potentially do.

"So Many Unmentionables About"
Parody, *Pride and Prejudice and Zombies*, and the Politics of Mash-up Fiction

In 2009, Quirk Books, a small publisher of odd humor and offbeat fiction, published Seth Grahame-Smith's *Pride and Prejudice and Zombies*. It became a runaway bestseller, hitting a million copies sold by early 2010 and becoming an almost instantaneous talking point. It also ushered in what has now come to be called zombie "mash-up" fiction (Voigts-Virchow 2010, Nelson 2013, Shapiro 2014, Wilke 2015). Its premise is simple enough: take an old favorite, out of copyright, and place within its otherwise undisturbed narrative newly written episodes of zombie mayhem. The resultant text copies large stretches of Austen's text verbatim: the sense of domestic life, of courtship, of familial dialogue which drove the Regency romance remains largely untouched. Yet interspersed among these events are scenes of zombie attacks, on the ball at which the Bennett girls first encounter Mr. Darcy, on their mansion, and on a carriage ride; the demise of Charlotte Collins, née Lucas, from a zombie bite; and the odd bit of information that transforms the world in which the romance is set. London, for example, is surrounded by a high wall to keep out zombies, and the army is out in force, trying to safeguard the countryside. The novel plays around with the backstory of the Bennett family, with their individual roles and fates, and yet it consistently remains faithful, for given values of the word, to its source materials.

Pride and Prejudice and Zombies became the forerunner of a series of formula novels whose chief claim to fame is that they plunder a reservoir of out-of-copyright but well-known and well-loved texts and repackage them to take advantage of the contemporary interest in zombies. Its ludicrous premise, its obvious attempt to profit off of both the recognition value of *Pride and Prejudice* and its out-of-copyright status, and its at best uneven execution all seem to rebel against a serious investigation of the work it does. When a critic generally sympathetic to the zombie phenomenon such as Jennifer Rutherford notes that "even the most avid zombie fan would be hard pressed to defend this as a book worth reading" (2014, 12), and Roger Luckhurst summarily avers that its "joke" of bringing together high literary culture and the zombie "rather overstays its welcome" (2015, 191), it bodes ill for any sustained engagement with what the novel might mean, both in the greater context of zombie fictions as well as a cultural phenomenon.

Part of the reason for this, however, is the very way critics have approached the novel—that is, as a mash-up. Much rests on the way we set out into the reading of *Pride and Prejudice and Zombies*: even the apparently neutral practice of terminological definition, usually undertaken in a half-sentence, becomes fraught with a danger of prejudicing the following reading, of substituting a term of analysis for an investigation of substance.[1] Recent criticism, as we have seen, has largely agreed to call *Pride and Prejudice and Zombies* a "mash-up," using a term initially used to describe a form of musical production in which two or more preexisting pieces of (usually pop) music were remixed. This form of cultural production notably did not require the inclusion of works original to the mash-up artist—in fact, it eschewed such originality in favor of simple reappropriation. The term has also more recently become used for similar techniques in digital media, such as the combination of Google's map service Maps with photographs (von Gehlen 2011, 206). What unites both uses of this term is the restriction to recombination, rather than the production of something original to the producer. If some recent discussions of the mash-up age have sought to expand this notion of the mash-up to include "found" medial artifacts with newly produced ones (Wilke 2015), two issues remain important for my purposes here. First, the heart of the idea of the mash-up is the recombination of preexisting cultural texts, without the addition of new material; and second, the fact that "mash-up" is a purely technical description, which does not speak to the purpose of this formal move.

To call *Pride and Prejudice and Zombies* a "mash-up," then, is certainly correct in an extended definition of the term; and one thing it does is to place the novel in a larger discourse, in what Stefan Sonvilla-Weiss has called the contemporary "mashup cultures" (2011). Yet it is not an interpretative move, and in fact seems at least tentatively to preclude such moves, suggesting, for example, that Grahame-Smith's additions to the novel are wholly derivative. This, as we shall see, is not the case.

In what follows, even though I agree that as a technical term, "mash-up" seems to work, I will prefer to call the *Pride and Prejudice and Zombies* "trilogy parodies," a term of much greater critical and interpretative power. As Jennifer Rutherford points out, the 2009 novel "parodied Austen and the entire genre of romantic regency literature" (2014, 13); I want to elaborate, however, on the sense in which the idea of parody needs to be imbued in order for this (somewhat throwaway) suggestion to be helpful. Indeed, it is probably impossible to use the term today without at least briefly noting the debate on the validity and scope of the term, especially as contrasted with the related practice of pastiche. David Castillo has made this point explicitly, arguing that Grahame-Smith's novel "functions as a pastiche, rather than a parody" (2016, 50). Jameson calls pastiche the "neutral practice" of parody, the "imitation of a peculiar or unique, idiosyncratic style, the wearing of a linguistic mask, speech in a dead language" (1991, 17).[2] It contrasts with parody, a similarly imitative form, in that parody still has "ulterior motives," which Simon Dentith has called the "critical distance from the urtext" (2000, 155). To use either term at the outset, then, is to imply already something about them beyond their merely formal conjunction of zombie and canonical text. The usefulness of the term "parody" emerges from this discussion in the delineation of parody and pastiche as particular forms of a similar practice. Both are essentially terms contingent on interpretation, in which pastiche names those parodies without critical distance. They are not distinguishable by formal elements (pastiche and parody share a cultural belatedness, engage in extensive direct quotation, and play with the linguistic imitation of a hypotext [Dentith 2000, 164–65]), but solely on the basis of a particular stance towards the hypotext (Gérard Genette's term for the original text being parodied). Parody's stance, as Simon Dentith points out, is one in which the combination of hypotext and contemporary engagement results in "politically and socially positive resolution" (2000, 174).

Thus, to read *Pride and Prejudice and Zombies* as a parody is to argue from the outset that it has ulterior motives—or perhaps less motives than privileged modes of reading. It emphasizes, as I will below, that as much as *Pride and Prejudice and Zombies*'s central gimmick is a joke, it also performs "evaluative and ideological work" (Dentith 2000, 14) on Austen's novel, contemporary readers of Austen, and the idea of romance in general. At its best, it "seeks to contain the new" and to "deflate the old" (185); at its worst, it recurs to being a somewhat overindulged gag. The existence of such bad moments (which I have no interest in denying) is not, however, sufficient cause to dismiss the novel and trilogy's capacity for useful literary and social critique. Indeed, perhaps the opposite is true, requiring us to at least briefly pause over the possibility that facile dismissals of all kinds of cultural texts cost us the opportunity of dealing with them on the terms they deserve.

Entailed in this discussion of pastiche and parody, and my own sense of the importance of understanding the various strands of critique that emerge from *Pride and Prejudice and Zombies*'s parodic play with Austen, readers, and the contemporary world, is an affirmation of the need for a close reading of the trilogy's texts, a challenge especially with regard to the "original" (as it were). Eckart Voigts-Virchow has claimed (and given the criticisms of Rutherford and Luckhurst offered above, it seems safe to say they would agree) that "[i]t is probably not worthwhile to subject *Pride and Prejudice and Zombies* to a close reading New Criticism-style" (2011, 48). Voigts-Virchow's point is, on one level, banal: even the most literary of contemporary fiction is difficult to read "New Criticism-style" today. On another level, it is simply wrong: *Pride and Prejudice and Zombies*, as I will go on to show, rewards close attention to what it does, and how it does it—perhaps not through regarding it as an autonomous work of art or by focusing on its formal ambiguities, nor by suggesting the novel's inherent unity of purpose, but certainly by suggesting the importance to it of parodic irony, and by highlighting the specific ways in which it does what it does, the ways in which it parodies its hypotext and this hypotext's readers, but also those in which it produces new readers, and new ways of reading its hypotext. To read *Pride and Prejudice and Zombies* closely reveals that its inclusion of zombies and their consequences permits a radically different view of *Pride and Prejudice* and remediates it for the contemporary.

Pride and Prejudice and Zombies modifies its hypotext systematically in four ways. It deletes passages of the original text, for what appear to be chiefly reasons of length. It adds and alters minor details to better fit, or at least more often mention, zombies. (As when Mr. Collins notes of his ascension to the rectory at Hunsford that it occurred when Lady Catherine "had been forced to behead the previous rector when he succumbed to the walking death" [56]; it had merely been "vacant" [Austen 2004, 52] in the original). It adds whole scenes and episodes of zombie attacks and related matter, such as the attack on the ball in the beginning of the novel or Charlotte Lucas's slow demise. And finally, it alters the novel in ways which are not related at all to zombies, or only indirectly, as when Mr. Collins, after Charlotte's death, commits suicide and so removes the threat of entailment from the Bennetts. These changes that are only vaguely or not at all related to what might be called the narratively necessary changes, are, as I will argue especially in the section on *Pride and Prejudice and Zombies*'s arguments about gender, perhaps even more interesting than the zombie additions. *Pride and Prejudice and Zombie*'s world is a schizophrenic one, in which the genteel balls, visits and counter-visits, dinners, walks, and idle chats, not to mention the preoccupation with marriage, sit uneasily against an increasingly dark background of England's "present difficulties" (77). The novel rests on a sense of the upper classes fiddling while Rome is burning. It suggests this in half-sentences and throwaway lines, from the "fall of Cambridge" (12) in Darcy's introduction through the discussion of London as a "fortress hardly fit for the fragile nerves of a gentle lady" (37–38), the "battlefields of Derbyshire, Cornwall, and Essex" (24), to the "recent troubles in Birmingham" (190).[3] The zombie plague, notably, appears as an entirely English problem, one with (as the sequel establishes) dire consequences: "England had lost its colonies, found its once-great navies unwelcome in any port, and could do nothing but watch as Napoleon Bonaparte put half the world under his little heel" (Hockensmith 2011, 232). In this radical reimagination of the Regency era lies, as we shall see, much of the trilogy's critical parodic potential.

This chapter will make three interrelated points. I will begin by offering a close reading of *Pride and Prejudice and Zombies*, highlighting the variety of ways by which the novel changes and expands upon Austen's original. My point here is that *Pride and Prejudice and Zombies* (despite appearances and a marked amount of critical disdain), its subsequently published prequel, *Pride and Prejudice and Zombies: Dawn of the Dreadfuls*, and sequel, *Pride and Prejudice and Zombies: Dreadfully Ever After*, deserve the kind of close attention which literary criticism gives. The three texts raise important points in the terms of their engagement with gender and power. If not always successful in updating the women in Austen's novel to the status of genuinely self-determined individuals marked more by their abilities than by their socially determined, narrow gender roles, the novels certainly set into relief the narrowness of Austen's fictional world; and they do so by way of parody.

Pride and Prejudice and Zombies emerges in this reading as a complicatedly layered narrative in which different interpretations necessarily clash: on the one hand, the zombies clearly can be understood as the appearance of the repressed lower classes which Austen's novels so largely elide. But if so, the remarkable act of empowerment which the Bennett girls undergo simultaneously means, as Andrea Ruthven has pointed out, "paradoxically fighting to maintain the patriarchical system that confines [them]" (2014, 347)—as well as the class system, of course. This, intriguingly, may be especially relevant given the gendered readerships of Austen's fiction today; as Stephen Shapiro has noted, *Pride and Prejudice and Zombies* does not merely mock any canonical literature, but a book "particularly beloved by women, who might allow their own emotional investment in Jane Austen to allow for learning the sense and sensibility of zombie codes." It thereby mobilizes this readership for "entirely different purposes and social problems" (2014, 208). Besides commenting on the difficulties of coordinating gender and social equality, and thus producing a deeper problem in their own right, the three novels in the *Pride and Prejudice and Zombies* series also engage with the lasting contemporary fascination with the novels, and the era, of Jane Austen: an engagement that highlights how problematical the lasting popularity of Austen is.

I will tie this argument back to a shorter reading of a different mash-up text, *The Adventures of Huckleberry Finn and Zombie Jim*, which will serve as what is no doubt a necessary corrective to my claims for the *Pride and Prejudice and Zombies* trilogy's critical usefulness. In the hands of Bill Czolgosz, the zombie mash-up of Mark Twain's great American novel emerges as an update that ultimately adds little to the already fraught racial commentary of Twain's text. In emphasizing how not just any out-of-copyright text can serve as the grounds of a powerful contemporary reappropriation, my discussion of *The Adventures of Huckleberry Finn and Zombie Jim* will simultaneously correct any notion that zombie mash-ups per se are politically and socially useful, and reemphasize the particular usefulness of the updating of Austen.

In sum, what will emerge from this chapter is an understanding of the parodic elements of zombie mash-ups as capable of performing a particular work: "to 'double-code' the present," a use of the "cultural past to unlock the complexities of the present moment" (Dentith 2000, 170). In the best essay on *Pride and Prejudice and Zombies*, Camille Nelson suggests that the "mysterious plague that the text envisions has less to do with the middleclass violence that the historical Austen does or does not depict, but is rather [...] a symptomatic representation of the violence of the American Empire today" (2013, 6). As I will go on to show, this kind of an either-or proposition is entirely unnecessary: the parodic work of the mash-up of *Pride and Prejudice and Zombies* acts on the historical Austen, the reception of Austen, and the contemporary moment's systematic exclusions and violences.

"Dead, Rendered Lame, or Married": Constructing Gender in *Pride and Prejudice and Zombies*

In one of the most famous opening lines in literature, *Pride and Prejudice* begins thus: "It is a truth universally acknowledged, that a single man in possession of a good fortune, must be in lack of a wife" (2004, 1). In *Pride and Prejudice and Zombies*, this reads instead: "It is a truth universally acknowledged that a zombie in possession of brains must be in want of more brains" (Austen and Grahame-Smith, 7). There can be little doubt that the alteration of *Pride and Prejudice*'s famous opening line is a somewhat lame joke—one which, admittedly, leads nowhere in particular. It removes the ironies of Austen's line, which plays with different readings of the "fortune" of having no wife, and which gives way to the idea that such a man will be considered the "rightful property" of the daughters of his neighbors. Yet this act, if it rightly seems somewhat silly, also highlights already some of the troubling aspects of Austen's novel. Marriage becomes a quest and a tournament for financially desirable bachelors, for whom the woman, in turn, is hardly a prize at all. In light of this, it is perhaps surprising that *Pride and Prejudice and Zombies* ends like *Pride and Prejudice*, with the marriage of Elizabeth Bennett to Fitzwilliam Darcy: despite Elizabeth's marrying for love, an entirely normative, ostensibly happy ending, which strangely counteracts Elizabeth's role in the narrative. After producing Elizabeth as a violent, willful, able, and above all independent protagonist, one with an independent role to play, Grahame-Smith's novel does not fully change the notion that women's lives are geared towards obtaining a husband (much more so than a man's is geared towards finding a wife). Indeed, as we shall see, Grahame-Smith's narrative reinforces the obvious problem with the surrender of female power to male in the act of marriage.

There can be little doubt, then, that gender roles are at the heart of any critical reading of either novel. They are important in Austen's, where the roles of (rich!) men as objects of desire and of women as somewhat mercenary creatures are only partially counteracted by the way in which Elizabeth Bennett behaves. Similarly, in Grahame-Smith's, where the centrality of the marriage plot as a whole is initially obscured, and its reintroduction, as we shall see, rests on slightly different premises than it does in Austen. In *Pride and Prejudice*, as Mr. Bennett notes, Elizabeth is "silly and ignorant, like all the other girls," if with "something more of quickness" (Austen 2004, 2); in Grahame-Smith's rewriting, Elizabeth is the "exception" (Austen and Grahame-Smith 2009, 8). *Pride and Prejudice and Zombies*, indeed, constructs Elizabeth Bennett as a far more vociferous opponent of marriage in general than *Pride and Prejudice* does: "I do not seek love" (109), she tells her aunt Mrs. Gardiner, a radical disavowal that in the original was a tempered discussion of her prospects with Mr. Wickham. In this disavowal, she echoes her father. As the Bennetts' debate early on the prospect of getting a daughter married to the extremely eligible Mr. Bingley, Mr. Bennett shows in how far his wife's concern for her daughters' marriage misses the point of life with the zombie menace around: "I would much prefer [my daughters'] minds be engaged in the deadly arts than clouded with dreams of marriage and fortune, as you own so clearly is." The narrator then adds what the issue is: Mrs. Bennett's interest in the rituals of courtship and marriage are "the comfort of traditions which now seemed mere trifles to others" (8). *Pride and Prejudice* thus very early lays in what becomes its two central concerns: the question of how appropriate Regency gentility is in the circumstances of the zombie threat, and how the particular patriarchal constitution of gender relations fits into this scheme.

In fact, *Pride and Prejudice and Zombies* radicalizes the options available to women in general, and Elizabeth Bennett in particular. If, in the Regency romance in general, woman's choices boil down to a defeated spinsterdom or marriage, these choices are also effectively determined by a man's willingness to take a woman to wife—a waiting game of sorts, in which womanly wiles may aid in the desired outcome but cannot actively open new avenues. This does not hold true for *Pride and Prejudice and Zombies*. Elizabeth Bennett—"Defender of Longbourne" and "Heroine of Hertfordshire" (23), in Caroline Bingley's words—is not merely a marriageable, disposable woman. She (like her sisters) has also sworn a "blood oath to defend the Crown" (185). She is "a warrior" (109), as she herself insists; and not only does this grant her an already more active role than she had in *Pride and Prejudice*, it also bodes well for her long-term prospects.

As in the original novel, the threat of entailment hangs over Longbourne, the family home, with Mr. Collins inheriting it on Mr. Bennett's death. The looming threat of homelessness which subsists through much of *Pride and Prejudice*, however, is early on counteracted in Grahame-Smith's version, where the sisters "could make tolerable fortunes as bodyguards, assassins, or mercenaries if need be" (50). Andrea Ruthven notes that "to have to work for a living would be a step down in the world for these daughters of the gentry" (2014, 348), but to argue this is to submit to the logic of *Pride and Prejudice*, rather than *Pride and Prejudice and Zombies*. Elizabeth, proud of her abilities, in particular is overtly willing to sacrifice the prospect of marriage, and to continue to "work" as a zombie slayer: there is no sense that this is in any way below what she feels is her position. But if that is so, then marriage becomes genuine sacrifice, substituting love for self-fulfillment, which in turn supports Ruthven's more general conclusion: "the libratory potential of the position of the heroine is undermined by postfeminist discourse, re-encoding the heroine as heteronormatively desirous and desiring" (2014, 347). *Pride and Prejudice and Zombies*'s Elizabeth Bennett thus at least in one sense merely sets out in more concrete terms one of the traits which Austen's Elizabeth already had—namely, a range of deeply "unconventional" traits of character, all of which set her apart from the traditional heroines of the romance. She "refuses the silence and subordination marked out for women" (Kaplan 1992, 186); yet where *Pride and Prejudice*'s Elizabeth will, probably, be perfectly able to retain her refusal of silence, *Pride and Prejudice and Zombies*'s Elizabeth will certainly not be able to retain her claim to independence or her status as a warrior.

There is, then, a certain radicalism to Mr. Bennett's position, and to Elizabeth's initial adoption of it, which underlies much of the novel afterwards. As it turns out, the number of people who do believe that the traditional way of upper-middle-class English life is trifling, as Mr. Bennett does, is itself trifling. Much time is spent by the characters at dances and dinners, as in the original Austen, and among people for whom the Bennett sisters' insistence on training in arms is, at beast, eyebrow raising. It is not correct to suggest, as Collins and Bond do, "that martial arts skill has come the hallmark of the 'accomplished' young lady" (2010, 197)—with the implication that society at large accepts and even demands training in arms. Muskets and katana swords, in fact, as the novel avers, "were considered unladylike" (*Pride and Prejudice and Zombies*, 27); and training in arms, as Darcy somewhat mischievously suggests given his own predilections, "must very materially lessen their chance of marrying men of any consideration in the world" (32). This dimension is somewhat more obscure in *Pride and Prejudice and Zombies*, where all of the younger women, with the exception of Charlotte Lucas, appear to have combat training, and most who appear not to have it do not have speaking roles; this is a dimension much more pronounced in the prequel. Here, with the zombie menace freshly returned after a decades-long hiatus, Mr. Bennett's decision to train his daughters in the oriental arts of warfare is immediately censored as "'unladylike,' 'uncivilized,' 'un-English'" (Hockensmith 2010, 137). In Mr. Bennett's parsing, his daughters throw off the "shackles of good manners and gentility" (31) in favor of survival—the same sentiment that he professes in *Pride and Prejudice and Zombies*.

This insight is crucial because on it is grounded the budding relationship between Darcy and Elizabeth in *Pride and Prejudice and Zombies*. Where in *Pride and Prejudice*, Darcy is initially introduced to the Bennetts as "having ten thousand a year" (6) and his attraction stems in no small part from this, in *Pride and Prejudice and Zombies*, this introduction is rendered as his "having slaughtered more than a thousand unmentionables since the fall of Cambridge" (12). The parody, as it does frequently, shifts the hypotext's rendering of relationships in terms of monetary security to an appreciation of ability. Thus Darcy's first glimpse of Elizabeth, as she and her sisters fight off the zombies who have attacked the ball at which they meet, lets his commentary rest on her "skill [...] grace, and deadly accuracy" (14)—an overt break with the sharply dismissive way Darcy treats Elizabeth in Austen's text.

The basis of Darcy and Elizabeth's relationship in *Pride and Prejudice and Zombies*, then, is an almost professional one, in which their mutual respect for their respective abilities, more than anything else, determines their attraction: as Darcy muses, "were it not for the inferiority of her connections, he should be in some danger of falling in love [. . .] for he had never seen a lady more gifted in the ways of vanquishing the dead" (42). In terms of their fighting prowess, they are equal: "warriors such as they" (143), as Darcy puts it to Elizabeth, and with which sense of themselves Elizabeth quietly agrees (200). It is very apropos, if suitably over the top, that Elizabeth and Darcy "consummate," as it were, their ultimate agreement to marry in a "fight side by side" (302) against a herd of zombies: brought together by fighting, engaging in fighting during their tempestuous early relationship, to fight with one another against a shared foe becomes symbolic of their newly shared social status. This redefinition of relations among the upper classes in fact extends to Lady Catherine, Darcy's aunt and archnemesis of Elizabeth's. Elizabeth finds her intimidating, not for her money or standing in society, but for her martial abilities: a "woman who had slain ninety dreadfuls with nothing more than a rain-soaked envelope" (124), Lady Catherine finally must be defeated in a duel to establish Elizabeth as her superior in no uncertain terms. If in *Pride and Prejudice*, Lady Catherine suffers the ignominy of a moral defeat in not being able finally to force Elizabeth to give up on Darcy, in *Pride and Prejudice and Zombies*, she falls to a more devastatingly personal one, replaced as the preeminent fighter in England by a woman who, startlingly, must soon renounce fighting forever.

This is the vexed problem of Grahame-Smith's narrative. As Mr. Collins notes when he first applies for Elizabeth's hand, no matter Elizabeth's "talents in slaying the stricken," he "will require [her] to retire them as part of [her] marital submission" (85). This is not, as the novel repeatedly makes clear, merely a fancy of Mr. Collins's, either. Elizabeth herself notes that her services to the Crown last only until she is "dead, rendered lame, or married" (225), a startling trio of terms indeed. Fighting zombies is a bachelorette's semi-profession, then, while Darcy, by contrast is, not similarly bound. The novel becomes still more problematical where it reproduces the hypotext intact. In agreeing to allow Darcy to marry Elizabeth, Mr. Bennett avers as in the original that Elizabeth would "be neither happy nor respectable" unless she "truly looked upon [a husband] as a superior" (308). Fully aware of the consequences of her decision to marry Darcy, then, Elizabeth squanders away not just her prized talents and ability, but also her status as Darcy's equal. It is, as Andrea Ruthven points out, an unsettling conclusion to a narrative that seems to have promised more: the Bennett sisters (Jane marrying Bingley, and Lydia eloping with a maimed Wickham) at the end of the novel, as at the beginning, appear "always subordinated to a patriarchal figure" (2014, 358), and in what must appear to be a shockingly more radical way than in the original, thanks to the quality of the two novels' endings when juxtaposed to their narratives. Elizabeth's decision to marry Fitzwilliam Darcy (like Jane's and Lydia's) has starkly different values in the two novels; Austen's Elizabeth, for all intents and purposes (like most genteel women in the 1810s), has a binary system of choices also reflecting a win/lose logic: marry, or do not and become a spinster. Grahame-Smith's Elizabeth has three choices: marry, and give up fighting zombies; do not and become a spinster, and give up fighting zombies (though the novel never entertains this possibility); or do not, and continue to fight zombies. *Pride and Prejudice and Zombies*, in other words, makes Elizabeth's decision a much more profound one, a sacrifice on her part which complicates the novel's conclusion.

Pride and Prejudice and Zombies treats this problem of how to judge Elizabeth's (and by implication Jane's) decision to leave their swords and their good words behind fairly ambivalently. The novel in fact concludes on a note of stagnation:

> England remained in the shadow of Satan. The dead continued to claw their way through crypt and coffin alike, feasting on British brains. Victories were celebrated, defeats lamented. And the sisters Bennett—servants of His Majesty, protectors of Hertfordshire, beholders of the secrets of Shaolin, and brides of death—were now, three of them, brides of man, their swords quieted by that only force more powerful than any warrior. (317)

The sheer inertia of this conclusion stands in sharp contrast to the changes which the novel wrought upon its hypotext. Yet the undoubted problem which this presents to readers desirous of finding a more meaningful exploration of feminism is one which is obviously imported from *Pride and Prejudice* (the romance needs to end with a marriage). It is thus owed to the occasionally uneasy connection between *Pride and Prejudice and Zombies*'s historical source material and its zombie-fictional additions, a formal feature of the gimmick which is operative in the design of the novel. The idea that marriage must stand at the end of the novel is indeed not overtly challenged by *Pride and Prejudice and Zombies* itself. Andrea Ruthven in fact suggests that the novel points to the "pervasiveness of postfeminism" in the way it produces Elizabeth Bennett as simultaneously physically strong and independent and yet "chained to the necessity of finding the ideal mate" (2014, 341)—indeed, one might add, not the necessity, but the desirability, which seems more damning.

I would contend, by contrast, that this is only one possible reading. It is also more than possible to read the conclusion of *Pride and Prejudice and Zombies* as an element of its strong parody of *Pride and Prejudice*, where all Elizabeth's wit and cleverness see her finally no better off, in terms of the independence for which she is often celebrated, than her sisters Jane and Lydia, or indeed even Charlotte Lucas. In *Pride and Prejudice and Zombies*, Elizabeth's far more incongruous decision to marry Darcy should be understood as a critique of Austen's novel rather than as a contemporary surrender to the logic of postfeminist discourse: in heightening the sheer discrepancy between Elizabeth's initial self-understanding, her role in the community, and the gains she makes from a marriage of love (which she had explicitly foresworn earlier), *Pride and Prejudice and Zombies* should leave readers uneasy with its ending. It gives us grounds to question Camilla Nelson's suggestion that this is one of "three decidedly happy endings in a row" (2012, 4) in the trilogy.

This reading may seem like a thin excuse at best for the novel, yet it is, I would argue, one that is endorsed by its sequel, Steve Hockensmith's *Dreadfully Ever After*. Set four years after *Pride and Prejudice and Zombies*, the sequel opens on Darcy and Elizabeth on the grounds of their estate, fighting zombies: Elizabeth, the novel notes, is finally again displaying "something that had been missing for a long time: joie de vivre" (7). "No longer a warrior [. . .] as the wife of a gentleman" (8), Elizabeth has clearly sacrificed too much for the "happiness" of their shared life. She professes herself relieved to be childless—a clear indication of the limits of her willingness to surrender to societal norms—and as if on cue, they encounter the zombified son of Darcy's steward, and Darcy is bitten.

Dreadfully Ever After represents Darcy's and Elizabeth's marriage itself as happy, but Elizabeth as inconceivably constrained by the arbitrary elements of life as a married woman. With Darcy in the process of succumbing to the dreaded disease, however, she now has a new task: the quest to find the serum that promises to restore Darcy's health. More attention is paid by *Dreadfully Ever After* to the interlinked problem of class and race, rather than gender (of which more anon); yet Elizabeth's role, and indeed gendered roles in general, remain important in two ways. First, Elizabeth's quest is itself a meaningful breach of her promises as a wife, and one which does her much spiritual good indeed; she cannot be expected, and indeed the novel does not expect her, to return from this journey into the restricted life of a wife. Besides this, it is her sister Mary—nearly nondescript in Austen—who has the most to say about women's lives. A vociferous adherent of Mary Wollstonecraft, Mary Bennett develops the trilogy's clearest vision of female self-empowerment, one which also starts to influence Elizabeth. Initially left behind in Hertfordshire as Elizabeth and her father depart for London to find the cure for Darcy's bite, Mary follows them on her own. Having traced the potential source of the serum to London and the somewhat eerie laboratory of Sir Angus MacFarquar in the city's Bethlem Royal Hospital, she then moves to retrieve it from there by direct means, rather than the somewhat circumspect ones the other Bennetts employ. As she informs Elizabeth in the letter in which she also gives the family word of her plans: "Independence, Mary Wollstonecraft informs us, is the basis of every virtue" (156); reading it, Elizabeth cannot but agree. Mary's proto-feminist position in the narrative sees her successfully retrieving the cure and discovering the horrible secret of MacFarquar's work. While Elizabeth and her father largely follow the rules of societal engagement in trying to come closer to MacFarquar, Mary's success at going it alone signals to the sisters, as well as to the readers, where the real position of female strength in the narrative lies.

For all that, little of *Dreadfully Ever After* is given over to an elaboration of gender roles, but, then, it hardly needs to be. The Bennett sisters' realization that their independent actions are capable of saving Darcy is the bedrock on which their characters rest at the end. To be sure, in a sense *Dreadfully Ever After* appears slightly ambivalent about this narrative of female independence. Elizabeth, whose fate as a wife remains important in the novel, obtains a strong sense for the need to ignore social conventions about women's roles. As she goes to cure Darcy, to see Lady Catherine finally be devoured by her own, zombified daughter, and to dispatch that daughter herself, too, Elizabeth ends up fighting zombies together again with Darcy; this time, however, they recognize that this is the life they want to lead. At the novel's end, this is what Darcy and Elizabeth have settled on, notwithstanding the fact that it "wasn't done" (284). *Dreadfully Ever After* retrieves the happy ending for Elizabeth that *Pride and Prejudice and Zombies* does not have, in making Elizabeth truly equal to her husband. It is with this in mind, too, that we have to parse the novel's decision to pair off the remaining Bennett sisters. While it seems easy to read this decision as a false return to heteronormativity, this element certainly is tempered. Neither of them, at the conclusion of the novel, is actually married (although Mrs. Bennett appears to hope they soon will be); and neither of them obtains a particularly eligible man, either. Mary is interested in the "man in the box," the Bennett sisters' former Master Hawksmoor from *Dawn of the Dreadfuls*, who has paid for his cowardice in that novel with his arms and legs and is now a mere rump; and Kitty's man is Nezu, one of Lady Catherine's ninjas—hardly the best English stock for either. What might be crucial here is that neither woman goes through the elaborate rituals of courtship: for either, this is a choice borne of a recognition of the other's talents and abilities, and, notably, their choice more than the man's.

Read as a trilogy, the *Pride and Prejudice and Zombie* books establish a remarkable narrative arc with regard to gender concerns. Early in *Dawn of the Dreadfuls*, with the undead suddenly returned after a long absence, Elizabeth and her sisters are still worried about even so meaningless a deed as sitting on the ground—"But what was proper?" (27), as Elizabeth agonizes—these "shackles of good manners and gentility" (31) are slowly worn down as the magnitude of the threat and the self-command accorded the fighting Bennett sisters becomes clear to them. That this is no easy transition is evident: both society and their own family are less than thrilled by this development. As Mrs. Bennett, conflating zombiehood and marriage, moans: "Instead of throwing my eldest in the path of eligible bachelors, they're to be thrown to the unmentionables" (76). This newly gendered perspective is reinforced, probably accidentally but remarkably, by the cover of *Dawn of the Dreadfuls*. The zombified female child on the cover suggests, on the first reading, the combination of the novel's engagement with the Bennett sisters' childhoods (although they themselves obviously remain alive) and the zombie (the cover in this sense is a kind of graphic portmanteau, or indeed a mash-up). But the cover (fig. 9) also shows the zombie girl's hands folded in her lap with blood oozing from them—it pictures, not to put too fine a point on it, menstruation and thus female coming-of-age. The picture represents womanhood, with all the attendant limitations and strictures under which women had to live. The juxtaposition of becoming a woman and becoming a zombie is suggestive here: both, it would appear, should at all events be avoided, indeed, perhaps they are not so very different from one another.

Dawn of the Dreadfuls largely centers on Elizabeth Bennett's avoiding both of these possible fates: she becomes wife of neither of her two suitors, nor does she succumb to the strange plague that has returned to savage the English countryside; rather, she and her sisters begin the hard work of making women's independent work acceptable. At its conclusion, the Bennett sisters' training, notwithstanding a clear lack of societal acceptance, saves countless lives when they successfully defend Netherfield Park, and thereby establish for themselves the beginnings of an independent role. But, as Mr. Bennett notes, "[t]his is no happy ending we have here. It's merely a hopeful beginning" (284). Indeed it is: *Dawn of the Dreadfuls* retroactively places *Pride and Prejudice and Zombies* in a longer narrative arc. The position obtained by the Bennett sisters at the end of *Dawn of the Dreadfuls* is, four years onward, still the position they inhabit at the beginning of *Pride and Prejudice and Zombies*: socially accepted as warriors within the boundaries of the societal pressures to otherwise conform, not to overemphasize their roles as Hertfordshire's defenders, and not to rock the boat of gender conformity beyond this initial step. Maaja Stewart, in her study of Austen's novels, points out that "female powerlessness," as she calls it, is laid in from the beginning of the novel through the narrative voice itself (40). What Stewart characterizes as the "*musts of social codes*" (41) persists in *Pride and Prejudice and Zombies*: despite suggestions such as Collins and Bond's that fighting the zombies has become a *de rigueur* activity for young women, *Pride and Prejudice and Zombies* in fact stylizes the Bennetts as outsiders precisely because of their activities. Elizabeth's marriage to Darcy at the conclusion

Fig. 9. The cover of *Dawn of the Dreadfuls*. In color, the black splotches covering the girl's hands and staining her dress are blood-red. *Pride and Prejudice and Zombies: Dawn of the Dreadfuls* by Steve Hockensmith. Copyright ©2010 Quirk Productions, Inc. Cover design and zombification by Doogie Horner. Cover art courtesy the Bridgeman Art Library International.

of this novel in that sense highlights the drastic limitations of the Bennett's choices: the more-or-less private decision to become katana-wielding warriors leads to societal exclusion, and the public choice of marriage must always conform to the rules of the societal game. This, indeed, is something that even Elizabeth Bennett, for all her violence and willful independence, submits to: marriage means, to her as to everyone else, the surrender of her status as a warrior and the surrender of her status as a free person.

As the last text in the trilogy, *Dreadfully Ever After* breaks this mold: here, Elizabeth and Darcy make their own choices for their married life. To be sure, it is still married life and thus awfully heteronormative, but it is a radical break with the kinds of relationships Regency romances offer. Read as a trilogy, read as parodies, the three novels' construction of gender identities and their depiction of the problems caused by shifting understandings of women's roles highlight the absurd fixity of gender roles in the Regency era, and with it, the celebration of Regency romances today as sublimely romantic texts.[4] The position of women in Regency society becomes the parodic mirror of the position of women in our own times, as well of the infatuation with happy-ending readings of Austen in *Pride and Prejudice and Zombies*. The novels establish the difficulty of changing the perception of gender roles in society, but also the possibility of effecting meaningful change, at least on a small scale. While far from revolutionary, *Pride and Prejudice and Zombies* thus is more than a mere affirmation of postfeminist discourses: rather, it meaningfully mediates between contemporary understandings of gender roles, Regency versions of them, and the act of reading.

Gender, if preeminent as a concern in the original *Pride and Prejudice and Zombies*, is not the only major category that the trilogy engages, however. Issues of class (far more obvious given the awkward upper-middle-class settings of the Regency romance) and race (deeply masked in the Regency romance) come to the fore as critical categories of difference and meaningful problems in their own right for both an appreciation of Austen's original novel as well as the events in the trilogy.

I Have Seen Him Savagely Beat But One Servant": Class and Race in *Pride and Prejudice and Zombies*

There is something awkward in my choice of speaking in a single section about both class and race, categories often loosely associated with one another in the famous triad of "race, class, and gender." Yet while race and gender are clearly identitarian categories—that is, difference categories—class is not; this, incidentally, is a lesson reinforced by the *Pride and Prejudice and Zombies* trilogy. That I am talking about these issues together is something of a convenience: I am more interested here in the way the novels use these two categories to destabilize parodically the strict naturalization of upper-lower class divisions and the expunction of race *as a concern in Austen's texts* (and, yadda yadda, by extension in contemporary readers' reception) rather than in the particulars of their different depictions. I am more interested, to adopt Camilla Nelson's words, in the way both of these categories invoke the "spectre of Otherness itself" (2013, 13). But it does bear pointing out crucial differences between the way the two categories work (see Michaels 2006).

Perhaps the most obvious difference for my purposes here is this: race comes into the novels as a specter of otherness through the presence of living human beings and cultural traditions. These include Lady Catherine's ninjas, the arts of fighting adopted from Japan and China, and finally the suddenly double-absent cause of English upper-class wealth, the various imperial ventures which, as especially *Dreadfully Ever After* makes clear, have an utterly different value in the context of the *Pride and Prejudice and Zombies* trilogy. Class, by contrast, enters far more strongly into the novels through the zombies themselves—through the undead, either in and of themselves or in the actions they necessitate. This, of course, is a time-honored tradition in zombie fictions, harkening back at least as far as the Romero films. Similarly, class issues are also easily more overt in the hypotext. Contra Raymond Williams's assertion that "where only one class is seen, no classes are seen," even absent the presence of a significant class difference (at least if you believe that the Bennetts' upper-middle-class status is less meaningfully different from the landowners like Darcy, or the noblemen and -women like Lady Catherine, than from the truly absent working class), the novels keep class in the foreground. Regardless of Austen's view "from inside the house" (Williams 1973, 117), Grahame-Smith's and Hockensmith's views can see class in the ways Austen does not. To name just one example, *Pride and Prejudice and Zombies* early on follows Bingley, Darcy, and Elizabeth to the kitchens of Netherfield Hall, where two zombies have killed "a dozen servants, four maids, two cooks, and a steward," whose death most unfortunately also makes a hash of dessert, "sadly soiled by blood and brains, and thus unusable" (80). As Darcy competently and without fuss dispatches the former staff, and the novel returns to the ballroom, where the peace of all present appears more disturbed by Mary's singing than the death of nearly twenty people nearby, the novel has clearly laid in a class dimension, a hierarchy of people whose value ranks from below dessert to the stratospheric.

Pride and Prejudice and Zombies makes this class dimension overt in the way the most hideous behavior of the upper classes receives only the most curtailed commentary. Thus, Darcy's housekeeper Mrs. Reynolds notes to Elizabeth, happily, how "affable to the poor" (198) Darcy is, and how she had "seen him savagely beat but one servant, and a most deserved beating it was. I dare say he is the gentlest man in all of Britain" (197). Readers discover that Lady Catherine's dojo has been "carried from Kyoto, brick by brick, on the backs of peasants" (129); and even the "recent troubles in Birmingham" (190) and the fact of "Manchester's collapse" (64) may be read against what the novel perceives to be the growing threat to the genteel life of the country squirarchy. Cradles of British industrialization and the nation's growing proletariat, Manchester and Birmingham stand for the shifts in Britain's societal structure in the early 1800s, an issue which the novel picks up in the zombie metaphor as well. Replying to Darcy's comment that in "a country neighborhood you move in a very confined and unvarying society," Elizabeth notes: "Excepting, of course, when the country is overrun with the same unmentionables as town" (37). Thus, this claim for the increasingly elusive difference between town and country is also a claim that what Darcy calls "unvarying society" is in the process of collapsing, a collapse driven by the zombies, those egalitarian "unmentionables."

Williams notes how Austen's writing came at a time when the "precise confidence of an established world gave way to disturbing, aggressive and conflicting voices" (117), and it takes little imagination to see these elided voices, safely tucked away in Austen's fiction, in the zombies of *Pride and Prejudice and Zombies*. Grahame-Smith's novel, largely caught up in other questions, parodies Austen's take (or lack of a take) on these shifts by introducing to it both radical change (the living dead, overrunning the nation) and a radical lack of change (polite society's insistence on business as usual). It puts this class dimension in the terms which polite society adopts in lieu of "zombie": "dreadfuls," and, more importantly "unmentionables," a term pointing more clearly still to the way in which working-class concerns and lives were left unmentioned in Austen's original novel. The problem with this lack of a role in Austen is, as *Dawn of the Dreadfuls* has it: "How can we face a problem squarely when we can't even bring ourselves to name it" (100)? As Camilla Nelson points out, *Pride and Prejudice and Zombies* itself only modestly changes this: the zombies, while present, are left indistinguishable from one another, mere herds of creatures that fall victim to the Bennetts' swords (2013, 7–8). Combined with the suggestion that the zombies might be read as symbolizing the forces of democratizing change in the early nineteenth century, the consequence is to read Elizabeth Bennett not merely as the defender of patriarchy but indeed also of the class foundations of Regency Britain. As Juliet McMaster has pointed out, Austen herself was extremely conscious of the workings of class in her times, and her novels mirror this consciousness. In McMaster's parsing, in Austen's novels "human worth is to be judged by standards better and more enduring than social status; but social status is always relevant" (1997, 129); and it is by no means the case that all classes are equally, or even at all, represented. While the various shades of a well-to-do middle-class reach into the lower ranks of the aristocracy and the higher ranks of the hard-to-do clergy and tradesmen, servants, for example, are largely there for their employers to shine as exemplars of good behavior towards them—which means, by and large, by their benevolent stewardship. As McMaster notes, "'The poor' are seldom mentioned, but they are there, for Lady Catherine to 'scold . . . into harmony and plenty' (*PP* 169 [original note]) or for Anne Elliot and Emma [of *Emma*] to visit compassionately" (128). This is, of course, on the one hand a consequence of Austen's realism: no lady or gentleman would be very likely to have contact with the laboring classes directly. On the other hand, however, it bespeaks the concerns of the novel, and should not be ignored as an elision of the foundation of upper-class wealth (like race, as we will see). Most importantly, however, such a parsing of Austen reveals again how *Pride and Prejudice and Zombies* makes overt in parody the way Austen's novels ultimately reinforce the status quo of class relations. In *Pride and Prejudice*, Elizabeth Bennett merely (and unexceptionally) does nothing to change it; in *Pride and Prejudice and Zombies*, she actively combats the grave threat facing the realm's (class) stability.

The zombie's violent intrusion, for example, into the ball visited early in the book by the Bennett family and almost all the other major characters—all of the upper class, or at least those genteel enough to be largely well off—suggests in no uncertain terms the detachedness of this upper-class practice from real-life concerns. The short episode features the literal break-in of those aptly named "unmentionables"—described in a tone of haughty detachment—into the lives of the upper classes, which causes much havoc before finally being repelled. The novel segues out with the laconic note: "Apart from the attack, the evening altogether passed off pleasantly" (16). As things fall apart around them, and even amongst them, the denizens of the upper class simply continue their business as usual.

Pride and Prejudice and Zombies, we might summarize, leaves class relations to the parodically heightened and sharpened depiction of upper-class privilege and detachment. Steve Hockensmith's prequel and sequel are certainly more overt and radical, but perhaps not necessarily more interesting (cf. Nelson 2013, 10). Yet again, as in the case of gender relations, they appear to signpost a larger narrative arc. In both novels, the upper classes become much easier targets of blunter satire: "cartoonish figures," Lord Lumpley in *Dawn of the Dreadfuls* and Bunny MacFarquar in *Dreadfully Ever After* serve merely to highlight the sheer ridiculousness of seeing them as in any way duly privileged. As Camilla Nelson points out, one of the ways in which Hockensmith makes the class divide and the zombie symbolism more overt is by giving them names and backstories, as with the first undead encountered, the former village apothecary (2013, 11–12). At the end of the prequel, such subtle changes fall by the wayside: fighting in beleaguered Netherfield Hall, the exigencies of the moment do away with class divisions: "[t]here was no division between upstairs and downstairs now. There couldn't be [. . .e]veryone was needed at a window or a door. [. . .] Tradesman, yeoman, gentleman, seamstress, fishwife, farmwife, lady—they all fought side by side, for sure the dreadfuls would be equally democratic" (262). Such democratic moments, to be sure, do not lastingly shift class relations, but the novel clearly lays out how the radical threat of the zombie needs to shift them, if anyone is meant to survive.

What also becomes evident here, then, is the way in which it is impossible (though possibly unnecessary) to give the zombie one straightforward symbolic meaning. In the defense of Netherfield Hall, the zombie is impossible to read as the proletarian forces of revolutionary change, even though in much of the rest of the text, it gives faces and power to the disadvantaged classes. The failure of Netherfield Hall's communal defense to shift the class discourse meaningfully going into *Pride and Prejudice and Zombies* suggests, however, why *Dreadfully Ever After* becomes more radical in the way it depicts the class element. As the London walls, interior and exterior, divide the city from the country and the upper-class sectors firmly from the rest, the novel gradually emphasizes the parallels between the zombies and the working class—and the somewhat blithe acceptance of proto-capitalist discourse that even includes Elizabeth. "What factory owner wants workers who insist on sleeping and eating and who complain when ground up in the gears" (117), she replies when asked about the possibility of using zombies for labor. As the novel goes on, however, it aligns the interests of the laborer and the zombie in no uncertain terms.

> Mr. Anthony Isaac Crickett of 23 Crabtree Row, Bethnal Green, Two East, London, did not lead an especially noteworthy life. A miserable childhood in a Whitechapel workhouse was followed by an adulthood stoking furnaces at the Hackney Crematorium & Glue Factory that was (fortunately) slightly less miserable but (unfortunately) rather brief. [. . .] Under normal circumstances, that would have been the end of Mr. Crickett and whatever chance he ever had of leaving some kind of legacy. Not so in the Age of the Dreadfuls! (246–47)

As the interior walls of London crumble, Crickett and a host of other zombies fall upon the "re-coronation" of King George III, and devour him and the crown prince and former regent, William. Avenging themselves upon the symbols of the class structure which condemned them to meaningless lives and early deaths, the zombies end Hanoverian rule and, since the novel does not make any attempt to establish consequences, leave us with a vacuum at the top of British society, as well as a more than merely symbolic end of the Regency era.

Class, then, is an issue permeating the trilogy, but one left dangling as an issue (even with radical implications). Of course, the problem here is that any genuinely radical vision of class is ultimately made difficult by the choice of protagonists inherited from the hypotext. If not exactly stable or condoned, the class differences persist between Elizabeth, Darcy, the Bennetts, and the now-increasingly "no longer nameless and faceless" (Nelson 2013, 11) but still ultimately voiceless lower classes.

We may draw some general conclusions from why this should be so by comparing the novels' treatment of class (ambivalent and open-ended) with their treatment of race. There are two major aspects in the way race is depicted in *Pride and Prejudice and Zombies*. The first is that it is depicted at all. This is especially notable given the way that it slumbers beneath a genteel surface in much Regency romance (see Said 1993), especially in Austen's *Mansfield Park*, where the Antiguan plantation of Sir Thomas Bertram always remains submerged as the source of all wealth, without being explicitly mentioned or discussed. Given the way much of Britain's wealth in the period depended on similarly exploitative relationships with the rest of the world and its peoples, the way *Mansfield Park* handles the subject is only the most overtly evasive one: little of the worlds of *Pride and Prejudice* or *Emma* or *Northanger Abbey* would have been possible without empire. To state this is not a dig at Austen's novels, or a call for them to make room for the various peoples suffering under British rule; this would certainly be misplaced demands to make on works that are comedies of manners and romances. Rather, it is to point to the way *Pride and Prejudice and Zombies* recognizes the need to place both its hypotext and its contemporary moment in a broader imperial context (the "American Empire," as Camilla Nelson has it ([6], as well as the nascent British empire of the early nineteenth century).

Race enters into *Pride and Prejudice and Zombies* overtly in the direct connection between the protagonists and the Far East: Japan, China, and later on Indian subcontinent. To be sure, the East Asia imagined in *Pride and Prejudice and Zombies* is indubitably clichéd, indeed stereotypical: a world of wise old masters imparting fighting techniques on willing adepts, of tea ceremonies, sushi consumption, and ninjas. This East Asia is not historical but fantastical; it isn't a useful image of geopolitical connections but the overdrawn Orientalism that spells East Asia in the capital letters of pulp fiction. But *Pride and Prejudice and Zombies* does not just draw on these images to suggest the mystery of the Far East, or to introduce the overtly other, as such figures as Fu Manchu did in the 1920s and 1930s. It makes them complicated as both representations of East Asia and as representations of the clichéd image of the Far East both in the 1830s as well as in pulp fiction. The complicated relationship between the levels of representation (in the original novel *Pride and Prejudice*, the stereotypes drawn not from the 1830s but recurring to a later popular imagination) has at least two dimensions in the *Pride and Prejudice and Zombies* trilogy. Some of the English returnees from the East, especially Lady Catherine and Fitzwilliam Darcy, adopt the cultural trappings of Japan and China, combining their English ways with the nonviolent aspects of their former host cultures. These appropriations bespeak the characters' respect for the East beyond the achievement of fighting prowess, even if, of course, this is still a reductive appropriation of vastly more diverse cultures. But if the "Oriental has often been imagined as an apocalyptic threat to Western civilization" (Hamako 2011, 115), here at least "he" becomes, if not exactly a savior, at least linked to successful models of resistance—especially, again, in the question of gender. It is never, of course, fully explained why the Asian fighting styles should be so completely superior to the English—why a Katana should be preferable to a broadsword, or a throwing star more useful than a brace of pistols. To send the Bennett girls to Asia for their training, in other words, is gratuitous, and in this gratuity it becomes especially significant. As Camilla Nelson points out, much of the engagement with race in the trilogy revolves around the category of "Englishness" (2013, 12), frequently invoked throughout the trilogy. In *Dawn of the Dreadfuls*, the attempt to cure a zombie is called "Re-Anglification" (231), and "fervent patriots" denounce this "turning to the East for guidance," demanding instead "an English solution to an English problem" (28).

Indeed, the trilogy's perspective of the Asian influence on events is by no means unambivalent: while their training allows Lady Catherine, Darcy, and the Bennetts to excel at killing zombies, it fails to instill in them a sense of cultural relativity. Elizabeth's deeply vicious streak, her sense of honor, and her often-voiced readiness to kill at the slightest insult is a consequence not of her Englishness but of the "instincts bestowed by our Oriental masters" (Austen and Grahame-Smith 2009, 95). It is in this sense, too, that we must read the radically over-the-top scene in which Elizabeth, fighting Lady Catherine's ninjas in her dojo, not merely kills them, but ends up strangling the final victim with his own intestines and then eats his still beating heart (197). We can hardly read this as an English, imperial disdain for the Oriental Other, showcased with parodic radicalness: the Bennett sisters' sense of ninjas as "[s]*neaky, deceitful little snakes* [. . .] *dirty, dishonorable, back-stabbing curs*

[. . .] *despicable, underhanded, pajama-wearing worms*" (144, original italics) as Kitty has it *Dreadfully Ever After* is a consequence more of their Chinese-Shaolin indoctrination than any more general disdain for the Orient. That this is the case becomes evident, for example, in the way Darcy speaks of the "proper Oriental education" (Austen and Grahame-Smith 2009, 159) which Wickham did not receive, or Elizabeth's sense that Pemberley House's gardens are a place where "the natural beauty of the Orient had been so little counteracted by English taste" (198). But most powerfully, the sense in which the Orient is a space of necessary hope for England's transformation—despite the various parodically heightened scenes of violence that impinge especially upon the life expectancy of Lady Catherine's ninjas—comes in the way *Dreadfully Ever After* finally analyzes the nature of the zombie plague. While it is true for some characters that "the Orient and its 'Orientals' continue to function within the text as sites of exploitation" (Nelson 2013, 10), it is less true for the trilogy as a whole. And indeed, the novels undermine the very idea of a monolithic Orient by the internal divisions they expose between the Chinese- and Japanese-trained Englishmen. Going to the Orient is not part of the kind of historical, mercantile or military expeditionary imperialism that was in the background of Austen's novel; rather, for those who go, it is more in the character of a pilgrimage, though not necessarily in the sense which Edward Said gave the term (2002, 166–97). Those English people who abhor the importation of "Oriental" training in arms, too, are confronted with the awkward fact that this training works, while their own, English ways apparently are less than successful.

The Orient, in other words, is a complex space in *Pride and Prejudice and Zombies*: it enables the depiction of the almost casual racism which much of the English gentility more or less openly demonstrate, but it also is a realm with its own complicated internal politics, as well as a source for solutions. It is this latter role that is most expansively explored in the final installment of the trilogy. Here, we are most explicitly informed that the "English problem" is genuinely a uniquely English problem: "It had always been a mystery why the plague never spread beyond Great Britain. It had something to do with their island isolation, some said. A peculiarity of English blood" (263). *Dawn of the Dreadfuls* insists on depicting English society as explicitly thinking in terms of blood purity, in as racist a dimension as it is possible to think, and on this thinking being at least the proximate reason for the plague's success in England. The novel offers three potential solutions to this dilemma. Two are related to the imperfect serum which keeps Darcy in a half-zombified state throughout much of the narrative, as it does Lady Catherine's daughter, Anne. Anne is an advocate for making this the solution, as she tells Darcy:

What good is purity? We English once fancied our blood so fine that it would be a crime to blend it with anyone else's. Yet did that spare us the strange plague? No. For all we know, it brought it upon us. And even now, when that curse could be turned into a blessing, many such as my mother lack the ability to see it, for that would require an acceptance—an embrace—of the very "impurity" they so hate. (192)

To be sure, Anne's solution, to become a half-zombie and a lover of zombies, misses the point because it misreads the zombies' status as an "impurity" of Englishness, and because she believes the immortality apparently (but not certainly) conveyed by the serum is a "blessing." It is a misreading of the situation that turns the English racial superiority complex on the zombies: the very act of refusing to mingle with outsiders bestows (if by complex and convoluted ways) an apparently tremendous benefit. Anne's death at the end of the novel, after she herself has turned more fully zombie in consuming her mother, also concludes this option.

The second option expands from Lady Catherine's decline-slowing serum to a full-blown cure: this is what Elizabeth is after and whose workings Mary discovers in MacFarquar's laboratory. It is much more radically based on racial exploitation. The cure lies literally "in the blood of foreigners" (263): men and women, but especially children, some "Indian, some Mohammedan, some African. Not one had blonde hair or blue eyes or fair skin" (257), who have been infected by MacFarquar and his assistants, and from the survivors of whom they draw the immune blood that serves as the basis of the cure. Hidden deep in the bowels of London's Bedlam Hospital, the dark secret of the vaccine cannot come out, even as it cures King George III (for a short while) of his own infection: despite it being such an obvious solution to a problem acknowledged to have been produced precisely by a "peculiarity of the English blood," it cannot be publicized. Camilla Nelson avers that there is "something exceedingly disturbing about the metaphors of contagion, vaccination, and cure" (2013, 15) in the novel; perhaps. The novel mobilizes the foreign (not just the Oriental) as the source of England's healing through racial mixing; by extension (in the conflation which King George's infection, cure, and death produces between the individual body and English body politic), it suggests the necessity for multiculturalism to the kind of radical decline undergone in England in the trilogy. MacFarquar and his ilk prefer to keep the basic facts secret, and to merely use, in the most horrible fashion, the resources (the blood) of enslaved foreigners; a simple metaphor, to be sure, but an effective one, both for a parody of Austen and Regency writing, as well as for our contemporary age.

The final option is the one ultimately advocated for by the novel and adopted (literally) by Darcy and Elizabeth: the bringing into English society the very Orientals misused by the production of the vaccine. At the novel's conclusion, Elizabeth and Darcy take in the orphans rescued from Bethlem, and not, as Mrs. Bennett slightly worriedly concludes, as "servants at all. They were guests" (284). Coupled with Kitty's relationship with Nezu, Lady Catherine's chief ninja, the Pemberley estate is suitably multicultural now—clearly a fantasy for the 1800s, though a possible model for the 2000s. These changes to the purely English order of life, and in countryside to boot, are reflected also in Mrs. Bennett's quizzing insistence that the children Elizabeth and Darcy have brought to Pemberley cannot be English and Punjabi at once, and Mr. Bennett's countervailing (and preferable) claim that they certainly can. As Mr. Bennett points out, in no uncertain terms:

> Mrs. Bennett, you may as well rail against the turning of the leaves or the rising of the tide. The dreadfuls came, and we looked to the East and to the deadly arts to save us. And save us they did—even as they changed us. England could have died, or it could become something new, and live. I, for one, am glad the latter path prevailed." (287)

As the children begin "a new game all their own" (287), the novel concludes with an idealized vision of the future in a multicultural, changing English society. It is an ending far less interesting on its own, conventionally liberal terms than it is as a parodic update of the stagnant conclusion of *Pride and Prejudice*. If *Pride and Prejudice and Zombies* can already be read on its own terms as a parodic update of this sort, emphatically insisting on the wrongness of celebrating *Pride and Prejudice*'s ending today, then *Dreadfully Ever After* makes this even clearer: *this*, it insists, is a happy ending in the twenty-first century. This is what readers should be looking for in their fiction.

Race and class thus figure into the *Pride and Prejudice and Zombies* trilogy's parodic critique of Austen's original novel and its contemporary readers, but it may appear surprising that it reserves so much of its radical demands on Austen's characters for the issue of race: almost a straw man, in a way. Where class relations were always overtly present if rarely thematized in Austen's writings, race was neither much present nor obviously neglected, most especially not in *Pride and Prejudice*. It is a contemporary concern—and here Camilla Nelson is correct to call on us to read *Pride and Prejudice and Zombies* especially in connection with contemporary concerns. Race relations figure only in the most distant fashion in *Pride and Prejudice*, in the specter of the foundation of English—imperial—wealth. They become intrusive in

Pride and Prejudice and Zombies, and in so being become revealing both of the trilogy's limits as of its successes.

Reading *Pride and Prejudice and Zombies* for class and race issues and the ways it handles them highlights again the constitutive difficulty of popular fiction to imagine genuinely radical changes to the social system. We already saw this in *World War Z*; *Pride and Prejudice and Zombies* is perhaps even more revealing for the sustained engagement given to the issue of race over the issue of class. The trilogy makes a big deal of race because it is an important topic to cover today, rather than because it is an obvious parodic target for its critique of Austen and Austen's readers (for while the exploitative nature of class relations in *Pride and Prejudice* is hard to deny, the distant relevance of race is fairly easy to). It offers a more radical "solution" to the problem of race versus the problem of class because it is so much more eminently solvable. It is not that the trilogy leaves an egalitarian restructuring of society as an impossibility: the issue is that it, in contrast to the way it reimagines race relations, does not similarly imagine a concrete future for the issue of class. In Walter Benn Michaels's words, the "problem of eliminating [class-based] inequality is not the problem of reorganizing the relations between the margin and the center, and the solution to the problem of inequality is not learning to love it" (2004, 158)—but these are the contemporary liberal solutions to the problem of ethnic difference, of race. And it is also the solution which the *Pride and Prejudice and Zombies* trilogy, in *Dreadfully Ever After*, settles upon: Kitty's love for Nezu and the Darcy's taking in of Punjabi children are certainly radical changes to the post-Regency (postmonarchical, perhaps) world, but they are reassuringly based on an acceptance of difference, not a complex restructuring of society. As Mrs. Bennett inquires of Mr. Bennett, will the "different England" that he espouses be the "kind where one's married daughter runs around with a sword collecting mahogany orphans, you mean? Or where one's unmarried daughters engage in disgraceful relations with the most inappropriate of men?" (287). Mr. Bennett's answer that yes, this is the kind of England he means, is certainly an easy acceptance of quite radical changes to the idea of Englishness and English identity. But it does not itself impinge on the social order of England. This is the limit of the imagination offered by *Pride and Prejudice and Zombies*: nowhere does Mrs. Bennett ask if this new England might also be the England where the privileges of the landed gentry will be done away in a democratic restructuring of an obviously broken social model.

I have now made what some might find to be somewhat over-ambitious claims for the often radical, sometimes ambivalent imagination that the *Pride and Prejudice and Zombies* trilogy brings both to Austen's original text and world, as well as for the work's status as an independent cultural artifact. The corollary to this is to ask whether any of this is structurally inherited from the very idea and practice of the mash-up: that is to say, if the addition of the sedimentation of meanings that is the zombie automatically enables such readings. It does not, as I will seek to show by contrasting the rather clever way the zombie is employed in *Pride and Prejudice and Zombies* with the less helpful way it figures in W. Bill Czolgosz's mash-up of Mark Twain's great American novel, *The Adventures of Huckleberry Finn and Zombie Jim*.

Mashing Twain Up: On the Limits of Zombie Mash-up Fiction

In *Huckleberry Finn and Zombie Jim*, the same mash-up technique that works in *Pride and Prejudice and Zombies* is used on Twain's novel but to far less persuasive effect. This is so in part because Czolgosz does not imitate Twain as closely as Grahame-Smith does Austen; it is also because of the novel's own choices about what to change narratively in Twain; and, not the least, because *Huckleberry Finn* itself, of course, already fairly foregrounds many of the issues traditionally added by zombies. Already subversive, *Huckleberry Finn* resists becoming more so or differently so by the addition of zombies, and in fact more than once appears to be regressive.

The narrative of Czolgosz's mash-up is easily retold: at some point before the novel's opening in 1839, a plague, which Huck calls the "fissythis," has started to turn dead people of all races into zombies—baggers, in the novel's parlance, a not-too-subtle replacement of the original novel's niggers. The novel sets out two categories of baggers: "good ones" are those like Jim, conscious but docile; bad ones—"full ones" (loc. 1518)—are those which, impossible to tame, roam the countryside and attack the living. The most radical consequence is that black slavery ends abruptly as those baggers who do not aspire to kill and eat humans take over for the slaves.

Much of the rest of the narrative, then, plays out as Twain's novel does: Huck escapes the civilizing impulse of his foster home, flees his abusive father, and encounters Jim on the Mississippi, with the two of them going down the river on a raft. As is perhaps to be expected, the division between malleable and violent baggers eventually breaks down. All baggers become equally hostile, society crumbles, and Huck has to decide if he can be friends with Jim, now a vicious monster; unsurprisingly, he decides he can, frees Jim from a holding pen of other zombies (who, apparently, do not rate saving), and the two of them float down the Mississippi as the world around them collapses.

It does not take much to spot the difficulties with this zombie version of Twain, most of which are related to the way the novel reimagines racial relations. In making Jim (who, in the original novel, was a black slave) a "bagger," the mash-up immediately sets the two categories—black slave and undead bagger—on an equal footing despite the pains to which Czolgosz goes to create a world in which race is no longer implicated in involuntary servitude. Slavery's replacement is, as our continued encounter with zombie Jim shows, not only just a little less onerous: after all, what makes a good bagger is being "gentle and still keeping pieces of [one's] former self" (loc. 1019)—that is, it requires at least partial consciousness of one's own condition. As Jim himself points out, "I uz a slave when I uz alive, an' then I get dead, an' I still gets to be a slave. The warld is a funny place" (loc. 947). This new slavery does not differentiate between black and white, only between violent and nonviolent, between being at least partially capable of thought or reflected action and being solely out to kill and devour. In this sense, it might appear to be redemptive, but the apparent egalitarianism can barely counteract the fact that the only zombie/slave we "get to know" is Jim—whose position essentially remains unchanged from the original novel to the mash-up. Whatever the social consequences of white undead slavery are, they remain hidden from us; and of course, the monstrosity of the slavery system becomes obscured by what, despite their remaining human traits, is now the evident slavery of non-humans and the at least tentative possibility that their enslavement is retroactively justified by their turn to violence at the novel's end.

I have argued above that a crucial element of *Pride and Prejudice and Zombies*'s parodic work is the way it tackles the readers of Austen and shoves them into the dark realities of 1810s Great Britain, to highlight the absurdity of reading it as a model romance today. It is from this vantage point that reading *The Adventures of Huckleberry Finn and Zombie Jim* becomes so problematic: no contemporary reader (beyond, perhaps, the young adult readers of abridged versions) is likely to have missed slavery and racism as constitutive elements of *Huckleberry Finn*'s narrative. Whereas the addition of zombies enables the highlighting of elided and repressed issues in Austen, it serves to obfuscate and destabilize *Huckleberry Finn*'s "explicitly anti-racist stance" (Smith 1999, 363). The ease with which, apparently, black slavery ends in the wake of the discovery that baggers make cheaper labor narrows black slavery down to an economic mode instead of a complex system of ideological, physical, and economic oppression and exploitation.

The point here is not simply, then, that *Huckleberry Finn and Zombie Jim* is a poor novel (though it is) but that its obvious aspirations to social commentary undermine the preexisting commentary already present in *Huckleberry Finn*. There can be no doubt that *Huckleberry Finn and Zombie Jim* has such aspirations. To pick one obvious example: at the conclusion of chapter eight, Huck references the arrival of the schooner *Amistad*, of slave mutiny fame, in New York, an issue that turns into a "farce" when Joseph Cinqué (or "Joe Sink," as Huck has it) discovers that "nobody wanted black slaves anyway." The "negros'd been reprieved by [zombies]" (loc. 955). The *Amistad* reference is clearly pop-cultural—it is much more about the 1997 Spielberg film of that title than the actual occurrences themselves—and quite bizarre, as though the slavery suffered by the Africans on the *Amistad* was less violent just because they were no longer a sought-after commodity. The novel's racial logic is facile at best, bound up in the simple equation that cheaper labor replaces cheap labor, without regard to the complexity of the edifice of slavery or its attendant violence.

There are many other examples of the overt interest the mash-up has in highlighting the consequences of the existence of baggers for black slavery and race relations, but I will reserve my attention here to its opening. Instead of opening with *Huckleberry Finn*'s famous first line, "You don't know about me, without you have read a book named 'The Adventures of Tom Sawyer,' but that ain't no matter" (Twain 1999, 13), the mash-up begins with a weird digression, in which Huck notes that "people used to own other people, an' they had a word for those people. Really mean" (loc. 25). For the use of that word (we are left to infer that it is "nigger"), the Widow Douglas actually hits Huck. This bizarre opening, which projects twenty-first-century liberal sensitivities onto the mid-nineteenth-century story, again serves to highlight the simple and ahistorical conception which the mash-up has of the constitution of American slavery. As David Smith points out, Twain "uses 'nigger' throughout the book as a synonym for 'slave,'" inclusive of all that this status brought with it in the antebellum United States: "an inferior, even subhuman creature who is properly owned by and subservient to Euro-Americans" (1999, 365). In turning it into a "mean" word, not for use in polite society, in the wake of the manumission of black slaves and their replacement by baggers, *Huckleberry Finn and Zombie Jim* once more puts the cart before the horse. It suggests that it is the fact that blacks are enslaved which causes whites to treat them as inferior beings, rather than the other way around.

More pertinently, the novel's decision to replace black slavery with zombie slavery has a number of insidious corollaries as we near the novel's conclusion. As the baggers, even the formerly docile ones, rise, devour the living, and send the world into chaos, the abolition of black slavery appears to be a disastrous mistake. Far better, it would seem, to have kept blacks enslaved, and ruthlessly hunt down even the docile undead, than to have free blacks be merely another item on the zombie menu. And, almost as peculiarly, by producing over and over the direct equivalence between zombies and black slaves, the novel also ends up suggesting that black slaves simply were too docile to throw off the shackles of slavery themselves.[5]

Conclusion: You Don't Add Zombies to a Romance

"[P]rofundity and depth of meaning is not what one seeks in this campy celebration of popular genres" (2012, 51) writes Eckard Voigts-Virchow of *Pride and Prejudice and Zombies*; he would have been more on the mark, as I have argued, to say this about *Huckleberry Finn and Zombie Jim*. Even for *Pride and Prejudice and Zombies*, it may be undoubtedly true for some readers—as much as any claim about readers in general is liable to be true for some in particular—but, as the readings I offered above should show, it is certainly not true if it is also meant to argue that no meaning can be found in these texts. What my discussions of gender, race, and class above have suggested *Pride and Prejudice and Zombies* does is make more overt what might (charitably) be said to be hidden beneath the surface of Austen's original novel. Austen, as Claudia Johnson notes, is more than just popular: her novels "hold a secure place in the canon of high as well as popular culture" (1997, 224). This overtness is certainly a parodic element of the latter novels, but it may speak to something more fundamental, too. If critics do not agree on a reading of Austen—for or against slavery, critical or supportive of patriarchy, willing to fundamentally critique the foundations of British society or not—it is hard indeed to expect the casual reader to make sense of these hidden possibilities. *Pride and Prejudice and Zombies*, in its blunt artlessness, makes these criticisms available: it does insist on the bizarreness of the "gentleman" who beats his servants rarely; on the casual violence dealt out to the "Oriental" ninjas; on the limits of female emancipation; on the outrageous detachment of the ruling class from the concerns of the people. *Pride and Prejudice and Zombies* does necessary work on a text whose politics, spoken, unspoken, and latent, are generally submerged beyond a superficial popular reading of the novel and its many filmic adaptions. It thus engages both in a quasi-literary critical discussion of the blind spots and empty spaces of Austen's novel as well as in their reception today, ultimately producing something akin to an updated version of Austen for our times. By way of its sometimes blunt but often inspired parody, *Pride and Prejudice and Zombies* provides new critical political and social positions, distinct from the original novel and yet similar enough to be recognizable as necessary updates. In this parsing, the very artlessness of the title of the novel asks us to pay attention to incongruous, unpopular readings of *Pride and Prejudice*.

To suggest that *Pride and Prejudice and Zombies* is new in its criticisms is not to say that Austen's work as such is not critical, but rather that its contemporary popular reception is; this is what *Pride and Prejudice and Zombies* immediately spotlights. Tony Venables has suggested that the zombies' "presence in the landscape of Regency England is patently absurd—an absurdity reflected in the jarringly incongruous tacking-on of the 'zombie' to the familiar title" (2015, 209); he is certainly correct to point to the sheer incongruity of the addition to the title. It is inelegant if pithy, doing violence (unlike *Sense and Sensibility and Seamonsters*) to the neat alliteration and the flow of Austen's title; it suggests, much as the text proper finally apparently produces, a simple additionality to the zombies, and a certain disregard for the venerated source text. But at the same time, to say that zombies in Regency England are absurd is to suggest that zombies elsewhere are not—and, more problematically, to suggest that Regency England itself, seen from the vantage point of today, is not already absurd very much on its own terms. To read a novel set in Regency England without noticing the many elisions, erasures, and evasions by which it is possible to submerge oneself in an upper-class love story, however fraught, is perhaps the most absurd of all.

Pride and Prejudice and Zombies thus must be read as successfully updating *Pride and Prejudice* by including social elements into the equation neglected by the novel in the first place, suggesting the artificiality, or at least the depth-lessness, of Austen's novel. This is true both for its original appearance but more importantly as a cultural artifact today: elements of social life in the 1810s studiously ignored by Austen's novel return with a vengeance. Austen's popularity—especially in the various film and TV versions made of *Pride and Prejudice*—points to her transformation into a writer of the kind of escapist, popular fiction in which readers find a certain solace, a way of imagining "truly" romantic love as well as a fundamentally care-free life: wouldn't it be great to be upper class and idle? Or at any rate, wouldn't it be great to be able to be idle (granting that few of us truly desire idleness)? Such a reading would imply a curious inversion between what is derogatorily called "popular," "paraliterary," or "junk fiction," and what is "literary" because it carries a social message. Adding zombies in this case does not make paraliterary or escapist what used to be literary, but it highlights the popular, in the derogatory sense, nature of Jane Austen's original novel *today* by emphasizing that it has itself become very much an escapist fantasy narrative geared towards allowing (especially female) readers a form of literary wish-fulfillment, what Martin Amis at the beginning of the contemporary, ongoing "Austenmania" called "forgetful toadyism" (1996).

Therein lies the crucial difference between such texts as *Pride and Prejudice and Zombies* and *The Adventures of Huckleberry Finn and Zombie Jim*, a difference based both on the different cultural valences of the respective novels as well as on their own critical stances. If to add zombies to *Huckleberry Finn* does not add much critical potential, to add them to Austen does. As Claudia Johnson points out, Austen enthusiasm has spurred both "campy anglophilia" and "antiquarian meticulousness," preferring "enjoyment" over what Johnson calls "hermeneutic mastery" (1997, 223). Austen's fiction thus mobilizes very much the same reading strategies that are employed for much popular fiction, and has readers not much different from the "trekkies, fans, and mass media enthusiasts" familiar from other cultural texts.

The contention here is, then, that *Pride and Prejudice*'s contemporary audience reads the novel (and views its numerous adaptations) as a romance in the same way it would any supermarket romance, or at least, as Jim Collins has argued, "as primers or guidebooks rather than expressions of transcendent literary genius" (2009, 183). As Janice Radway points out, this is not quite true—the complexity of early nineteenth-century prose gives readers pause (1984, 197)—but it appears to be largely true enough. As Marie Sørbø points out, the highly successful 1995 BBC adaptation, for example, made Elizabeth and her sister Jane both into "romantic dreamers from the start" (2014, 139). In this version of the novel, focused "on the beauty of [. . .] the world that was gone" (159), on "dreams of love," and a "happy ending" (160), much of the undoubtedly available critical potential of the novel becomes subordinated to telling a love story for viewers to indulge in. These popular readings are not fully exhaustive of Austen's more complex novel, but neither are they entirely off the mark. Readers of Austen have, of course, always been able to draw different conclusions about *Pride and Prejudice*. Elizabeth, as Dorothy Kaplan notes, has been the subject of various interpretations over the past two hundred years, owing to the "changing context of literary criticism and the social ideologies that influence that criticism" (1992, 185). She has been read as offering a counter-position to the prevailing patriarchal sentiment of her times through her witty repartee, as well as a merely superficial opponent to patriarchy who repudiates this wit. She has also been seen as a figure of silent opposition to the happy ending of her marriage—Marie Sørbø suggests that Austen "sacrifices the standard happy ending for her preferred statement of human complexity" (2014, 162) in marrying Elizabeth to Darcy—as well as "endorsing marriage as a patriarchal institution" (Kaplan 1992, 199). In this latter reading, *Pride and Prejudice* becomes an ancestral example of those "Victorian novels where social upheaval is prevented how? By staging a marriage!" (Brown and Szeman 2014, 40): whatever danger Elizabeth might have posed to the society in which she acts, the novel ultimately abolishes this danger behind the recuperative power of a wedding, the consummation of what Juliet McMaster has called Austen's penchant for the "Cinderella plot" (1997, 117).

There is no need to come down here on any section of the spectrum of possible interpretations of *Pride and Prejudice* and its heroine: the point is not to argue what Elizabeth's position is, but to highlight the very spectrum of these readings, and most especially their limits. It is not that Austen's own vision of her times was especially conservative: it is that no matter how progressive Austen's vision of women in the 1810s was, it is radically outmoded today. Yet it is radically outmoded and immensely popular, and this is the basis from which any discussion of *Pride and Prejudice and Zombies* must develop. The point is that the regressive happy ending of a novel in which marriage is all along understood to be the only viable life option for a woman is both immensely popular, frequently and uncritically adapted—indeed, even reduced in critical potential, if we follow Sørbø—and no more, in fact less, feminist than the version offered by *Pride and Prejudice and Zombies*.

The BBC production's influence in the creation of "Austenmania" in the late 1990s and 2000s has yet to abate, and its focus on reading Darcy and Elizabeth's marriage as an undoubted, unadulterated happy ending has become standard, a fact to which numerous slash-fiction texts and the 2005 film can also attest. Contemporary popular reception has thus narrowed the possible readings of Austen's novel down to one, in which the intricate courting and verbal sparring between Darcy and Elizabeth leads (much in the vein of contemporary romantic comedies) to an expected but at least ostensibly surprising coming together that appears to be fulfilling for both parties. This cultural reading practice of Austen that focuses on the banal to the detriment of a potentially more complex understanding of the author's writings is parodied in *Pride and Prejudice and Zombies*. This lies behind the self-aware thoughts which Kitty offers in *Dreadfully Ever After*: "One didn't add oil to water or axle grease to tea or zombies and ninjas to a romance. Like belonged with like" (209). It refuses to accept *Pride and Prejudice* as a romance for the contemporary by adding ninjas and, especially, zombies: you really cannot have a (Regency) romance with zombies. *Pride and Prejudice and Zombies* thus becomes something more, something that takes direct aim at the romanticized adaptations and superficial readerships of contemporary Austen. The novels' parodic stance towards the BBC production, as well as the banalized, sexualized, trivialized reception of Austen, begins with *Pride and Prejudice and Zombies*'s repeated insistence on Darcy's "most English parts" and the way that "his trousers clung" to them (305), but it is actually much broader than that. The target of this parody is what Martin Amis has called the "disembodied snobbery and vague postimperial tristesse" (1995) of Austenmania: its cheerful submission of all that is awkward and gray about Austen's world to the plot of a romantic comedy. In doing so, it retrieves what is to be criticized about Austen, too, and it irretrievably changes what we read when we read *Pride and Prejudice*.

There are perhaps the first signs of something more important here: China Miéville has suggested (perhaps a little surprisingly) that the zombie mash-ups I discuss in this chapter may be understood as harbingers of a new era of the novel proper, if, as Miéville has proposed, the future of the novel lies in becoming an open object (cf. 2014, 44) capable of constant reappropriation and modification—or, in a non-pejorative sense, a post-postmodern form of sampling, in which reader-producers create their own versions of fictional texts through techniques of selection and recombination. Under such a premise, an attentive reading of the work that zombie mash-up fiction undertakes may even offer us a genuine sense of the future of literary fiction.

Will we, then, be able to read *Pride and Prejudice* again *without* zombies? The question is not quite as facetious as it may seem. Grahame-Smith's (it should be said again) entirely mercenary, publisher-driven, hack-in-the-best-sense work allows us to see with different eyes the very construct of the Regency romance in current times. There is, as Camilla Nelson notes, something odd about the fact that *Pride and Prejudice and Zombies*, a text which is "seemingly so resolutely about the 'capitalist grotesque' is also in complex ways a product of that same market process" (2013, 15). Very much open to question is whether this is any odder, however, than the similar situation of most contemporary cultural artifacts, from a Jonathan Franzen novel to a Mark Millar comic or a Stephen King short story collection, or, more pertinently for my argument here, the Penguin Classics reprints, illustrated editions, BBC TV series, and film adaptations of Jane Austen. Indeed, contrasted with the politically emptied shells which often stand in for Austen, it appears to be infinitely preferable. Tony Venables has claimed that "postmillennial zombie literature is not just about mash-up and parody" (2015, 209), as though those were bad things: as this chapter has shown, it is precisely mash-up and parody that mobilizes the critical potential of *Pride and Prejudice*. It would be an easy play to suggest that *Pride and Prejudice and Zombies* is Jane Austen, zombified both literally and figuratively (as Eburne does; 2014, 409; see note 21): it's just out to eat your brains, a dumb, shambling mass that once was a lively, living thing. It's far more suggestive to say, as I have tried to above, that *Pride and Prejudice* itself is the zombie: whatever actual life as a complex work of literary art it once had, it has become a brainless sort of entertainment, one which required the radical intervention of the zombie mash-up to render it meaningful again.

Sadie and Allison in the Apocalypse
Zombies and Gender

> Maybe this is Utopia in a way—a tangled, difficult way.
> A paradise of infinite possibility.
> ALLISON HEWITT IS TRAPPED, 337

Let me begin this chapter with what amounts to a fairly banal observation: The books I have so far discussed have at least two features in common—zombies, and the fact that their authors are men. This predominance of male writers is not a question of my own selection so much as a simple fact of life: male writers dominate the field even beyond my selection so far. Among the many which I have not touched upon are J. L. Bourne, M. R. Carey, Scott Kenemore, S. G. Browne, Brian Keene, Joe McKinney, and Isaac Marion. We should not be surprised about this: in being written and read mostly by men, zombie fiction is simply like most genre fiction, at least outside of romances. As Theodore Martin has recently noted, "the conspicuous gendering of genre [. . .] continues to dictate [. . .] how (and which) genres are allowed to be transformed from objects of popular entertainment to subjects of serious study" (2017, 11). Martin has a point, and part of this chapter is aimed at countering this trend, even as I suggest some ways in which genre writing is structurally bound not just in critical reception, but also in authorial production.

Some of the texts produced under these circumstances cater more obviously to the kind of clientele associated with male genre fantasy. J. L. Bourne's *Day by Day Armageddon* series, for example, follows a navy officer (Bourne himself is a naval officer, and holds oddly predictable conservative views, as his Twitter account proves) through a zombie apocalypse, and is crowded with detailed information on guns, military lingo, and patterns of speech, and all the paraphernalia usually found in a Tom Clancy military thriller. In this series, problems are solved through acts of violence, and other characters than the main one, especially women, remain rather nondescript.

Even when it does not so wholeheartedly endorse a stereotypically male set of interests, most zombie fiction may seem unlikely to harbor feminist or gender-progressive potentials. Yet such potentials in fact appear in the least likely of places, such as Bourne's books. On the one hand, *Day by Day Armageddon* is an overtly stereotypical zombie novel/military thriller, with its lone military officer-protagonist/narrator solving the problem of postapocalyptic survival with practiced male skill and an eye for the uses of weapons and violence. He finds himself by default in charge of civilian survivors, and leads them safely onward, despite mishaps and challenges; all this requires very little attention or imagination. The novel's political world is simple: do not reduce military spending; do not take away people's guns; do not believe that the government will be there to help you. Its protagonist-narrator fits perfectly into this mold: he takes over the reins of a small group of civilian survivors, whose initial rejection of things military turns into grudging admiration; he goes about dubbing the women in the group "girls" (2004, 147), despite their acknowledged survival skills.

Over long stretches, *Day by Day Armageddon* reads as a frequently chauvinistic fantasy of alpha-male dominance. Even so, the novel's very same "girls" also (with some training) eventually become capable fighters, markswomen even, as the narrator without qualification describes. Despite its deeply conservative worldview, *Day by Day Armageddon* thus presents an at least ambivalent place for women in the apocalypse: still subject to the diminishing vocabulary of patriarchy, but capable on their own in ungendered roles, the exigencies of survival trumping any more simplistic gendered role models.

This, then, is my point of departure in this chapter: even the most stereotypical (not to mention badly written) zombie fiction frequently offers unexpectedly egalitarian visions of gender relations and surprising subject positions for women. Indeed, there appears to be a critical consensus that zombie texts are destined to open to view new conceptions of gender relations and alternative subject positions for women, an idea going back to the genre's origins. One notable feature of at least the original trilogy of George Romero's zombie films, as Steven Shaviro has pointed out, is that all three films have "women or blacks as their chief protagonists, the only characters with whom the audience positively identifies as they struggle to remain alive and to resist and escape the zombies" (1991, 88).[1] More recently, Kinitra Brooks has argued, with an especial regard to the role of black women, that zombie narratives are "pregnant with opportunities for exploring modern race and gender relations" (2014, 462).

I will be making three somewhat related points here. Most importantly, I will investigate a claim made explicit by Natasha Patterson, namely, that "the zombie narrative *in particular makes possible* alternative versions of femininity" (2008, 111, my emphasis). My interest here lies in two parts of this claim. On the one hand, the emphatic "in particular" suggests that what zombie narratives are *especially good at* are constructions of alternative femininities, as compared to other subjects (such as race); but it also, at least in part, seems to claim that this is something that *zombie narratives* are especially good at, as compared to other genres. This is a claim which relates to the particular nature of the zombie as a monster and to the apocalypse which it engenders, which echoes, in other words, my continued insistence herein to see the zombie as a formal constraint in zombie fiction. On the other hand, the cautious "makes possible" signals a problem: if, formally and thematically, zombie narratives are well-situated to develop alternative versions of femininity, they do not always do so, and in fact occasionally do the opposite; why and how they often do not will be a key issue below, as indeed it has been throughout this book. I will presume, as an organizing hypothesis, that there is indeed something about the particular constitution of zombie narratives that suggests them as ideal grounds for the investigation of alternative models of gender relations, and perhaps even of gender, period. I will discuss what is entailed in reproducing patriarchal systems of gender relations, rather than creating alternatives to them, against the generally progressive possibilities inherent in the genre. Offering up feminist opportunities, zombie fiction often resigns itself to a particularly unhelpful version of postfeminist outcomes.

Around this central aspect of this chapter, I will cluster two related issues. One is again the question of form, which, I will argue, tends to play a role in the writing of gender relations in zombie fiction. In seeking ways to conclude long narratives following the exploits of strong women, the heteronormative coupling as the ideal happy ending appears often as if by default—a default far less often assumed necessary for male protagonists. One way to circumvent this, it appears, is a shorter, episodic structure—one which even formally reneges on the need for closure. In the conclusion, I will more broadly survey the relationship between form and female empowerment as zombie fiction presents it, and think through the structural violence of the genre, which necessarily involves female protagonists in stereotypically male pursuits—sometimes, as in the case of *Allison Hewitt Is Trapped*, beheading zombies with fire axes. This will allow me to make a minor point on the nature of women's zombie fictions itself, as genre writing, what we may perhaps call the question of "genrécriture feminine."

In investigating these points, I want to begin by sketching a few general points about the nature of the relation between gender and zombie fiction, most especially those items which appear to militate towards reading zombie fictions as particularly suitable for progressive gender narratives. These are, chiefly, two: the nature of the zombie and the nature of the apocalypse that nearly always accompanies it. For one thing, as Natasha Patterson points out (slightly obviously but usefully nonetheless), strict delineations between the genders seem to immediately lose some force in a world where "everyone is capable of becoming a zombie" (2012, 108), and, with a bit of tongue-in-cheek, in consequence of the fact that one is not born but rather becomes a zombie. Once zombified, gender, as a category of identity and difference, becomes decentered both as a concern for the former individual's own sense of him- or herself, as well as an issue for those around, in the face of its absolute otherness. These are two related but separate points: as Marcus Harmes points out, "zombies are traditionally asexual and gender traits are sublimated by their undead state" (2014, 37). It simply does not matter whether a zombie used to be a man or a woman, male or female, or anything else; as a zombie, it is no longer any of those things, merely a threat to the surviving humans. More starkly put, "[t]he zombie has no gender" (Venables 2015, 215). It does not have a gender in the way that ants, tapirs, or blue whales do not: despite sexual differentiation (which we might say the zombie also lacks, in most narratives, given that it usually entirely asexual), given the lack of social construction which makes gender and constructs gendered difference, the zombie remains merely Other.

One consequence of this, in more theoretical terms, is that as Patterson has suggested, the categories of "woman and feminist" are "meaningless when confronted with zombie invasion" (2008, 114). Patterson's point here is, of course, a negative one, in which the (politically and ideologically) useful positions of woman and feminist are annihilated, and pleasure is experienced through self-abjection in the process of viewing a zombie film: zombie films establish "genderless identificatory viewing positions" (115). Yet this extradiegetic position hinges upon a diegetic realization of the meaningless of gender identities, suggesting that these (otherwise) meaningful identities become radically superseded by the only lastingly meaningful one, that of survivor, that in the face of a radical Other, all other Others become immediately Us. At the same time as becoming a zombie annihilates gender in the victim (even as gender may have been part of the train of events that has caused the victim to become a zombie), it also opens spaces for imagining alternative versions of gender relations. Patterson's gender reading of the zombie film, then, is doubly redemptive: it enables progressive reading positions and shows a world in which gender identities have become muted. Some recent films and novels have moved beyond this, either by giving zombies narrative agency and gendered, or at least sexual, identities, as in Isaac Marion's *Warm Bodies* or Scott

Kenemore's *Zombie, Ohio*, or by giving zombies sexuality without agency, as in M.R. Carey's *The Girl with All the Gifts*. But the majority of zombie fiction still treats the zombie, a creature without society, as a creature without the gendered strictures of society as well.

There are, then, two major ways in which the zombie complicates gender discussions: it can act as an ever-present foil for traditional gender relations, constantly reminding characters and readers of the essential egalitarianism of its being and the social constructedness of their own gender relations. There are limits to this: the not-inconsiderable sacrifice involved in achieving this equality (you cannot have it until you die) militates against any too happy reading of the zombie as a foil, and it seems little different, in fact, from simple death. On the other hand, the zombie can become the unifying Other against which surviving humans can aim to recalibrate themselves, with its very threat posing the possibility of rethinking the binaries of human existences.

The zombie is, however, a special Other, capable of making the differences between humans seem minor the face of the more radical, more fundamental difference of them to it, which is not just an issue for zombie narratives (it is also true for, say, aliens, inhuman monsters, demons, or what have you). What is interesting in Patterson's formulation that "everyone is capable of being a zombie" is the idea of "being capable" of being a zombie: the notion that even in the defeat of humanity that is death/undeath, there can be a sense of egalitarianism achieved, of similar capability being similarly rewarded. Much like the notion that it is easier to imagine the end of the world than it is to imagine the end of capitalism, the awkward echo here of a resolution of gender troubles which occurs only in the complete annihilation of humanity is hardly reassuring. The idea, however, that the quest for and achievement of equality may be found at the heart of zombie fiction is worth pursuing.

On the one hand, then, the formal narrative preconditions of zombie fiction contain, in the very figure of the zombie, something peculiarly egalitarian (unlike, say, the aristocratic vampire). As importantly, however, the particular form of the zombie apocalypse appears to lay in structurally a sense of gender-equal opportunities—it exists as a matter of form. The zombie apocalypse almost always sees the complete collapse of hitherto existing society, including at least in theory a breakdown of the gendered boundaries of contemporary life. These breakdowns of boundaries are otherwise, at the very least, rare. I have noted in the introduction the importance of recognizing that the very nature of the zombie as an apocalyptic horror trope is crucially different from the vampire, the werewolf, the ghost, aliens, and so on. The possibilities opened by this collapse set into sharper relief the persistent structures of oppression and hierarchy that can outlast even the rest of the social order, while also giving opportunities to re-order gender relations as they are actually, fictionally, enacted.

Between them, the two structural preconditions of zombie fiction—the nature of the zombie and the nature of the zombie apocalypse—are less generic constraints than generic opportunities, then: if you can't have a realist novel in which radical change to society occurs, likewise and contrarily, you cannot have a zombie novel that does not necessitate such radical change. It is against this background of formally necessary possibility that gender relations in zombie fiction must be read. I will do so, in contrast to the previous chapters, in the form of a broader, less in-depth survey of a variety of key texts—some of which I have already discussed.

In what follows, I will first draw together some strands from those texts in an effort to locate the discussion of gender and the zombie in a broad field. Gender obviously played a major role in my discussion of *Pride and Prejudice and Zombies*, so I will not repeat this discussion here; but it is also a valuable perspective to put on a number of other texts, notably Brooks's *World War Z*. I will also glance, at least *en passant*, at two texts I do not otherwise discuss, M. R. Carey's *The Girl with All the Gifts* and Jesse Peterson's *Married with Zombies*. The gender politics of these texts will serve as an introduction to the two main texts I will read in this chapter: Madeleine Roux's duo of zombie novels, *Allison Hewitt Is Trapped* and *Sadie Walker Is Stranded*. These two novels will illustrate what I take to be at the heart of feminist and gender-related zombie criticism: the availability (in the zombie apocalypse) of opportunities to imagine a fundamentally different relationship between men and women in contextually reappraised gender constellations, but also the inadequate use made of these same opportunities. In a (too-small) nutshell: the feminist and progressive insistence in *Allison Hewitt Is Trapped* on Allison's leadership role, capabilities, self-control, and the corresponding lack of emphasis placed on her being a woman fails at the novel's end, when Allison's story becomes subsumed by a romance plot of deeply uncertain narrative utility. This final failure is only reinforced by the second novel, in which Sadie Walker comes to rely both on her sense of what her hero Allison would do and ultimately on the capabilities of her male fellow survivors, while largely reducing herself to the role of a surrogate mother to her orphaned nephew. The narrative ends in the restitution of the nuclear family by recourse to a romance plot.

Combined with the blunt fact that Roux herself is a woman, the two novels' different narratives can stand as exemplary engagements (for better and worse!) with the question of gender, representation, and the zombie apocalypse. The argument here is not so much a qualitative one than it is one about genre form and gender-progressive literary form: whatever the genre's necessary formal opportunities, their realization is not easily reducible to either—form enables but does not necessitate, and certainly does not guarantee, visions of a more equal postapocalyptic life. Still, the very fact that the genre form does enable such a life should be noted. What I am offering here is an exploration of some expressions of the form's possibilities—with some trepidation, a feminist appraisal of zombie fiction. I take from Toril Moi the conviction that feminist criticism must be political: that "it seeks to expose, not to perpetuate, patriarchal practices" (1985, xiv). Within this broad remit, feminist reading practices span a wide gamut from reading stereotypical females figures in male texts to the specifics of female writing practices to contestations of the canon as a whole. This is not the place to reiterate them beyond noting, as Ellen Rooney does, that "no approach can summarize this protean body of work or claim to represent it in its totality" (2006, 9).

My own approach in this chapter will be comparatively simple. Zombie fiction is hardly amenable to recanonization, given that it has no canon. It offers some scope for debate on whether we can trace something like a "gen-récriture feminine" in the few examples of woman-authored zombie texts, but hardly enough to warrant a full chapter. It does, however, show a broad array of representations of female subjectivity, all of which can be explored. At their best, zombie narratives use their formal leeway to explore, consciously or unconsciously, the contemporary boundaries of gender roles and to offer versions of life that are less strictly regimented by patriarchy, or indeed by too facile and diametrical backlash against patriarchy, and to end up successfully deemphasizing the social need to think in strict gender categories. But this best is often not reached; too often, a limited sense of narrative logic acts against a more progressive stance than seeing the happy-ending for a woman in the successful heterosexual coupling with another capable survivor: a return to the narrative logic of the romance. As Steve Jones and Shaka McGlotten point out in their introduction to *Zombies and Sexuality*, "many zombie narratives reproduce or even celebrate norms tied to romance, gender, ability, and heterosexuality" (2014, 6). Capability, not ability, is one of the key issues I will be addressing below (especially in the comparison between *Allison Hewitt Is Trapped* and *Sadie Walker Is Stranded*, in which the respective mediations of female and male capability play a key role), but the general point addressed by McGlotten and Jones should be understood to inform my (measured) criticism below: the "possible alternative versions of femininity" which Patterson sees at work in the zombie narrative all too often remain unrealized.

Gender and the Zombie

Gender issues have been part and parcel of zombie narratives at least as far back as *White Zombie* (1932; for an exhaustive reading, see Klippel 2011). *White*

Zombie, hardly surprisingly, does not question the gender stereotypes of its times; in fact, it reinforces male anxieties about female behavior and roles. It offers an inauspicious start to the zombie film genre's gender narrative: its female lead, Madge Bellamy's Madeleine Short, becomes a voodoo slave to Murder LeGrange—at least some necrophilic overtones are present here. Zombiehood merely amplifies Madeleine's stereotypical female helplessness and her presence as a mere object or a prize; she is saved in the nick of time by her fiancé, escaping one form of bondage for what is perhaps just another. As Kyle Bishop points out, *White Zombie* is closely related to the Gothic melodramas, such as *Dracula*, "in which a single menacing figure threatens the safety of a helpless female character" (2010, 19); later films of the 1940s and 1950s, by contrast, more strongly echoed the fears of colonial revenge and anti-imperialist movements.

If *White Zombie* offers no particularly empowering view of female agency, we should probably be leery of criticizing too much a low-budget B-movie of the 1930s for its lack of innovation in depicting gender relations. Thirty years later, in George Romero's *Night of the Living Dead*, the depiction of Barbra, the female protagonist, is already more ambivalent. Her instincts, for instance, unlike her brother's, point her to the impending danger lurking in the graveyard, but her flight to the farmhouse ends with her essentially becoming agency-less, a mere ward of the more active and commanding male protagonist, Ben. Nor is it just Barbra who embodies "negative female stereotypes" (2006, 38), as Kim Paffenroth points out, the other women in the film, too, are not depicted as either capable or independent. This has been read by several commentators as a reflection of "cultural anxieties concerning the liberated status of women during the 1960s" (Bishop 2010, 126). Natasha Patterson understands Barbra as "symbolic of everything that is wrong with patriarchy and male-defined notions of femininity and womanhood" (2008, 110). Understanding Barbra as symbolic, notably, rather than symptomatic, her depiction is thus a critique of "behaving in a way appropriate for a woman at that time": "Her investment in, and performance of, a passive (and therefore respectable) femininity literally hurts her" (2011, 230). Such a reading, which sees Barbra's abandonment of agency as a critical intervention, rather than a repetition and affirmation of stereotypes, also squares well with the later installments of the *Dead* series. Fran, the female protagonist of *Dawn of the Dead*, vocally insists at one point on being treated no differently from her fellow male survivors, and at the end of the film, flies herself and Peter away from the doomed mall. Sarah, the female protagonist of *Day of the Dead*, shows the kind of leadership which finally achieves the survival of at least a few of her fellow humans.

What these examples highlight is the divergence in critical interest from the voodoo zombie to the Romero zombie. In the voodoo zombie, the issues of gender and zombification are strongly conflated, with one (the zombified state) easily capable of metaphorically standing for the other (woman's roles in society); in the Romero zombie, by and large, it is the human reactions to the zombies that are of interest to gender critics. Both of these perspectives, of course, can produce meaningful interpretations. The first perspective concerns what Steve Jones calls "the gendering of zombies" (2011, 41)—that is to say, a reading of how the zombies themselves may represent gender beyond a simple abnegation of it. Unsurprisingly perhaps, this, too, is a many-sided issue. Jones argues that "the generic zombie" must be read as female, given the way the stereotypical characteristics of women are reflected in those of zombies and therefore grant a measure of female empowerment (43). By contrast, to offer just one example, Bock, Isermann, and Knieper argue that zombie fictions (their example being *Resident Evil*) "generally reinforce existing clichés" (2011, 161), despite the initial appearance of an equality based on the fact that "the female zombie kills as brutally and emotionlessly as its male counterpart" (153). The radical openness of the zombie figure thus enables, here as everywhere else, a space for the development of alternative patterns of gender that is not always, perhaps not even often, used.

As interesting as the gendering of zombies is, my own point of departure in this chapter will be, as throughout this book, the belief that it is not about the zombies, but rather about the humans facing them. I will largely follow Bishop's and Patterson's lead here in not talking about the gendering of zombies; instead, I will focus on issues of gender reflected by the human protagonists of the novels I will be discussing. These gender issues develop from the apocalyptic scenarios imbedded in most zombie narratives. As noted, the collapse of hitherto existing society and the reorganization of survivors into new groups, collectives, communities, and societies brings with it the opportunity of reshaping conceptions of gender roles and relations. Yet a struggle for survival, which is at the narrative core of so many zombie narratives, brings with it a reshaping of what it "means" to be woman or man. Zombie fictions refract this point symptomatically: a radical break with the heteronormative patriarchal past and present that at least potentially opens avenues for reconceiving these relations.

This also brings me to what is probably the most fraught issue at stake in this discussion of gender and the zombie: what to call the reconceptions of gender relations offered by the texts I discuss below. As Judith Butler points out, "the very description of the field of gender is in no sense prior to, or separable from, the question of its normative operation" (2006, xxii); speaking and writing on gender and about gender thus always happens within preformed discourses, and to speak about gender may always imply a sense of normativity. In what follows below, I will largely equate "progressive" models of gender relations with struggle against the subordinate position of women; and consider "subordination" here to mean such things as following male leaders, surrendering agency to male compatriots, and to willingly adhere to traditional roles: mother, wife, and domestic support.[2]

For the remainder of this section, then, and before reading more exhaustively two novels whose paralleling sheds more light on the ways zombie fiction enables but does not necessitate progressive gender narratives, I will briefly sketch gender depictions in a number of texts that I have already discussed, plus a few notable examples from new texts. My point here will be essentially this: narrative form structures in a number of remarkable ways the extent of a progressive gender position. Or, to put it more bluntly: long form narratives frequently struggle with finding a conclusion for its female characters that does not envisage a romantic relationship, unless it is the end of the world. By contrast, shorter forms, often more open-ended, are also more capable of imagining different ends for their female characters.

Perhaps the text that most obviously allows for this conclusion is Max Brooks's *World War Z*. Its major lasting thread of narrative, the loss and ultimate reconquest of the continental United States, features no important female characters: its politicians, generals, and other top-level characters are all male, leftovers from the structures which *World War Z* does not generally disavow, as I have argued in Chapter 1. *World War Z* thus appears to broadly reaffirm patriarchal structures in refusing to depict radical alternatives to them; but in its less immediately connected vignettes of individual struggles, women become both centerpieces of narrative action as well as (obviously) survivors of their own. *World War Z* has more vignettes narrated by men, to be sure. Only four women get to tell their stories of the Zombie War: Jesika Hendricks, a child at the time of the outbreak and now a part-time volunteer at a Wilderness Reclamation Project; Mary Jo Miller, mayor of Troy, Montana, a newly built safe community; Christina Eliopolis, an air force colonel; and Maria Zhuganova, formerly a Russian soldier and now little more than a human incubator.

Like most men, women in *World War Z* remain sketches. What is important is that these sketches are not, in fact, particularly strongly imprinted by gender roles. In some of the stories, like that of Jesika Hendricks, gender apparently plays no role at all: Hendricks's family's journey into the safety of Canada's frozen north hinges nowhere on gender issues, and Hendricks's own survival is not correlated with gender. Her current role is clearly ungendered; she is merely one of a number of people doing the same job in the wake of the zombie apocalypse (121). The same holds true, to a slightly lesser extent, for Mary Jo

Miller, for whom the apocalypse at least has brought a shift away from the purely domestic (and certainly stereotypically female or maternal) concerns of financial worries, sick pets, the need for new children's soccer cleats, and so on, towards her new role as a mayor of the new community. Neither the narrator nor Miller feels obligated to nod towards Miller's gender with regard to this role or her experiences (even though Miller herself explains that when the family first encountered zombies, she was unloading the washing machine), but it does more or less firmly situate her position on a before-after spectrum, in which Miller's pre-apocalyptic concerns, role, and behavior are not worthy of comment: they merely are "who I was" (65), as she herself notes in a slightly different context.

In other vignettes, we do get to a point where gender and sex become relevant, but only late in the game or very tentatively. In the case of Christina Eliopolis, the transport pilot whose struggle to survive after bailing out of her plane serves as an illustration of the persistence of human will in adversity, a similar gambit of briefly noting gendered pasts but then quickly ignoring them as, indeed, safely *past* plays out. Eliopolis is not a transport pilot because she is a woman (that is, relegated to the less challenging tasks because of her gender) but because this is what is needed: she used to be a fighter pilot. Eliopolis briefly recounts the lack of female solidarity at the Air Force Academy (174), and we get hints that her difficulties at the academy are not least related to her being a highly capable woman, but there is no insistence on this. The heart of her story is the relationship between her and her contact—the possibly imaginary "Mets"—and their self-sufficient survival out in the wilderness. More strongly than Mary Jo Miller's story, Eliopolis's suggests that bygones are bygones; the gender-related troubles at the pre-apocalypse Air Force Academy are in the past, now replaced by a genuinely egalitarian system based on individual capabilities and achievements.

Maria Zhuganova's gender, at least initially, also apparently plays no role at all. A Russian soldier, Zhuganova initially finds herself an equal member of a rebelling battalion; she narrates the facts of her experiences without suggesting at any time that her gender was important. Explicitly included in the numbers counted towards the violent decimation of Russia's rebelling military, *World War Z*'s choice of a female soldier in fact initially seems to highlight more strongly a version of female life that has all avenues open to (it is certainly remarkable that two out of four female characters in the novel are military personnel). But as the novel ends, we discover her current circumstances—Zhuganova is in what amounts to a breeding program: "Our leader says that the greatest weapon a Russian woman can wield now is her uterus" (330). Zhuganova ends, then, sexualized and objectified, even as she herself apparently accepts this as merely another service to the state. More notably, perhaps, Zhuganova remains the only woman in *World War Z* to be sexualized like this—an echo of the novel's light cautionary insistence on seeing Russian recuperation as a militant theocracy as an outlier to its deeply liberal vision of the postapocalypse—and thus sets into even sharper relief the more general progressive message the novel brings across.

World War Z has nearly reached its end when it hits its highest gender-political note: in Arthur Sinclair's final appearance, he notes: "When the new president asked me to step back into my role as SEC chairman, I practically kissed her on the spot" (337). The first female American president has come into office, but it is an event that does not warrant anybody's comment in *World War Z*, or indeed more than a single pronoun. This is typical of the novel's conception of change: whatever changes it presents it presents as given, as natural, as barely worthy of comment, at least in the aftermath of the apocalyptic events it recounts. In refusing to comment on what must still be regarded as an extraordinary shift, *World War Z* offers a dually progressive vision of gender roles: in terms of the characters' self-conception, they become naturalized, and the same holds for the narrative perspective. Both the novel and its characters, then, would like to depict these female positions (with the exception of Zhuganova) as the identitarian equivalent of their politically progressive, liberal vision of the future.

At least in part, however, I would suggest, the ease with which *World War Z* establishes women as fully equal in (most of) the postapocalyptic world is precisely due to its vignette structure. With only the sketchiest of backstories and descriptions of their current situations, the women in the novel are hardly well-rounded characters, but this also prevents them from being forced into the usual circumstances of well-rounded female characters in genre fiction: without the need to depict their love lives and relationships as part of an effort of full characterization. To be sure, that *World War Z* uses its vignettes to speak not about such issues as losing one's husband or finding true love in the midst of carnage are choices not demanded by the structure. Yet, in abandoning the need for narrative closure, the novel's structure also leaves behind the temptation of the kind of romantic closure provided female characters ("I survived, and now I'm happily married again, too!").

M. R. Carey's *The Girl with All the Gifts* offers the opportunity to make a different point, one focusing on the conjunction of text and reception. At the center of its narrative is Melanie, one of a number of what quickly are revealed to be zombie children who nevertheless retain cognitive powers, consciousness, and are (or, at least, Melanie is) gifted with great intelligence and strength. Held on a research base twenty years after a mutation in the *Ophiocordyceps* fungus responsible for the so-called "zombie ants" has spread to humanity and wiped out most of civilization, Melanie and her fellow children are taught in classrooms designed to quantify their intellectual and emotional responses, and then dissected to find a cure for the fungus. She bonds with one of her "teachers," the psychologist Helen Justineau. Melanie is the most high-functioning of the children; she thus becomes a target for Dr. Caroline Caldwell's dissections, from which Justineau can barely save her; as she does so, the base falls to an assault by human survivors leading a horde of zombies. Melanie, Justineau, Caldwell, and two male soldiers, Sgt. Parks and Pvt. Gallagher, escape and head for the community of survivors at the south England enclave of Beacon. The group's solidarity is narrowly balanced between Caldwell's desire to retain Melanie as a specimen, Justineau's desire to keep Melanie safe, and Sgt. Parks's increasing acceptance of Melanie as more than just an ordinary "hungry" (as the novel calls its zombies). On the way, they discover that the zombification fungus, which has so far only spread through contact with body fluids, is fruiting in an immense rhizome and threatening to spore; and then find a mobile research lab that had been lost twenty years earlier, which allows Dr. Caldwell to discover the real workings of the fungus. Melanie, it turns out, did not become infected by the fungus through a bite: she is the actual offspring of two hungries who have retained enough vestiges of their former selves to engage in sexual activity. Dr. Caldwell's conclusion is shattering: there is no chance for survival for the other humans, and no cure. Melanie, agreeing, sets the rhizome of fruiting fungus on fire, releasing the spores and dooming the rest of mankind to death: only the half-zombie children, in whom the fungus has become a symbiont, will survive, and they will go on to create a new civilization. In the final scene, Helen Justineau, temporarily protected by a hazmat suit, teaches a group of feral zombie children the alphabet.

There are a number of interesting aspects to Carey's novel, from its Matheson-like argument that humanity's time has passed to the mode of zombification chosen; for my purposes here, I am interested in the depiction of women, in particular that of Dr. Caroline Caldwell, the head scientist and the paratextual apparatus. Caldwell's chief function as presumed antagonist throughout the book is her desire to treat Melanie and the other children as specimens, as routes to the solution of the problem of (human) survival. She is an able scientist: not the most able, as she herself is forced to acknowledge, having not been chosen among those top scientists who twenty years earlier were sent out with the mobile labs to discover a cure, but clearly capable, working assiduously within her limited means. Strong-willed and single-minded, she ultimately does work out both how the fungus works and why Melanie does not suffer death by it; and accepts, with comparative good grace, what is simultaneously her greatest discovery and her greatest defeat. All of these characteristics, including her deep curiosity, make her an eminent scientist; and yet, as the book depicts her, she is also the human antagonist, whose success, at least by the methods she has chosen, we are supposed to root against.

It is therefore not a little striking that among the questions which the novel offers for reading groups is this: "Caroline Caldwell would have been a more sympathetic and likable character if she was a man. Do you agree with this statement?" (loc. 5545). I don't want to discuss whether or not Caldwell is likable, of course, but rather the question's implicit understanding of female and male roles, which makes it a less meaningless question than it might appear at first glance. There is the kernel of a meaningful exploration of Caldwell as a character here: she is the epitome of the mad scientist figure—and, in this, already a surprising choice, given that, as Cherilyn Lacy has noted, "Western conceptions of science have frequently relied upon gendered metaphors that characterize science as a masculine enterprise that manipulates Nature and coerces *her* secrets out of *her*" (2004, 57, original italics). The fact that Caldwell is a woman, then, already places her against conventional expectations. But what the question implies, of course, is more than that. Set against Helen Justineau's empathetic and emotional relationship with Melanie, Caldwell's cold, meticulous, and above all emotionally detached single-mindedness signals a masculine hardness which, if we take our cue from the readers' question, makes more of a negative impression coming from a woman: she is apparently out of her place. Yet even if this were true, two issues complicate this simple reading.

The first is that this is the perspective of someone cognizant both of the way women should *be* and be *represented* under the normative conditions of contemporary society as well as the way scientists usually get depicted. We must take for granted the existence of this reader and his or her reactions, yet in doing so, we should not miss that this is possibly not the novel's stance on this. The second issue is that while the novel clearly, and fairly overtly, sets the "likable" Helen Justineau, who hugs and protects Melanie, against the "unlikable" Caroline Caldwell, who cuts open children and rummages through their brains, the novel also defies easy moralizing. Caldwell, it turns out, is simply much more *right* than anybody else in the novel. Her view of the fungal parasite is that an infected is already dead: "though its heart may beat [. . .] and though it speaks and can even be christened with a boy's name or a girl's name, is not the host. It's the parasite" (loc. 561). As it turns out, this is not wholly correct—there is a symbiosis between the fungus and the host in the children—but given the immense danger which emanates from the children, it is also a far safer course of action than Helen Justineau's. In setting the arbitrary boundary between mostly human, and mostly not, Caldwell errs on the side of caution, and Justineau, on the side of compassion. Neither position is ultimately fully validated, but it is Caldwell's discovery of the ultimate hopelessness of searching for a cure, and her establishment of the fungal life cycle, that permit Melanie to finally choose a new future for the planet.

It is not, then, that Justineau's inferences about Melanie—conditioned by stereotypically feminine attributes such as warmth, attachment, compassion, and even love—are correct: in fact, the first time she breaches the appropriate distance between herself and Melanie, she almost gets killed, and from there, it is largely Melanie's ability to control herself that keeps her from attacking Justineau. By contrast, results follow from Caldwell's rational working through of the scientific method, her repeated endangering of herself and others in her quest to understand the various "hungries" they encounter, and even her hijacking of the research lab. These results, as Caldwell correctly insists, would have required the dissection of one of her children-subjects' brains at the research base, and those only become less important because she has obtained suitable other specimens in the field. In its depiction of two vastly different women, both of whom, in their own ways, contribute to the modestly hopeful conclusion of the novel, *The Girl with All the Gifts* refuses to take clear positions on what women "should be like."

At the same time, the novel also avoids a heteronormative conclusion to its incipient love—or, at least, sexual attraction—plot, if we except the brief dalliance between Sgt. Parks and Ms. Justineau shortly before the novel's end. It does so largely by making Justineau the last woman on Earth. Even then, the role which she adopts, that of teacher, is perhaps more stereotypical than the researcher's position she held at the novel's beginning. It is not that Carey's novel suggests it is easier to imagine the end of the world than the end of heteronormativity; it is that it appears to suggest that it takes the end of the world to imagine the end of heteronormativity. On the way to that conclusion, however, *The Girl with All the Gifts* offers a rather remarkably gender-progressive vision of a future in which gender plays no role when set against individual capability, and in which the easy opposition of male science versus female emotionality is avoided. The novel's characters neither accuse Justineau of surrendering to her female sensibilities in getting closer to Melanie, nor Caldwell of a lack of ability; gender really plays no role in the narrative's evaluations of its characters. *The Girl with All the Gifts* also spares us the moment when the successful male scientist, with all the pathos of the dying genius, can stand up against the woman teacher and tell her how right he was not to be so emotionally involved by the simple expedient of making both characters female. It does so not just because there is no male scientist (though this is a rather remarkable fact in its own right): it does so chiefly because in its ultimate conclusion, both Justineau and Caldwell play important roles. Justineau's teaching is what enables Melanie to bridge the gap between the old human civilization and the new one to be ushered in by the zombified children: through her, the knowledge of the old world will, at least in parts, be saved and transferred, but it is Caldwell's discoveries that enable Melanie in the first place to accept that this will be the necessary future. *The Girl with All the Gifts*, notably, does not end up censuring Caldwell: her efforts do not end in scientific failure (although her desire for a cure is thwarted) but in success; her hijacking of the research lab, her illicit obtaining of brain tissue, of a fungal seed pod, and other things she does behind the back and against the explicit desires of the rest of the group are thus at least partially validated.

To discuss whether or not Caldwell is "likable" or not, then, as the readers' question has it, is less interesting for what it reveals about Caldwell than it is for what it reveals about the implied readers of zombie fiction and possibly all genre fiction. They are assumed to read female characters along an emotional axis, judging them for their likability rather than for their capabilities—or for the way their capabilities might make them more likable; they are also assumed to judge men less harshly for emotional coldness and calculation than they do women. The readers' question thus reveals something like the dark underside of progressive gender narratives, namely, the danger that they are read, as Judith Butler implies, with an inappropriate normative lens that precludes the very seeing of a successful, albeit robustly uncaring, woman such as Caldwell as being more than merely likable or not.

Jesse Peterson's *Married with Zombies* is perhaps the most revelatory example of awkwardly gendered zombie fiction, and its focus on marriage as an institution sets the stage for my discussion to follow of *Allison Hewitt Is Trapped*. The novel's plot is quickly retold and thoroughly, perhaps overtly, conventional. It follows Sarah and David as they make their way from Seattle to Longview, in the wake of a zombie apocalypse that began in a lab at the University of Washington. On their way, they are joined by their neighbor, the vapid Amanda; encounter and leave behind a teenage girl survivor; engage and are nearly killed by a religious repopulationist cult; and finally arrive at Longview only to have David's in-denial sister be killed by her love interest-become-zombie. Little of this is remarkable, then, with the exception of its central gambit, the overt way in which the novel presents the coincidence of zombie apocalypse and a saved marriage. Sarah and David encounter their first zombie in marriage counseling; and its chapter headings are all styled like the pithy one-liners one expects from self-help books, such as: "Give each other compliments every day. Even when the undead attack, it's nice to feel pretty. Or badass" [78]. Sarah and David occasionally remind us of how their marriage stood on edge; and, of course, in the end, their shared survival also saves their marriage. As Sarah, the book's narrator, bluntly concludes, if there "isn't much good to say about the zombie infestation," at least "I have to say, the zombie plague saved my marriage" (2011, 241).

Prizing one's marriage is one thing, but foregrounding it in juxtaposition to the collapse of civilization is quite another. As Kay Steiger notes of *The Walking Dead*, for people to behave the same in a world where priorities have radically shifted seems, at least, strange (2011, 105). To insist on the importance not of the emotional bond but on the institution (not: saved my relationship, but: saved my marriage) in the midst of the dissolution of all other civic institutions is no idle choice (readers, after all, do not yet live after this collapse, and must perforce read "marriage" as more than just shorthand for "love"). Given this, the novel might be one of two things: an unrepentant affirmation of heterosexual marriage as an institution worth saving even in the face of zombie hordes, or a more-or-less clever sendup of precisely this notion, as well as the connected idea of self-help. The only thing which can save marriage, this parsing might suggest, is the zombie apocalypse—hardly a resounding affirmation. *Married with Zombies* is, of course, a comedy, and it does not pay to think too much about it, but it bears pointing out how the novel leaves its own stance both apparently open (and thus permits it being read as a sendup of traditional discourses on marriage, including the tendency to assume to need to "save" it) even as narratively, it provides no position from which to validate any of the alternate subversive readings: if it is satirical in intent, then it does not signal this intent through either form, plot, or paratext.

None of this would bear mention, and neither would *Married with Zombies*, were it not for the way this analysis works on the rest of my argument: whether or not a zombie narrative opens progressive gender positions hinges on matters of form. If *Married with Zombies* is read as a satire—as a sendup of self-help books, exemplified by Sarah's concluding remarks highlight the bizarreness of (especially the reader's) caring for the stability of a marriage in the face the collapse of civilization—then it critically reflects on the limits of heteronormative coupling and the possibility of accepting the end of such arrangements gracefully. If it is not read as a satire, then it is hardly a very progressive narrative at all. Even without taking into account its penchant to depict women as silly (Amanda), intransigent (the teenage girl), manipulative and mad (the repopulationist cultists), or thoroughly overwhelmed and unperceptive (David's sister), Sarah's callous conclusion—sorry for all the death, but hey, at least I have a husband—is more than a little problematic.

Married with Zombies is overtly suffused with concerns about gender roles—David's failure to be a provider, Amanda's general failure at life, and the repopulationist cult's subordination of women's freedom to the exigencies of making babies, to name a few—but breezes past all of them. It ends, of course, in the indeterminate affirmation of marriage that serves as its happy ending, and thus as a first marker of my central argument here. *Married with Zombies* is only the most radically overt of zombie fictions when it comes to imagining what counts as a happy ending, and as the "right" way of life for men and women.

Married with Zombies, *World War Z*, and *The Girl with All the Gifts* offer different readings of the possibility of progressive gender relations after the zombie apocalypse: most notably, they highlight the difficulty of imagining, despite all the radical changes which the apocalypse brings, narrative conclusions that do not reaffirm or at the very least nod to traditional heteronormative relationships. Even *The Girl with All the Gifts* cannot avoid a heterosexual coupling, narratively inconsequential and gratuitous though it is. The novels share the possibility of radical revised gender relations. None of the them suggests, at any time, that there are structural, or even formal, limits to the way their actual or potential reformed societies can operate. The failure to provide radically different gender relations is thus a failure of the imagination, one which highlights the persistence of contemporary patriarchal structures. For all their potential, zombie fictions often find it difficult to avoid the trappings of the marriage plot. Departing from this baseline, I now want to talk at greater length about two novels which explore these issues more fully: *Allison Hewitt Is Trapped* and *Sadie Walker Is Stranded*, both written, not coincidentally, by a woman, Madeleine Roux. As I will go on to show in the following, *Allison Hewitt Is Trapped* offers a remarkably ambivalent take on women's roles after the zombie apocalypse, while *Sadie Walker Is Stranded* refuses even those advances in the representation of female characters made in *Allison Hewitt*. Together, they suggest again the limits of the gender imagination of zombie fiction.

"A Paradise of Infinite Possibility": *Allison Hewitt Is Trapped*

Two opposing impulses are at work in Madeleine Roux's *Allison Hewitt Is Trapped*. On the one hand, the narrative is one of female empowerment, in which Allison, a graduate student and bookstore clerk, slowly comes to gain a sense of her own capabilities, her capability to lead, and her unusual strength while facing a zombie apocalypse. This part of the narrative suggests the novel's debt to feminist discourses, its effort to present a female heroine that is not primarily female but primarily a heroine, its sense that individual capability will trump whatever predisposed sense of gender roles lingers in the wake of society's dissolution. This progressive narrative of a woman's successful struggle to cope in a world fraught with infinite dangers is clearly foregrounded. But on the other hand, set against this progressiveness is an uneasy relationship with the patriarchal structures which it appears to be on the verge of overcoming, most especially marriage. Marriage, as I will show in what follows, recurs in *Allison Hewitt Is Trapped* as a marker of the structures that persist, and the novel, for all its progressiveness, cannot shake a sense that this should be so.

This is a point about the novel's content, of course; but *Allison Hewitt Is Trapped* begins by drawing attention to its form, and this form is the second crucial point to identify, given its importance to where the narrative ends. The novel is in its own fashion a found narrative; a description which might also apply to the process of its publication. In real life, half of it was originally posted online as a blog (still at https://helptheyarecoming.wordpress.com/). Roux was contacted with an offer to turn the blog into a book, which preserves the blog structure of semi-regular postings. The novel version adds a historical frame narrative, in which the blog becomes a historical document, submitted for publication a hundred years after the events of the novel (that is, in 2108) by a literature professor who has painstakingly reconstructed it, to become part of an anthology on notable female survivors of the "Outbreak," as the novel terms the zombie apocalypse. Historicizing the Outbreak, establishing a firmly and safely reconstituted, postapocalyptic society (so stable that it can afford literature professors and spats about book publishing) on the one hand certainly lowers the narrative stakes of the novel somewhat. At the same time, it emphasizes from the outset that whatever achievements the characters in the novel attain, gender- and otherwise, at least potentially remain constitutive of the new society. The novel's frame suggests that Allison Hewitt's story is meaningful—historical, even—and that it has something to say to survivors. This is the vantage point on Allison's story that the novel wishes to lay in for readers, and it is against this that we must read the subsequent narrative, which we must then judge against the conclusion of the frame narrative in which Allison's story is rejected.

The frame narrative also reveals the mechanics by which Allison's blog was written and survived the collapse of society; the blog itself forms the main portion of the book. The story details Allison's experiences during the Outbreak; it is written by herself and posted online by recourse to a military-made wireless network (SNET) still curiously operating and keeping her in contact with other survivors. Allison begins the novel trapped in a safe room of the bookstore at which she works with three co-workers in the never-named city that is identifiable as Madison, Wisconsin.[3] As supplies run low, the four survivors are forced first to seek out supplies in the bookstore itself, and then depart the store for the apartments above it, settling down for a while in them. But three things compel them to leave: first, a man they encounter in the apartments, Zack, turns out to be a thief, stealing from them the vast majority of their supplies. At the same time, Allison finds a broadcast on the radio stemming from the university campus, which offers a tantalizing hope for safety. Finally, Allison has been contacted by her mother in a comment on her blog. When she fails to reach Allison at the apartments, Allison decides to search for her.

Allison Hewitt Is Trapped is also a quest narrative, then: a narrative of journeys aimed at securing first safety and then Allison's mother, whom Allison now expects to find in Liberty Village, Colorado, leading her and a changing cast through the American Midwest in the latter half of the novel. The novel hits all the standard tropes of the genre: the bookstore survivors need to abandon their safe room for food and hygiene; they are tricked and robbed (by another survivor, of course) in their alternative hideout, and almost killed by the university survivors in a case of mistaken identity; and then brought to the university compound, which in turn collapses from internal strife. As part of an ever smaller group, Allison and her fellow survivors barely escape from the clutches of a radical cult; heading out to the apparent safety of Liberty Village, they encounter still more human dangers on the road, and finally make it to Liberty Village only with further losses to finally live in comparative safety. Allison herself is at the core of a shifting and changing group of survivors, whose only other constant is her colleague, Ted; the group's episodic encounters with by-now almost clichéd threats—zombies, of course, religious cults and violent militias—serve to frame the growth which Allison undergoes in the course of the narrative.

Various moments highlight significant shifts as well as significant continuities in the perception of gender relations, both for Allison herself and the various characters she deals with. Allison quickly becomes a leadership figure to her small group of survivors, but initially in the curiously gendered fashion which Zack describes as the "mother hen" (71), a role which Allison easily owns. But this maternal role does not last: when the group discovers that Zack has robbed them of their tools and food, and fled, they set off in pursuit, with Allison taking a leadership role. Catching up with Zack, Allison, brandishing her favorite weapon, a fire axe, cuts off his foot, and leaves him to the zombies. The action marks a significant break: with her group reduced by losses, and her trust shattered by Zack, Allison becomes less of a "mother hen" and more of a fighter for her own survival and that of those whom she cares about.

This fact becomes sharply evident in the juxtaposition between her and the group of survivors she now joins: the university group whose broadcast Allison had been listening to. On the campus, a mixed group of survivors has established themselves, with one subgroup standing out: a religious cult called the Black Earth Wives, an all-female group of survivors who believe that they have been tasked with repopulating the Earth. In a novel which, narratively, simply plods forward, this, too, would be unremarkable, were it not for the fact of the group members' sex, which contrasts sharply with the familiar version of the religious sex cult (for example, the version presented in *Married with Zombies*, where the cult leader is male, though his wife is also involved). The group members are all women, and they are all in the cult by choice; in fact, they are even willing to rape males to generate the offspring they believe they need. In a lesser book, this situation might be read as a misogynistic fantasy; yet in being set against Allison's straightforward opposition to them and offered with an at least partially relatable genesis, the Black Earth Wives function as a useful foil for Allison's development. As Allison describes them caring for a heavily traumatized fellow female survivor: they "enfold her in a tangle of arms, rocking her, clucking softly at her like a brood of giant mother hens" (129). In the aftermath of the drama of Zack's betrayal, Allison has changed: no longer herself a "mother hen," she recognizes in the female bonding and the largely gendered activities of the Wives (stitching blankets, cooking, praying) are at odds with her own sense of herself.

The Black Earth Wives's version of gendered life after the apocalypse is clearly meant to be read as an offense against good sense: religiously overcoded, the Wives call their preferred candidate for repopulation activities "Adam" (192), an almost overbearing biblical literalism that suggests the deep, indeed archaic, conservativism at the roots of their beliefs. The Wives take over the university campus and force Allison and her friends to flee, thus fully setting themselves apart from the version of postapocalyptic life that Allison stands for. In offering such a radical foil, the novel makes the life choices Allison makes appear progressive—but this is a bit of trompe l'œil, as it turns out. At the same time as the novel develops Allison into a fairly self-assured and capable survivor, a leader even, it lays this onto a background canvas in which negotiations of marriage take place. None of these negotiations hit upon the most obvious point: that marriage, as an institution, seems ill-suited to the postapocalyptic world in which the characters act. What comes out here is that despite the undoubted advances in Allison's portrayal, *Allison Hewitt Is Trapped* is hardly at odds with heteronormativity or the patriarchal structures that the postapocalypse has inherited. Its depiction and discussion of marriage and long-term male-female relationships are an ambivalent meandering between its overt claims about female independence and agency and its concrete narrative developments. Symbolically, perhaps, halfway through the novel, Allison notes: "I'm not some huge proponent of marriage necessarily—my mom got along well enough after my dad died and never felt like remarrying." It's not just that this is a half-hearted disclaimer of marriage but that it is a disclaimer of re-marriage rather than marriage—more of an argument, in its way, for marriage as an everlasting bond that cannot be recuperated after a spouse's death. Allison's point, such as it is, is that while she need not defend marriage as such, she "can't [. . .] see the point of divorcing someone like Ned" (158), of whom more below. This is no principled position for female agency, then; rather, it is a point which sets obscure personal sensibilities (her mother's getting along well, her own sense of who Ned is) against the problematic nature of marriage's civil bounds.

The novel's ambivalence and curious attachment to marriage as an institution comes up several times, but two examples stand out. The first mention of marriage occurs in the early parts of the novel, while the first group of survivors is still stuck in the apartments above the bookstore, with Allison still in the "mother hen" mode. Two of her fellow survivors, Holly and Ted, are in a relationship and have been for some time; now, a distraught Holly confesses to Allison that Ted has asked her to marry him. Allison notes that they appeared destined to be in "for the long run" anyway, to which Holly replies that the problem lies elsewhere: the fact that Ted would not have asked her to marry him except for the circumstances in which they find themselves. Afraid of his parents' rejecting Holly, she believes "[i]t means he doesn't think we'll ever see his parents again. I think he's given up" (83–84). Marriage in this short passage becomes a signal of surrender, something that is not, apparently, worth fighting one's parents for, but a possibility once one has given up on seeing them again. At the same time, however, Ted's choice reminds readers of the sheer persistence of the concept of marriage. In the desperate straits of uncertain survival, Ted's proposal of marriage is meant, of course, to signal love and commitment, but this sits uneasily with Holly's complaint. Indeed, Ted's proposal and Holly's complaint both sit uneasily against the situation in which they find themselves. In practical fact, marriage (the religious or civil contractual obligation) has lost its value; there is no institution capable of making it binding. What remains is its latency as a reminder of the past. Instead of complaining about the idea of marriage, Holly complains about the motivations Ted has: she accepts, then, the patriarchal heteronormativity implicit in a marriage proposal. The episode is a reminder of the persistence of these patriarchal structures of thought; not the last one.

The second example brings us back to Ned. In the middle of the Black Earth Wives subplot, he and Corie, a married couple with kids, arrive at the university campus. As it turns out, they have brought their marital problems over into the postapocalypse. Corie's drifting towards the Black Earth Wives, her refusal to eat, her increasing distance from Ned and the rest of the community soon begin to puzzle Allison. Then, Corie confesses to Allison: "[w]e were going to try a separation. I wanted to divorce him but he convinced me to go for a separation first" (158). Allison takes this as a sound enough reason to go weird; "a divorce, especially now, would be more than enough to test anyone's faith" (159), she avers. "Especially now" signals, despite her protestations to the contrary, how Allison feels about the vestiges of patriarchal structures: it anchors her and her fellow survivors to a more stable past. This would be less worrying if not for the fact that Corie becomes part of the Black Wives cult, participates in their violent takeover of the university campus, and later becomes an accessory to the collapse of the campus, dying in its destruction. Allison, in other words, was completely right in her evaluations of both Ned and Corie: divorcing Ned would have been a literal madwoman's move, completely unfathomable in the novel's sense of things.

Marriage is seen in these scenes as an intensely private, stabilizing force, one which retains its hold over the survivors of the apocalypse, and more importantly, *should* retain this hold. Perhaps the most puzzling version of this in the novel is the way the novel depicts Allison's relationship with Collin, the leader of the university settlement. Collin's own interest in Allison appears to be largely due to Allison's abilities and capacity for action, and so suggests something beyond mere sexual infatuation; but this needs to be shaded further. Their budding relationship—which Collin early sees as something he cannot do without—becomes endangered when Collin's missing wife, Lydia, turns up at the campus; Collin and Allison become more distant, with Allison retiring to the belief that, since Lydia represents something stable from Collin's past, he should stay with her. They take separate routes to Liberty Village, their shared destination; upon arriving, Allison discovers Collin safely there and queries him about Lydia. It turns out the two have separated; Collin and Allison end up happily together.

This is, in many ways, a gratuitous addition to the story: Collin's disappearance for much of the final third of the novel, the final reunion, the way Collin tells Allison that his wife is (alive but) out of the picture (in fact, has abandoned Collin for his friend Finn). The whole romantic subplot is narratively detached from the main story. It drives nothing, it heightens no stakes, it necessitates nothing, and most importantly, it serves as a comment on nothing: it simply is. And, as I have tried to suggest above, it is there because of the narrative logic of female-centered genre fiction. What it does do, after all, is code the ending as happy. Allison, as it happens, does not find her mother at Liberty Village; she loses additional friends on the road; and the frame narrative's assurance that some people still think highly of her may appear as an insufficient ground for the novel to declare a happy ending. Collin and Allison's relationship, on the other hand, as insubstantial as it is, *reads* as a happy ending: because it is the inlaid structure of long-form narrative fiction that they lived happily (married, or at least together) ever after.

Notably, it is Lydia who has made the choice to separate from Collin: as with Holly, as with Corie, it is women who disturb the solidity of marriage, women who are, to put it mildly, not commended by the novel for it. To sacrifice one's holy bonds to men (or to be anxious about forming them in the first place) is fraught ground in *Allison Hewitt Is Trapped*, something that is more than a little surprising given these relationships' deep fissures in the first place. This becomes even more puzzling given the fact that the novel is much concerned with Allison's journey and growth, as well as, crucially, the way it refuses to make much of Allison's womanhood, at least on the narrative surface. Allison describes herself thus after reaching the university campus: "I want to be the person I was before all of this started: Allison Hewitt, Graduate Student, Student of Literature, Faulkner Enthusiast, Field Hockey Player, Daughter, Normal Person" (120). A gendered identity, significantly, comes in only in the fifth place on that list, a list which even begins with the gender-neutral "person"; Allison, who at this point has already shown herself as a capable leader—strong, effective, and decisive—does not reduce herself to a gendered role (unlike Sadie Walker, as we will see), and, in fact, as the next line establishes, does not reduce herself to any role at all. "Those titles don't exist anymore," she notes—a disavowal which includes, strikingly, whatever was encoded in the concept of "daughter" beyond the mere biological facts. Allison replaces these "titles" with the simple designator "survivor," an inclusive and ungendered term that describes her status effectively without tapping into residual societal roles. As a survivor, Allison neatly fits in among the rest of the people she encounters—a shared identity under which new life could be ordered. In becoming Collin's partner, she does not, of course, surrender this identity, but especially in replacing his wife, she does add an awkwardly sexualized, gendered identitarian category to the humble idea of the "survivor" that sits uneasily with the rest of the narrative.

It is too facile, of course, to suggest that Allison's relationship with Collin, affirmative of heteronormativity as it is, is also necessarily a step backwards: after all, she neither marries him nor abandons her newfound skills and capabilities. But the juxtaposition of these with the profoundly traditional male-female coupling is reminiscent of what Diane Negra has called the "popularity of re-casting traditionalism as innovation," with a twist: as Negra points out, the contemporary real life "frequency of this gambit [. . .] is derived from a sense of paralysis about the prospects for innovation and reform in American life that is in turn closely connected to the insularity and fear that currently predominate in so many features of national experience" (2009, 50). No such strictures apply, of course, in *Allison Hewitt Is Trapped*: with the zombie apocalypse sweeping all before it, such a conservative retrenchment signals more than a sense of paralysis. It is a conscious return to the hitherto existing models of male-female relations. Rather than trying to solve a real-life problem of framing one's life choices in the most positive terms available, the novel surrenders utopian possible solutions to the question of gender relations to a postfeminist sense that no survival can be complete without it ending in a heterosexual relationship.

It does so despite its overt references to a feminist literary tradition, most importantly in its repeated references to Kate Chopin's *The Awakening* (1899). Chopin's complex novel of a woman's search for her own place in a society which offers only a limited amount of choices is not just Allison's mom's favorite book (and Allison's most treasured success during a quick scavenging in the bookstore early on): it is also one of the texts which Allison hears read on the radio at night during her stay in the apartment above the store, and one of the books which lend their titles to chapter headings in the novel. Indeed, the themes of *The Awakening* linger in the background of *Allison Hewitt Is Trapped* throughout even as *The Awakening* itself disappears halfway through. So, one might facetiously argue, does its main thrust: it seems significant that *The Awakening* is Allison's mother's favorite book, rather than her own, a suggestion perhaps of the generational split between feminism and postfeminism. Allison's treasures *The Awakening* for its emotional appeal, whereas her mother (we may assume) did so because of its content, the latter of which seems at times to mirror (but at other times is at odds with) *Allison Hewitt*'s thrust.

Edna Pontellier, the protagonist of Chopin's novel, progresses "from disengaged wife to autonomous subject: in control of her body, she becomes aware of its potential for pleasure and learns to claim her right to self-determination" (Heilman 2008, 87). The sexual dimension of Chopin's novel is largely elided in *Allison Hewitt Is Trapped*, but the concern for female self-determination remains prominent. Like Edna, Allison at times appears trapped by her sense of societal proprieties, chafing at them but unable to really refuse their hold. Yet in more important ways, Allison is wholly unlike Edna. It is especially in the chapter "The Awakening" that this becomes apparent. Its overt appropriation of Chopin's title stands against the chapter's content: Allison and Collin's mutual admission of their love, and Collin's wife's return to the compound. Edna's sexual awakening heightens her own sense of what female independence would be like; Allison's emotional awakening to her love for Collin, by contrast, binds her to the kind of relationship Edna seeks to escape.

Where Edna finally surrenders to the impossibility of acting upon her awakened desires, committing suicide by drowning, Allison is spared the stark choices which undo Edna. Her major problem is solved for her: Collin's wife of her own free will abandons him. For Allison, marriage is not a state without agency, but mainly an affirmation of an emotional bond. If it would be going too far to say that *Allison Hewitt Is Trapped* misreads the power of *The Awakening*, its update of the dilemmas of Chopin's novel speaks to the different sense of difficulty as understood by postfeminism: how to square one's personal development with still being a loving, caring girlfriend or wife. *Allison Hewitt Is Trapped* in that sense seems to be an example of literary "postfeminist girl power" (Ruthven 358): showing their agency in the development of martial or other strengths, this is power that does not ultimately challenge the structures in which it is embedded.

Allison Hewitt Is Trapped does not, in fact, simply end with Allison's happiness in her relationship; it concludes in its frame narrative, which restitutes at least some of the progressive potential of the novel. In the novel's final pages, Allison's story is rejected from the anthology of survivor's lives; "vulgar, bloodthirsty," it is deemed inappropriate for a book that is "designed to laud what is best and most noble about our species" (339). Allison's rejection as an object of celebration, however, is emphatically not motivated by misogyny. Plenty of women are explicitly named as being centerpieces of the anthology—including a famous scientist. Allison's rejection as unsuitable for the editor's vision of a celebratory publication, as unfortunate as it is for her public memory, is paradoxically a positive sign for women's roles: in being dismissed for behavior, rather than gender, her rejection emphasizes the egalitarian treatment of men and women in the aftermath of the apocalypse. For a book so thoroughly steeped in literary references, this glance at historical canon formation bespeaks a value-oriented choice instead of dead white maleness: a matter of excluded genres rather than excluded genders. Roux's novel, assuming the acceptability of a heavily female-centered zombie story suggesting simply en passant the equal capacity of a male and a female protagonist to carry it, breaks a staff for genre-equality; it simply assumes—and thereby, I would argue, actively promotes—gender equality. It does not make this into a persuasive argument, largely because of its own ambivalence about the structures of patriarchical gender relations, especially marriage. But despite these ambivalences, it is a far more progressive narrative than its sequel.

"One Small Step for Feminism": *Sadie Walker Is Stranded*

In *Allison Hewitt Is Trapped*, the eponymous protagonist's journey through the zombie apocalypse and her trajectory of personal development is set against the counterpoint of traditional conceptions of marriage. In *Sadie Walker Is*

Stranded, Sadie Walker's anxieties over her mother-role are set against a far less persuasive and far less impressive narrative of personal development. Motherhood becomes far more central to *Sadie Walker Is Stranded* than marriage ever was to *Allison Hewitt Is Trapped*. The result is a narrative that is far more deeply affirmative of given patriarchal structures. *Sadie Walker Is Stranded* ends up celebrating romantic love and the nuclear family—a deeply regressive fantasy embedded in a narrative where women play major but faulty roles. In this, the novel participates in a larger representational trend, in which a reinforced sense of motherhood as a crucial element of being a woman becomes "the central justifying ideology of what has come to be called 'postfeminism'" (Douglas and Michaels qtd. in Negra 2009, 31).

Even compared to the plot of *Allison Hewitt Is Trapped*, *Sadie Walker Is Stranded* is unexceptional as a zombie narrative. It follows Sadie, a former illustrator and Outbreak survivor living in Seattle, through the consequences of a second collapse of what had already been a stabilized city (and we should note here the echoes of Žižek and Wegner, although it is not immediately apparent what is finally achieved by this second death). Sadie cares for her nephew, Shane, whose parents died in the Outbreak: at the beginning of the novel, she finds that Shane, whom she has left with her boyfriend, has been kidnapped. Pursuing the kidnappers, she finds herself in the middle of the collapse of Seattle, engineered by a radical group of survivors called repopulationists, whose purpose is to have as many children as possible to repopulate the world. Managing to save Shane, Sadie is brought on board a small boat in the harbor by her friend Andrea with an assortment of other survivors: Cassandra, a traumatized nurse; teenage Noah; and Moritz, a somewhat enigmatic Swiss. The group flees the city for the comparative safety of Puget Sound. They end up shipwrecked on an island, where they encounter another group of survivors. Led by Whelan, a former police officer, this group has been on the island since before the second collapse of Seattle. They are amply stocked with food and medicine, live in solid if sparse huts, and appear altogether much better prepared. Joining together, however, proves of little immediate value: two young girls with Whelan's group disappear, the food store goes up in flames with one of the survivors, Cassandra, apparently burning with it, and the surprising number of zombies present on the island seem to act strangely.

Whelan's group, as Sadie finds out later in the novel after spending the night with Whelan, were at least for a while themselves repopulationists: although they have since withdrawn from that group of fanatics, this discovery and apparent betrayal of trust leads Sadie to flee the camp with her foster child Shane. Separately, Sadie and the rest of the group then discover to their shock that Cassandra is both still alive and has been an impostor: a former inmate of a mental asylum, she has killed her nurse and escaped. She bears a physiological secret, too, as Sadie discovers: having been clinically dead for three minutes at some point in the past, she is not registered by the zombies as an object of attraction and can wander freely among them. She has been responsible for the killing of the two children, wanting to make them and some of the other survivors into a "family" (315) for her by killing them and letting them turn into zombies. Sadie returns in time to save some of the others at least; she, Shane, Whelan, and Andrea eventually make it off the island. An epilogue set a year later reveals that Whelan and Sadie have become a couple.

The novel interweaves a number of other, smaller concerns into this basic narrative. It is concerned about the question of the value of art in the apocalypse (Sadie is an illustrator eking out a living by drawing children's books, and Moritz, as it turns out, is on a quest to preserve works of art for the future; indeed, the epilogue sees Sadie and Whelan rescue Moritz's art cache in a Seattle bank before taking it with them on their journey to safety further south). It nods to the story of Allison in *Allison Hewitt Is Trapped*, who has become a byword at least for Sadie of the right way to act in the apocalypse: "What would Allison do?" (109, 116, 123) turns into a refrain in her thought, and the planned journey south at least tentatively looks to Allison's Colorado as a destination. Yet the most interesting issue in *Sadie Walker Is Stranded* is its awkward picture of woman in the zombie apocalypse, an awkwardness that begins with the characters and extends to the details of the plot, most notably the focus on motherhood in Sadie's choices. The novel is, putting it charitably, interested in exploring the concept of family (juxtaposing the mindless procreationism of the repopulationists, Sadie's insistence on the importance of her family bond to Shane, and Cassandra's twisted desire to make an obedient zombie family out of everyone), but its ultimate choice is to celebrate the heterosexual couple-with-child. This is especially notable since, as Jennifer Rutherford has noted, zombie fictions generally see the disintegration of the family as an inevitable occurrence (2015, 6–7). She relates this to Ulrich Beck's notion of the family as a "zombie category"; as she notes, Beck's point is that "with the breakdown of traditional social identities the antagonism between men and women over gender roles emerges at the very heart of social relations" (6) in the contemporary moment. *Sadie Walker Is Stranded* in this sense abandons the contestation of those "traditional social identities" and substitutes a simple affirmation.

The novel includes a surprisingly large number of female characters: Sadie, Andrea, and Cassandra in Sadie's group; and Danielle and the curiously named Banana in Whelan's. Yet this near-equal representation vis-à-vis men becomes problematical as soon as the individual characters come into focus. I will put

Sadie herself in the focus of my analysis momentarily, but the more minor characters already tell a somewhat questionable tale of how survival in the zombie apocalypse works. Andrea, Sadie's best friend, is fixated on the sexual attractiveness of her male compatriots, circumstances notwithstanding, from teenage Noah and the mysterious Moritz to the other survivor groups' Whelan and Nate. As a character, Andrea is not without redeeming features: she is strong and capable, with a flourishing medical drug business of sorts while still in Seattle, and a supportive friend to Sadie. Andrea's objectification of men is, certainly, something of a progressive stance if read as the inversion of the stereotypically male gaze. Andrea acts on her sexual predilections only once, with Nate, one of the three males in the other survivor group, during which act she also discovers the sectarian roots of the other survivors, which she, probably wisely, chooses to ignore. But at the same time, the insistence on foregrounding Andrea's sexuality over other possible traits in the first place, no matter what partially redeeming qualities this sexuality has, reduces Andrea to her heteronormative desires.

With slightly more narrative motivation, the two women with the group of former repopulationists are also curiously chosen: Danielle is a former stripper with "the biggest, fakest tits" Sadie has "ever seen outside of a porno" (159); Banana is a former burlesque dancer (179). As much as the novel repeatedly draws attention on both women's breasts, and as much as Sadie reduces Danielle, in particular, repeatedly to them, it makes surprisingly little of the past that, apparently, functions to explain these women's appearance in the novel in the first place. Only ever implicit, the suggestive link between their female attributes and their connection to the repopulationist cult means nothing to the novel's plot. As with Andrea's characterization, a charitable reading would be to suggest the novel's insistence on the unimportance of these pasts in the first place and to focus on these women's present capability and survival; but at the same time, the lack of a necessary narrative connection between the present and the past makes this past seem especially gratuitous. Why does a woman stripper whose past does not matter to the plot need to be a stripper in the first place? Presumably to suggest the need to get rid of various stereotypes about strippers and the reducing of women to their bodies in the way their old professions inevitably did. In so doing, however, the novel itself inevitably also reduces its characters.

Sadie Walker Is Stranded offers us a woman caught up in her substitute mother role (Sadie); a woman interested in appraising men for their eligibility as sexual partners (Andrea); an exotic dancer and a stripper (Banana and Danielle); and an insane murderer (Cassandra).[4] The most crucial element of this, and the one which is most clearly set off from *Allison Hewitt Is Trapped*, is

Sadie's role as a substitute mother to her nephew Shane. To become a mother, in Sadie's case, is less than a decision: her sister and brother-in-law "never made it home and voilà, just like winning a twisted game show, I became a mother" (11). "I became a mother" highlights the way the novel represents this role: it naturalizes both the act itself as well as its status. For Sadie, the mother role comes both naturally and inevitably, and in lieu of other ways of perceiving the relationship: foster parent, aunt, guardian, or what have you. This early assumption of the mother role shapes Sadie's character throughout: the "weird [. . .] swelly feeling, like my heart was trying to beat too fast or there was too much blood in it" (96) she has when thinking about Shane indicates her emotional involvement. Motherhood shapes one side of Sadie's character, and it is a traditional form of motherhood, too, as much as one is possible in the apocalypse. Even towards the end of the novel, she worries about "the kind of male influence I knew I was never very good at giving" (243), a curious juxtaposition of the innately male and female given that the novel, up to that point, had been fairly insistent that such traditional distinctions are no longer of importance. Her insistent focus on Shane lead her, shortly before the novel's grand finale, to abandon the rest of the survivors, feeling it safer for Shane to be with her alone—a decision at least in part legitimized by her discovery that Cassandra is not who she claimed to be, thus unraveling the mystery of the deaths the group has suffered.

"Crisis and fulfillment" for the postfeminist woman, argues Diane Negra, "center upon the discovery of personal destiny, the securing of a romantic partner and motherhood, and the negotiation of the problem of paid work (seldom its rewards)" (2009, 47). Paid work, of course, is no longer is an issue in *Sadie Walker Is Stranded*, but the other three issues remain vital to Sadie's role, their absurdity in the face of apocalypse notwithstanding. Sadie is still firmly attached to the way one was a woman before the collapse of civilization: even, in this instance, the *second* collapse. Despite this, when Sadie reflects on "things that should've crushed my spirit, anyone's spirit, but didn't," she points to this memory as proof of remaining unbroken: "I could still remember what it felt like to wear lipstick, the decadent way it made you want to pout and the waxy taste when it accidentally touched your tongue" (113). This is certainly impressionistic, and not necessarily indicative of something like a hedonistic emptiness on Sadie's part. But it sits in a series of data points about how the novel reflects on female subject positions. When Sadie injures herself in crossing a stretch of water, Whelan helps her with her injuries, and again, the way Sadie renders these events appear to foreground precisely the concerns Negra lists: "Woman purposely trounces through sea urchin bed to get a gruff but handsome man to bend over her feet for two hours. It did seem vaguely romantic, actually, the fact that someone I had known for less than a day cared so deeply about what was—more or less—my own fucking problem" (2009, 149). Sadie's reflection on how "romantic" Whelan's painstaking removal of the urchin pins is, and her note on her previous (postapocalyptic!) boyfriend Carl ("brought me a stale muffin once from a Dumpster" [149]), again seems to suggest something deeply banal about Sadie's thoughts.

In her insistence on romance, love, and make-up in the very dire situation the survivors find themselves in, Sadie appears wholly reflective of postfeminist ideology. This ideological surrender is matched by the novel's conclusion, in which Sadie, having seriously endangered her fellow survivors and required rescue from the outside, reflects on past events. As Whelan and she exchange her stories, she surrenders to watching Whelan's apparently enchanting dimples ("O dimple of ultimate destruction, you will be the death of me" [332]). It's hard to read this without the image of a love-struck airhead coming to mind: but no matter such idiosyncratic readings, the novel lays in the focus on Whelan's and Sadie's romantic love as the happy conclusion to what is a far more bumbling, inept tale of survival than *Allison Hewitt Is Trapped*.

This, then, is the problem with the novel. It is not that it is uncritical of the romance plot; it is that its romance plot is almost literally the sole concept of a happy ending offered by the novel. Whereas *Allison Hewitt Is Trapped* ended with its protagonist in the safety of a town that (from its frame narrative) we know will last, and thrive, for at least a hundred years more, *Sadie Walker Is Stranded* ends with the nuclear family setting out on their own quest for safety (possibly in Liberty Village). Together, the novel argues, whatever comes next may be mastered; as long as the nuclear family, established through romantic love, persists, we should not worry about leaving them in the medias res of the ongoing apocalypse. If, at their best, as Diane Negra suggests, even avowedly postfeminist texts depict "empowered heroines [who] investigate alternative systems of support that might be more accommodating of female independence" (2009, 138), *Sadie Walker Is Stranded* must be regarded as at least reactionary. Even if its nuclear family is not biological, it is the most traditional possible system of support imaginable. Sadie, Whelan, and Shane, brought together by Sadie's romantic love for Whelan and her unfailing maternal instincts, reconstitute a social nucleus around which it is possible to imagine a return to old conditions. To be sure, it never overtly enacts this return to the old, just as it never enacts the successful establishment of the survivors in safety. It is precisely this that makes it so insidious, however: leaving open all possibilities, and masked by its patchwork nature, it appears to offer something less traditional than it actually does.

Conclusion: The Formal Limits of Zombie Gender

Allison Hewitt Is Trapped and *Sadie Walker Is Stranded* stake out the limits of zombie gender narratives: stuck between feminist aspirations, encoded so neatly in *Allison Hewitt Is Trapped* through its references to *The Awakening*, and their own postfeminist realities, put in a nutshell by the easy slide into the heteronormative family unit at the finish of *Sadie Walker Is Stranded*, they highlight the difficulty of transforming the potentialities of zombie fictions into progressive gender realities. But at the same time, they also highlight the constitutive ambivalence of much zombie fiction when it comes to gender portrayals.

This is, as I have noted, an issue inseparable from form. I have already highlighted above one version of this claim: that it is the zombie's formal aspects, its own nature and the nature of the apocalypse it always engenders, which open the opportunities for investigating alternative versions of gender relations, which form the ground on which the claim that zombie narratives are inherently geared towards progressive visions of femininity rests. As Natasha Patterson notes, "[t]he presence of zombies renders the patriarchal-capitalist social order obsolete as both men and women are called on to step outside their prescribed gender roles to ensure the survival of humanity" (2011, 229). One of the ways in which it does so is by legitimizing the use of violence, which is significant for gender representation especially in those books where women are the protagonists. Much horror fiction indeed insists on violence as a counter to the monster: Ellen Ripley in the *Alien* franchise, the many final girls of slasher films, and *Buffy the Vampire Slayer* all bespeak the empowering possibilities inherent in violence. Zombie fiction conventionally requires not only the killing of humans by zombies, and of zombies by humans, but usually also the killing of humans by humans. To be the protagonist in such fiction is by necessity to play by its rules, and thus to become at the very least an agent of violence, a slayer of zombies, but also very likely of other humans. Inasmuch as the exercise of violence is still an apparently stereotypically male pursuit (its horror fictional history notwithstanding), zombie fiction thereby formally appears to require a progressive breaking of gender roles by the very act of making a female character the protagonist. We should also note, at least in passing, the way in which this relates to the construction of gender in *Pride and Prejudice and Zombies*: the sheer, and mere, capacity to take on a violent role contrasts with the roles potentially open for the female protagonists in Regency fiction. Zombie fiction foregrounds the possibility to promote versions of female agency through the need for violent activity very much in the way Regency fiction does not.

There is a second formal claim to make here, however, which is its paradoxical obverse: that the genre's particular genre-form acts against progressiveness. As Nicholas Brown has observed, genre's "requirements are rigid enough to pose a problem, which can [...] be thought of as a formal problem" (2014, 161); in Brown's parsing (to which I will return more fully in the conclusion of this book), this is an opportunity for literary autonomy. But in being a problem, it is also a potential stumbling block. The issue is that even those narratives offering strong female protagonists—focal figures or even first-person narrators—ultimately seem to require for them the kind of romantic closure both ill-suited to the zombie apocalypse and, more importantly, not usually deemed necessary for male protagonists. This insistence may in fact be somewhat more striking coming, as it does in the cases of *Allison Walker Is Trapped* and *Sadie Walker Is Stranded*, from a female writer. The particular problem illustrated in the various texts that I have used above to illustrate the failure of progressive gender narratives face in ending a zombie narrative centered on a female protagonist; their default choice is to put that protagonist in a heterosexual relationship. This constraint, I would argue, is largely imported from the most powerful female-centered genre fiction, the romance: this is the model on which female genre characters are usually built.

This analysis yields insights more generally into feminist discourses in popular fiction, and what I have facetiously called "genrécriture feminine." There is already a considerable body of critical work on feminism and popular culture (e.g., Savigny and Warner, eds., 2015; Munford and Waters 2014; Moody 2006; Fenton 1998) that does, however, largely focus on television, cinema, or music, rather than popular (written) fiction (for which see Radway 1991). What seems striking in my (limited) analysis of zombie fiction is that male-authored narratives, especially *World War Z* and *The Girl with All the Gifts*, appear to have a stronger sense of how to write progressive gender narratives. This is not to make any claims about male and female writers and their respective abilities to write such narratives, to be sure: rather, it is to make a suggestion about the very limits of genre-form which Brown speaks about. Tentatively, I would suggest, we need to consider the possibility that there is a different set of requirements for women writers of genre fiction, the most important of which is the inclusion of a female protagonist: a requirement stemming from the surfeit of male protagonists in genre fiction otherwise. Yet the extension of this requirement is, I believe, the idea that such a novel also needs to include what are stereotypically "women's concerns," precisely the kind of interest in love, relationships, marriage, and kids which (probably inadvertently) repudiates the otherwise hopeful role of the capable female protagonist. The texts I have discussed thus speak to the dilemma which Natasha Patterson notes, that "merely inverting gender roles" may not in fact be "the answer female viewers [and readers, too] are seeking" (2008, 110) to the overbearing male-centeredness of horror fiction (and, of course, society). What, then, is that answer? Patterson's own investigation of Romero's films leads her to conclude that the tensions she detects in Romero's films "cannot be easily answered by assuming that certain genres revolve in 'feminine' orbits and others in 'masculine' ones" (116–17)—and while this is certainly true, it appears to be similarly true that certain "feminine" and "masculine" traits (here, a heavy focus on romance) exist in texts written *by* and, one assumes, also *for* women.

To stay with Nicholas Brown's terminology, the rigid requirements for a woman's zombie novel may be more rigid than those for a man's and, in a sense, represent a genre of their own. So, while male writers like Max Brooks and M. R. Carey achieve a signally more progressive vision of women's roles in the aftermath of the zombie apocalypse than Jesse Peterson and Madeleine Roux, and while formally, Brooks's choice of the short narrative is happier than Carey's choice of the long in avoiding romance altogether, this may in part be because, in simple terms, nobody expects Brooks or Carey to hold with the conventions that Roux and Peterson are restricted by. Roux's and Peterson's female protagonists need to be successful both as zombie novel protagonists and as women circa 2010—a far more serious charge than that placed on Brooks or Carey (or Fingerman, Kirkman, and so on). This gendered explanation may or may not hold, since there is another, simpler option. Both Carey and Brooks have written books which are far less conventional, far less generic, than Roux's and Peterson's; it may simply be that the more generic novels also bring out the more generic gender systems. Thus, if zombie fiction as a genre can be rightly said to formally permit progressive gender narratives, its permissiveness needs to be tempered against the various things that militate against it becoming, in practice, capable of sustaining visions of alternative femininities.

Such, at least, may be a possible conjecture. What is certain is that female subject positions in zombie fiction run the gamut, conditioned by a variety of formal contingencies and choices, restrictions and opportunities. This should, at least, give us pause, simply because a similar (non-) point might be made about almost all fiction, even the much maligned romance. Janice Radway, in her groundbreaking *Reading the Romance*, concluded that "it will be impossible, then, to use this conclusion to bring a single, large picture into focus simply because there is no context-free, unmarked position from which to view the activity of romance reading in its entirety" (1991, 210): a similar point holds for zombie fiction's construction of gender. Yet, like Radway, I believe that the glimpses offered of individual positions along the broad spectrum are useful: they should give critics pause in claiming too much from zombie fiction, or even genre fiction overall, without noting the embeddedness of their discourses in larger systems. And they should point to the need not to lose sight of the formal conditions of genre-literary production, which heavily bears upon what appears, at first glance, a purely thematic concern with female subject positions.

There is a final, purely formal (indeed, almost more than formal, entirely constituted by the exigencies of written language) point to be made here, whose importance I find difficult to evaluate. It is far easier to supersede racial categories in fictional writing than it is to supersede those of gender, simply on account of the pronominal necessity of identifying sex. There is no identifying speech marker for race, but there is, in the simple "she said," an almost unavoidable speech marker for sex, and thus an almost inescapable fall back to the existing, normative perceptions of gender on the part of the reader. Far more than race, then, gender is a necessary part of any narrative; and it pays to recall Judith Butler's note that any talk about gender necessarily occurs within preformed discourses on gender, so that even a simple "she said" carries far more theoretical and conceptual baggage than it may appear at first sight. This point provides the point of ingress for the next chapter: recall Kinitra Brooks's suggestion at the beginning of this chapter that zombie fictions are "pregnant with opportunities for exploring modern race and gender relations" (2014, 462). In the final chapter of this book, I will explore zombie fictions' depictions of race relations; and, as we shall see, the easy equivalence made by Brooks's claim between the two identitarian categories of race and gender is quickly deconstructed by the formal and historical capacity of zombie fiction to speak about race in a way it simply cannot about gender.

The Postracial, Postcapitalist Zombie
Colson Whitehead's *Zone One* and Junot Díaz's "Monstro"

> Identity sprouts on the graveyard of communities, but flourishes thanks to the promise of a resurrection of the dead.
> ZYGMUNT BAUMAN, *Community*, 16

Many of the texts discussed in this book so far have points to make about race in the zombie apocalypse, often ending up with a common progressive point of view: "The only races that mattered now were humans versus zombies. Skin color was passé" (Fingerman 2010, 189), as *Pariah* puts it. This moral can be found, implicitly or explicitly, in virtually all the texts I have discussed above; if race is mentioned at all, it is to set off pre-apocalyptic racism against the larger narrative of us-vs.-them that now preoccupies survivors. Zombies may not initially appear to stand out in this: apparently any narrative which sets humanity against a larger Them will draw upon this trope, suggesting racism to be easily relativized. But there is a crucial difference between the zombie and those other monsters. The zombie stands out precisely because it is always already racially marked, not so much as an individual, but because of its historical roots. The zombie is a historical monster, and as such, it drags history with it wherever it goes. As Roger Luckhurst has pointed out, "it remains connected to the meaning of Haiti and the islands of the Antilles to the modern world" (2015, 15). This meaning inevitably ties it to the history of the black Atlantic, to slavery, to early twentieth-century labor exploitations, but also to the successful Haitian revolution under Toussaint L'Ouverture, and includes its later mobilizations as a means of resistance to imperialism. Race, then, is in many ways a fundamental issue in the discussion of the zombie, seeing as how its historical roots and its transmission into popular Western culture were intimately bound to narratives of black agency, of slave revolt, of fears of miscegenation, and a particular clarity about the desirability to racialize the zombie itself. After all, *White Zombie* already explicitly marked the zombie as a usually non-white creature. Thus, the first fictions of this version of the zombie, and indeed much of the sensationalist pop-ethnography of the 1920s through the 1940s, also had a particular threat in mind. As Kyle Bishop notes, the real threat which figures in these texts is "the risk that the white protagonists—especially the female protagonists—might be turned into zombies (i.e., slaves) themselves" (2005, 65–66), thus turning upside down the natural order of power between white and non-white.

This is why discussions of race and the zombie fall into two broad camps. On the one hand, critics turn their gaze to the historical and cultural origins of the zombie as a creature of Caribbean Vodou practices. Here, the zombie becomes racially encoded once through its embeddedness in a black African diaspora, as itself a (usually) black creature, but also as the object of fascination by a white metropolitan society whose interest is caught by the threat and exoticism of both these practices and their setting. Focusing on the ways in which the voodoo zombie is inscribed onto colonial and contemporary images of Haiti (Degoul 2011; 2014) and the Caribbean, and on the lasting impact of the cultural history of the zombie, this view of race and the zombie is broadly postcolonial. Indeed, Cory James Rushton and Christopher Moreman, in a collection which focuses on the lasting Caribbean dimension of the zombie, suggest that it is "best understood in the postcolonial mode" (2009, 1), and its historical roots "remain the first and perhaps best way to explain and explore all modern manifestations of zombieness" (2). This connection, of course, inevitably also involves (black) slavery. As Edward Comentale puts it, "[i]n talking race and zombies we begin with the deathliness dispersed everywhere through slavery and colonial power" (2014, 278). In extended form, such a reading includes the notion that "the zombie-human war compulsively enacts the biopolitical distinction between life and anti-life," a distinction which is "always a racial one" (Hurley 2015, 312).[1]

The second line of critical inquiry into race and the zombies begins with the films of George Romero and their importation of a version of the zombie, and a different concern for race, into the United States. When Romero made the protagonist of his 1968 *Night of the Living Dead* black and had him killed by a sheriff's posse at the end of the film, zombies entered the civil rights movement. In Romero's films, race remained important, even if, as in *Night*, its impact remained restricted to the subtext: race is never explicitly foregrounded by the characters, even though, of course, Ben's race is out there for everyone to see. Romero continued this trend: in *Dawn* (where the characters "never once think of their respective races," as Kim Paffenroth points out [2006, 63]), a black policeman is one of the main protagonists. *Day* features both a Hispanic and a black protagonist. And in *Land*, both the Latino protagonist and the black zombie gas-station attendant and revolutionary leader Big Daddy highlight the interest Romero has in speaking about racial issues and in intertwining them with class, suggesting the deep divisions in contemporary American society.

Land also highlights two internal strands of division in this second line of critical inquiry, readings which focus on racial issues as represented by the human characters and the racial symbolism of the popular cultural zombie itself. As Jessica Hurley points out, for example, "when the zombie moves from its original Afro-Caribbean location onto the American mainland it becomes almost exclusively white-skinned" (2015, 317). Criticism has engaged this, and related versions, of race and the zombie, focusing on the question of how the zombie is racialized, siting it within larger systems of racial thought and racist ideologies, and stressing the specifics of depictions of race and racism within zombie fictions. As Kinitra Brooks puts it, such discussion focuses on questions such as: "What worlds are constructed after the initial attack that brings on the zombie apocalypse? What power dynamics continue? Does Western hegemony continue?" (2014, 426).

Colson Whitehead's 2011 novel *Zone One* and Junot Díaz's 2014 short story "Monstro"—the two texts which I will focus on in this chapter—serve to illustrate the respective reach of these approaches. *Zone One*'s concern for race is less usefully related to the zombie's history (but see Hurley 2015 for a reading that does this), but rather sees race as subsumed by a larger and more persistent political and economic problematic, that of neoliberal capitalism. It is true that the novel speaks directly about racial stereotypes on a number of occasions, but, as I will argue below, this is heavily problematized by the way these stereotypes are introduced by the (black) protagonist himself. *Zone One*, in its fleeting direct engagement with race, probes the workings of racial stereotyping as something in which readers are necessarily complicit. "Monstro," on the other hand, set in contemporary Haiti, all but forces one to reconsider the older cultural and historical concerns. It brings back to Haiti, in a world imagined at the edge of complete collapse, the zombie as a figure of revolution, one ignored by imperialist and neoimperialist powers at their peril. Finally, these texts will form a segue into the Coda, where I will seek to draw some broader conclusions about zombie fiction's relevance for the contemporary literary situation.

What is at issue in both these texts is not simply their engagement with race: their own literary cross-connections are vital to understanding the way these texts work on fiction, genre, and the zombie. On the one hand, Díaz, a

Pulitzer Prize winner, and Whitehead, a MacArthur fellow, are highly regarded, profoundly literary writers; neither is white, and as with the argument in the previous chapter about gender, it will be necessary to read this biographical fact into the way the two texts represent the zombie. Both of these writers have already written in a speculative mode (Díaz's only novel, *The Brief Wondrous Life of Oscar Wao* [2007], and Whitehead's earliest, *The Intuitionist* [1999]); their turn to the zombie nevertheless remains intriguing. In both cases, the narratives themselves are quite unexceptional as zombie stories: their power lies in their depiction of what race means after the apocalypse—and, in no small part, in the way their choice of genre is significant as part of two turns. The first, the generic turn in literary fiction, has seen a broad field of writers turn their attention to the potential of various forms of speculative fiction in order to explore our contemporary moment (cf. Lanzendörfer 2015c): the other, which bears more discussion, I think, is the specific turn of what Ramon Saldivar has called "post-race aesthetics" (2011, 2013). Díaz's short story, in fact, may be more significant for its relation to these extrinsic factors than for its narrative: written by a Dominican-American, drawing on the colonial history of the zombie figure which Roger Luckhurst has emphasized recently (cf. 2015), it was published in the *New Yorker* in the fashion of many early chapters of future novels, which is what Díaz apparently intended it to be. But the project of a zombie novel was abandoned and only later resurrected. The open-ended Haitian section of this novel thus remains its only published part: it will, I think, form a fitting conclusion to this study to end on the question of how we can read this reappropriation of the zombie figure by a Caribbean-rooted writer in one of the most significant American literary venues.

My aim in this chapter thus is twofold: on the one hand, to tease out what *Zone One* and "Monstro" have to say about race, a question which quickly and necessarily extends to greater questions of neoliberal capitalism's persistence; and, on the other, to determine the place of their arguments about race in the context of contemporary literary and ethnic fiction. Using the zombie to explore race appears to involve a conviction that "it may well be necessary first to imagine the end of the world before we may imagine the historical end of racialization and racism." Saldívar argues that "[wi]th the near-total annihilation of humanity has come as well the near elimination of racial difference and of racial strife, as if only a complete and total destruction of contemporary life will allow for the end of the color line" (2013, 13). My own short discussion of race in *Pride and Prejudice and Zombies*, *Pariah*, and *World War Z* has already shown that this is in fact not so remarkable a phenomenon in and of itself. But, as I will go on to show below, it is not a good description of what happens in *Zone One*, which complicates notions of "the end of the world" in its twofold apocalypse. The postrace scenario of *Zone One* is one brought about by the initial limited changes consequent on the (first) zombie apocalypse: only the later collapse of *Zone One*'s reconstructed world at the novel's end is truly radical in its consequences. *Zone One* goes one step further than other zombie fiction, in which the act of dismantlement which the zombie apocalypse brings is inevitably followed by a longer period of (gradual) adjustment to the new world. Whether this final apocalypse will end up hopeful for humanity, or its final demise, is unclear, but in affirming the need to think radically, and only radically, with regard to swiping away the overarching structures of capitalist society, *Zone One* suggests, here at the end of this book, a potential utopian imaginary.

Capitalism, Postrace Aesthetics, and *Zone One*

Zone One is set in the aftermath of a zombie apocalypse which has started some indefinite time before, on what is throughout the novel called "Last Night." Its three-day narrative—Friday through Sunday—follows Mark Spitz, from whose perspective the novel is narrated, and his two colleagues in Team Omega, one of several three-man sweeper teams tasked with clearing blocks of real estate in the eponymous Zone One, the lower part of Manhattan Island, of zombies. In *Zone One*, zombies fall into two distinct groups: "skels," the familiar roaming and aggressive undead, and "stragglers," who do not move from places to which they have become accustomed in life. "Their lives had been an interminable loop of repeated gestures; now their existences were winnowed to this discrete and eternal moment" (50) in which they, "a succession of imponderable tableaux" (48), seem like the last vestiges of life before the collapse. It is these symbolic stragglers that Team Omega is largely engaged with in the novel.[2] As we follow the experiences of Mark Spitz and his colleagues, Kaitlyn and Gary, interspersed with his reminiscences of life both before and after the zombie apocalypse, the novel layers more and more information about the nature of the recovery undergone by the US. Sharply satirical, the novel traces a world in which a resurgent, state-sponsored neoliberalism sets corporate interests and commercialism before all other considerations. But even as the contours of this world became progressively sharper, so does the threat faced by it. The country's new capital at Buffalo disappears from radio contact, as do many of the various safe zones that have been established; the wall protecting Zone One from the rest of Manhattan starts to crumble; and, as Team Omega sits by, one straggler, a long-dead fortune teller, suddenly becomes animated, and bites Gary. As Zone One falls in the aftermath—though perhaps not as a consequence of what appears to be a general awakening of stragglers everywhere—Mark Spitz finds himself alone again, faced with an anguishing decision about what to do as zombies swarm around him.

By now, this narrative will seem utterly familiar: starting in medias res, slowly revealing details of the past, leaving the origins of the apocalypse in shades, focusing more on the human characters than the zombies themselves and ending openly, *Zone One* situates itself firmly within the traditional narrative structure of zombie fictions. A second glance, however, reveals much that needs unraveling. To start with, *Zone One*'s short three-day narrative revolves around two apocalyptic moments: the first, "Last Night," which remains outside the narrative proper and is only available in recollections and reflections, took place at some point in the past and is of somewhat vague constitution, as the constant references to "accursed" (111), "repugnant" (116), and "mephitic" (138) Connecticut (also imbued with any number of other unflattering adjectives) indicate. Much that is revealed about the new postapocalyptic world in the three-day narrative is only hinted at, but all of these details, so crucial to most other zombie fiction in its reconstitution of a new postapocalyptic life, are reduced to meaninglessness in the second, now apparently total collapse of human defenses and the overrunning of Zone One. *Zone One* here, of course, forcefully enacts the Wegnerian and Žižekian theme of the "second death" that finally effects real change, which I have already mentioned a number of times above—though, of course, it also refuses to spell out the exact nature of this change. The outcome of this second apocalyptic moment is left open, its consequences uncertain: *Zone One* is thus concerned with an eminently transitional and ephemeral moment, while leaving final conclusions open.

What interests *Zone One* is the particular form recovery takes after the apocalypse, and what it foregrounds is the problematic conflation between corporations and the resurgent state, the recovery of civilization couched in the terms of commercial advertising and operating under the logic of a thoroughly neoliberalized society. As Marlon Lieber has put it, in the transitional phase between crashes, *Zone One* represents "a fantasy of a *temporary apocalypse*" (2015, 7, original emphasis), foregrounding a desire and expectation that a return to the old normal is possible. This is, in and of itself, not particularly surprising; it is, after all, also what *World War Z* does, and it is also at least implicitly the way most zombie fiction frames their narratives, even if, as in the cases of *Pariah* or *Dying to Live*, the ultimate end of the apocalypse is implied or deferred. What is more striking is that its representation is decidedly a critical one—indeed, one that heightens the existing structures of contemporary life in the peculiar recovery after the initial apocalypse.

As we follow Team Omega, we become aware that state-sponsored corporatism stands behind the entire process of postapocalyptic "reconstruction." In the world of *Zone One*, it is the logic of brands and advertisements that become the focus of much governmental thought, in ironic counterpoint to the very real and very basic problems which exist in the world. In this world, names must reflect the upbeat mood and cheerful associations usually produced by commercial advertising: thus, for example, survivors' camps are renamed "Happy Acres" or "Sunny Days" (Whitehead 2011, 24). Reconstruction itself has a snappy tag, "the American Phoenix," which gives rise to the derogatory term "pheenie" for the believer in reconstruction (although in the last analysis, almost all the characters we meet are believers in the need for a form of reconstruction). The logic of governmental action follows the perceived "wisdom of rebranding survival" (79), a pseudo-wisdom replacing thought about the actual act of survival with decisions about the symbolism of its naming. Survival itself is clearly not enough, in that it lacks that chief requirement of capitalist societies, the promise of perpetual growth. Along with the new name for the act of survival comes a feature film with its own, apparently memorable theme ("Stop! Can You Hear the Eagle Roar?") and encouraging T-shirts (110–11)—in other words, all the paraphernalia of merchandising.

In representing a world in which survival is synonymous with the survival of capitalism, *Zone One* presents us with an apocalypse that is not. Or certainly one in which the world has ended but corporations have not—there are shades here of the Great Recession's too-big-to-fail banks and destitute homeowners. Indeed, *Zone One* might be said to enact key features of the Gramscian moment of crisis which Wolfgang Streeck has recently adopted to describe the contemporary moment. *Zone One* narrates a symbolic interregnum, "a period of uncertain duration in which an old order is dying but a new one cannot yet be born" (2017, 14). Here, in Gramsci's phrasing, the zombies may easily be parsed as the "morbid symptoms" (1971, 276) of a declining system, the very kind of neoliberal corporate state system which *Zone One* satirically heightens. In Streeck's parsing, these symptoms are, after all, also operative in our moment. In such a symptomatic reading, Streeck sees the various seismic political events of 2016—Brexit, Trump, the demise of Hollande—as the dismantling of the "old order" by the "onslaught of the populist barbarians" (2017, 14). We may certainly read the zombie figures in post–Great Depression *Zone One* as prefigurations of such a specifically right-wing opposition to resurgent globalized capitalism (cf. also Ehrmann 2014 for a reading that suggests the metaphoricity of the zombie in this context).

Whether one subscribes to such symbolic readings or not, *Zone One* certainly heightens contemporary narratives of unrepentant capital satirically. Even as the reconstituted US government, operating from Buffalo, adopts the mechanisms of commercial advertising in its dealings with survivors, the pre-apocalyptic structures of business are strikingly unaffected by events. Reconstruction has "official sponsors": companies that make available part of their merchandise for use by survivors, often without any lasting benefit to those same survivors (31). These companies' support is hardly disinterested: most of their goods, stranded in deserted cities and at the mercy of both zombies and marauders, are not under their supervision anyway, and companies can expect major benefits from donating them:

> Buffalo created an entire division dedicated to pursuing official sponsors whenever a representative turned up, in exchange for tax breaks once the reaper laid down his scythe and things were up and running again. . . . [The companies] generally put a price cap on their goods or specified a particular product in their brand family, one not too dear, but their sacrifices were appreciated nonetheless. Pledge all your tiny cartons of children's applesauce, in all the nation's far-flung groceries and convenience stores? It was a no-brainer: they were expired anyway. (39)

Zone One critically juxtaposes the interests of society and of corporations: there is no voluntary engagement by corporations here, no freely willed desire to help out, no connection between society and its industry. There are only "tax breaks," financial motivators (indeed, future financial motivators) to get corporations to acquiesce in what even in the face of apocalypse cannot be imagined as anything but a problem of business: how to make sure one's goods remain commodities. The novel expands this narrative point symbolically in the very fact that Zone One gets established in the lower part of Manhattan Island, south of Canal Street, not merely a convenient place to begin but also encompassing the heart of New York's financial district, Wall Street. If nothing else, there is an echo of the exclusionary power of modern corporate finance in the "wall" that seals off the still-plagued northern parts of the borough from the south. Also symbolic is the first sweep we witness the protagonist and his group make, which takes place in the Human Resources department of a large law firm. The action makes Mark Spitz reflect on the "pandemic of pheenie optimism that was inescapable nowadays and made it hard to breathe, a contagion in its own right" (13). What is worse, the novel seems to ask: the apocalypse or the cheerful hope for a return to how things were before?

Zone One offers sustained commentary on the broader sociopolitical implications of the form that its reconstruction, apparently inevitably, takes. Towards the end of the narrative, a simple juxtaposition brings to the fore the constitutive relationship in the new postapocalyptic world, that of "sponsors, patriots" (235), selfishness rendered as selflessness, in which the support of one's fellow citizens is firmly tied to the *quid pro quo* nature of corporate sponsorship. Indeed, the novel affirmatively ties this unfortunate conflation of government and business to our contemporary life: "it was almost as if the culture was picking up where it left off" (79). Thus, unsurprisingly, the survivors clean out Manhattan fully expecting that what they are restituting is the *status quo ante*: "'You think we're going to end up here? We ain't special. They're going to put the rich people here. Politicians and pro athletes. Those chefs from those cooking shows'" (72). Behind the process of reconstruction stands the logic of the old and collapsed but now inevitably resurgent capitalist world, unassailable even in an otherwise total breakdown of society. In its righteous drafting of government-work force for corporate goals, it is more strongly and obviously geared towards capitalist interest even than before.

In this light, the two variants of Whitehead's zombies increasingly seem like they have the two possible answers to an unchangeable system. The ultraviolent skels and the acquiescent stragglers come to appear as the only possible solutions to the problems of the corporatized neoliberal state: either apathy and complete surrender or unmeasured rage and destructiveness, either individual resignation or communal action.[3] This essential split holds true for much of the book, but then something changes as the novel narrates what amounts to the kind of "second death" which Phillip Wegner has theorized as a precondition for real change. As the wall that shuts off Zone One from everything north of Canal Street collapses, allowing a newly resurgent mass of skels to pour into the zone, Gary gets bitten by a formerly docile straggler—a fortune teller, no less (223–28; see Bishop 2014 on the question of "fortune telling"). *Zone One* arguably exposes the way "chains of *surprising* events take the place of *predictable structures*" (Streeck 2017, 15, original emphases) in the interregnum it narrates. After having spent so much time with the certainty that stragglers are not aggressive, they suddenly turn violent, Zone One is found to be under final assault, and the team to which Mark Spitz belongs to breaks apart. Everything collapses at once in this: we understand that the lack of news from without Zone One indicates the destruction of the reconstruction camps and the demise of the Buffalo administration. As everybody is once again forced to fight for themselves against newly aggressive stragglers and masses of skels, Zone One is revealed to be little more than a "public relations stunt" (249), rather than a genuine attempt to make New York habitable again. Although the narrative never makes the point explicit, the concurrent awakening of the passive stragglers and the overpowering of the defenses of the Zone suggests a connection between them.[4] Together, the various zombies of Whitehead's world are irresistible, but when split into two distinct groups, they are not.

This reading of *Zone One* foregrounds a set of profoundly political concerns: the novel diagnoses, explicitly as a contemporary problem, a variety of structural relations that inhibit society, to the extent that even an apocalyptic event cannot shake the foundations of the existing social relations. Despite its clearly ironic tone throughout, therefore, this reproduction offers no vision of change. Little of this appears to be much concerned with race, and indeed, a cursory reader might miss the issue completely. If there are nods to the history of race in America, as in the novel's choice of the term "reconstruction" for the efforts at restoring the pre-apocalyptic United States, and its description of "untold Americans [who] still walked the great out there, beyond order's embrace, like slaves who didn't know they'd been emancipated" (39), these moments do not amount to a sustained engagement. Its chief issue as far as race is concerned, in fact, remains largely hidden. Mark Spitz, the everyman protagonist of Whitehead's novel, goes through postapocalyptic life with a nickname, one that we only discover late in the text is racially marked and, indeed, is a possibly less-than-gentle mockery. About halfway through the novel, Mark Spitz explains how he got it. Caught, in one of his previous jobs, by a horde of zombies in the middle of a viaduct, beneath which a river offered a means of escape, Mark Spitz decided not to jump, instead opting to fight. He later justifies this decision by admitting that "he couldn't swim" (147). His gleeful teammates dub him Mark Spitz, in reference to (perhaps still?) the most famous Olympian swimmer of all time. It is only later, when the novel is almost at an end, after Gary has been bitten, that we become privy to "the subordinate ironies in the nickname." What is ironic about the nickname is that Mark Spitz is a mediocrity and the real Mark Spitz a record-holder; "[p]lus the black-people can't swim thing" (231). The novel's protagonist, it turns out, is black, the more striking irony perhaps given the way the most famous photo of the real Mark Spitz shows him with a bare torso, seven gold medals around his neck: obviously, nakedly white.

The question is, of course, what this might mean: both in the fact that the novel takes nearly its entire length to reveal the protagonist as black (why so late? why so casually?), and in the fact that despite it being so late, it still bothers to do so. In fact, as I will argue here, *Zone One*'s relationship to the question of race is a far more ambivalent one than the one Saldívar suggests in his essay: that, essentially, we may not imagine a postracial era outside the complete victory of the living dead. To do so unduly privileges both race as a marker of identity (a marker which *Zone One* sees as comparatively unimportant) and mischaracterizes the nature of the novel's engagement with the "near elimination of racial difference and of racial strife" (2013, 13). Implicit in Saldívar's argument is a sense of race that is not too far from the satirical take offered by comedian Stephen Colbert when he suggests to a black man that he does not see race—it suggests, in other words, that he does not see his skin color or that skin color does not translate for him into race (the latter the far more subversive stance). In terms of *Zone One*, it suggests that because black men are (belatedly) identified as having dark skin color, and because they are quizzed about racially coded stereotypes, there still exists "racial strife." More particularly and puzzlingly, Saldívar himself speaks of race in those terms in which he considers the novel to express the persistence of "racial difference." For Saldívar, "racial difference" cannot merely mean different skin colors, because if that were the case, he could never possibly speak of its "near elimination" as a hopeful goal (or indeed a goal at all); but if it is not mere skin color—if we mean something altogether more sinister, a set of encoded beliefs about the nature of a person held simply on account of his skin color—then paradoxically it is Saldívar's expectation that such beliefs are encoded by the novel, more than the novel itself, that perpetuates the notion of essential racial differences.

In fact, we should argue that the novel is simply not concerned with race, although it may be with the use of race in reading it. *Zone One* gives race enough room to appear to matter, but not enough for it to matter unless it is already assumed to matter. "On a second reading, [. . .] with the knowledge that Mark is African-American—Mark Spitz's avowed averageness becomes legible as a recognizable means of black survival in a white world" (Hurley 2015, 322). The need to assume such a second reading suggests, however, that on a first reading, without knowing Mark Spitz's race, this insight is unavailable, literally turning the entire reading of the novel on an affirmative self-identification of Mark Spitz as black. But if the detection of all the various and ostensibly racially marked actions of the novel become available only on a second reading, after we know our protagonist is black, and therefore that we should read the novel through the lens of race, are we not doing the stereotyping ourselves? This becomes even more problematical if we recognize that it is in fact Mark Spitz himself who introduces the stereotype that brings him his name: he suggests that he cannot swim, even though later, when Gary quizzes him on the nickname, he claims that he can.

The novel's focus lies more broadly on the commodification of everyday politics and the apparent impossibility to imagine significant change within a totalizing economic system. Race plays a role in this, but it is a different one than we might expect. In simple terms, the point is this: to argue that *Zone One* imagines the end of the world as a precondition for the end of racism depends on a sense of "the end of the world" which the novel, far from endorsing, in fact heavily questions. To be sure, the world which Mark Spitz and his fellow survivors inhabit appears in some respects fundamentally different from ours. It has zombies in it, for one, and many of the ways in which life functions are radically at odds from how they did before. But the economic, neoliberal heart of it beats on as ever, though its changed circumstances have also changed the role of race.

Every action taken by Mark Spitz and his team in the course of the novel is geared towards an overarching goal: the rebuilding a particular form of society. Race has been eliminated as a marker of identity, but class remains alive and well; one misses this, I believe (as Saldivar does when he speaks of a more generalized "near total leveling of difference that occurs among the surviving humans" [13]) when one's sense of what constitutes the end of the world has already naturalized the persistence, even after the end of the world, of the "state system of global capitalism" (Streeck 2017, 14) and state-sponsored neoliberalism that is the real target of *Zone One*'s satire. The first apocalypse in *Zone One* is not in fact the end of the world: it is a satirical heightening of our world. But what is curious about this satirical heightening, and its insistence on the persistence of the basic economic and political structures of the ostensibly ended older world, is that racism has apparently vanished nevertheless. After all, not once in the whole course of the book does there appear to be any sense that Mark Spitz is anything but an equal member of the team or that his race is noticed or matters. In other words, while it appears to take something to make racism all but disappear, that something is not "the end of the world," at least as *Zone One* sees it.

Zone One's postracism exists in any meaningful sense only in so far as it acknowledges the capitalist subsumption of race under the category of exploitation and uses its intermediary apocalypse to stress the conditions for such a subsumption. If capitalism has created race in the first place as a tool to reconcile, as Immanuel Wallerstein has it, the objectives of minimizing production costs and political disruption while maximizing capital accumulation, then it is hardly surprising that race can become less important in a situation where different priorities prevail. "If there are no Blacks or too few to play the role, one can invent 'White niggers,'" as Wallerstein points out; the possibility to shift the boundaries of race is a necessary part of the capitalist construction of race (cf. Wallerstein 1991, 34). The drudgery of menial work done by the sweeper teams in *Zone One* must be read as a shift towards the invention of a differently constituted but structurally similar outcaste of workers. In the world of *Zone One,* racism has ceased to matter because the government mobilizes all identities equally in the service of a capitalist reconstruction effort. The deconstruction of race in *Zone One* is contingent upon the construction of a broader base of workers. This, too, is how we should read Mark Spitz's belated musings on what he significantly calls "prejudice," rather than racism. "If they could bring back paperwork, [. . .] they could certainly reanimate prejudice, parking tickets, and reruns" (231), as Mark Spitz says. By conflating generalized prejudice with the minor nuisances of parking tickets and reruns, Mark Spitz significantly reduces his investment in an already more limited problem. More importantly, perhaps, the whole thrust of the narrative thereafter is that "they" cannot, ultimately, bring back paperwork; and most importantly, Mark Spitz here implicitly recognizes the way racism is bound up in a larger bureaucratic and economic system, capable of returning due to governmental fiat.

In lieu of race, the novel frames Mark Spitz through a different, and new, identity category: his mediocrity. Spitz himself insists upon this mediocrity, carrying it before him as a sign of his necessary survival. As the narrative of his obtaining his nickname concludes: "He was a mediocre man. He had led a mediocre life exceptional only in the magnitude of its unexceptionality. Now the world was mediocre, rendering him perfect. He asked himself: how can I die?" (183). There are a number of issues bound up in this sense and fact of mediocrity. On the one hand, of course, it functions as a replacement identitarian category, one which, as he himself points out, places him firmly in the mainstream of the postapocalyptic moment. Yet more pertinently, Mark Spitz's mediocrity itself should be read as a necessity of making *Zone One* meaningful: it is, as Franco Moretti makes clear, par for the course of monster fictions, in which the human "antagonist—the enemy of the monster—will always be [. . .] a representative of the present, a distillation of complacent [. . .] mediocrity" (68). In Moretti's argument, mediocrity is the necessary precondition to making the defeat of the monster universally meaningful: it cannot require the exceptional, because the exceptional is, well, exceptional, and so cannot offer guidance to the (non-exceptional) reader. Most tellingly, perhaps, because mediocrity replaces blackness for Mark Spitz, *Zone One* here also speaks to a more complicated issue: that of the black protagonist of monster fiction, whose very blackness precludes him from being also mediocre, from standing in as the everyman who is "representative of the present." To raise the question of Mark Spitz's race, then, even as late, or perhaps especially as late as the novel does, is a means of starkly setting out this condition of horror fiction: if you have identified, in a sense, with Mark Spitz so far (perhaps even, thanks to his nickname, identified him as white), what does the shock of understanding this misrecognition produce? It reveals the need to read averageness—which is, after all, the fate of most of us—across racial divides: what sticks is Mark Spitz's mediocrity, which allows us to place ourselves beside him.

Zone One's single most important moment here, then, is its finale, when Mark Spitz "walked into the sea of the dead" (259). On the one hand, Spitz reenacts the famous conclusion of Kate Chopin's *The Awakening*, in which

Edna Pontellier, unable to overcome the structural prejudices against women (and herself in particular), chooses suicide over lingering in a society in which she feels stifled. Edna's decision harkens back to the remarkable freedom in swimming which she had experienced earlier in the novel: she had learned how to swim, and swimming becomes symbolic of her awakening sense of her own powers, her own body. The final scene of the novel plays with two different senses of how we can understand Spitz's inability, if it even is an inability. Stuck in an apartment building, Spitz recognizes that the efforts to rehabilitate Manhattan are doomed. The undead outside his door are not

> stragglers, transfixed by their perfect moments, clawing through to some long-gone version of themselves that existed only as its ghost. These were the angry dead, the ruthless chaos of existence made flesh. These were the ones who would resettle the broken city. No one else. (258)

Spitz realizes that his chances to reach the terminal from which the evacuation is, he hopes, taking place are minimal, and that he is closer to the river and wonders if he should go there and swim for it. The suggestion leaves the final lines in limbo: "Fuck it, he thought. You have to learn to swim sometime. He opened the door and walked into the sea of the dead" (259).

The conflicting versions of Mark Spitz's ability to swim come into contact here with a repeat of the situation in which he found himself when he got his nickname: to literally swim, or to dive into the middle of a horde of zombies, are conflated here. If Mark Spitz can swim, if he has willingly submitted to the racial stereotype, rather than just said the truth, his "learning to swim" must refer to the "sea of zombies," rather than the river. If he cannot swim, if he has lied to Gary, then the line is ambivalent, and the conclusion of the novel even more open. Yet there is more: the last time this choice came up, as Andrew Hoberek has pointed out, Mark Spitz survives because, like an action hero, he fights the zombies alone and prevails against them (2012, 410). Now, perhaps, his joining the zombies, his swimming with them, even at the possible cost of becoming one of them, signals his true mediocrity. If the skels, then, represent the final catastrophe and the end of the world that is the only imaginable alternative to existing capitalist structures and their inevitable reproduction, Mark Spitz's decision to join them suggests his identification with their violent overthrow of reconstruction and everything that it represents. Significantly, of course, the possibility of death at the hands of the zombies remains only that: a possibility, explicitly not spelled out but rather implied as one of a number of possibilities, the most tantalizing of which is Mark Spitz's becoming part of the zombie hordes in a more meaningful sense.[5]

Race in *Zone One* is a deeply problematical construct, rendered through a character who introduces racial stereotypes himself, only to deconstruct them later. Racism becomes an issue which thus intrudes more through the lens of criticism than anything the novel does; and where the novel does actively reflect on race, it does so through the perspective offered by the logics of neoliberal capitalism. *Zone One* brings this book into a first full-circle from Max Brooks's *World War Z*. In both, the apocalypse appears temporary: not a full-scale destruction of contemporary society, but rather a check. In Brooks's novel, reconstruction takes place on progressive, liberal, and utopian terms: capitalism survives, perhaps fairer now than it was before; this no doubt extends to the issue of race, which has been radically exposed as irrelevant in the face of the zombie other. *World War Z* is satisfied with this: its world is one where sensible people can, faced with clear evidence of their misbehavior, come together to create a more equitable world on the ruins of the old. *Zone One* contrasts sharply, not so much in the particulars of is vision, but in its interpretation of them. Its own sense of the possibilities offered by reconstruction highlights race not as a category abolished for what might be termed the intellectual acknowledgement of its defects, but as a consequence of the logics of an intensified neoliberal capitalism, one which it then sweeps away in a second apocalyptic moment whose outcome is uncertain. The two novels, as I have argued elsewhere (see Lanzendörfer 2014), thus symptomatically represent two moments of the twenty-first century: Brooks's 2006 novel reflects a moment where its internationalism and liberal progressive belief in a unified society contrasted with the neoimperialist politics of the George W. Bush administration; Whitehead's 2011 novel reflects the post–Great Recession realization of the depths of neoliberal connections between state and corporations, and the way these economic issues might easily subsume the category of race.

"Monstro": The Zombie Returns to Haiti (Perhaps, Briefly)

This chapter will conclude with a second full circle, the one which has brought the zombie out of Haiti, into American popular culture, into American literary culture, and thence back to Haiti: Junot Díaz's 2012 short story "Monstro" (for a longer and somewhat differently focused discussion, see Quesada 2016). "Monstro" appropriately concludes this book. It returns us to the origins of the zombie in Haiti and to people we prefer to keep invisible. "Monstro" is set somewhere in the near future, a world of runaway global warming that sees rich people (or certainly, rich Dominicans) living in climatized "domes" (2012, 118) even as "the planet [is] cooking like a chimi and down to its last five trees" and coral reefs have gone "adios" (107). China's renminbi has replaced the dollar as the international currency of choice, "hypercapitalism" (109) has produced a "General Economic Collapse" (108), and instead of texting or tweeting, people "glypt" (113). A curious disease breaks out in Haiti: its symptoms initially appear to be restricted to black pustules and buboes, but progress over the course of several months to behavioral changes. The "infected" (108) desire to remain together; they die when removed from one another; they stop communicating before starting to regularly utter hideous shrieks in chorus. It appears to mutate: detectable as fluctuations in body temperature, it has silently and without being noticed spread to much of the population of Port-au-Prince by the time it is noted. As the WHO tries to discover what is going on, the infected suddenly turn violent: they slaughter anyone who comes into their path. A conventional military response fails to stop them: Haiti is placed under quarantine, the border with the Dominican Republic sealed, and a US bomber wing drops "enough liquid asskick to keep all of Port-au-Prince burning red-hot for a week" (117). As they do so, they, in some fashion, appear to create an electromagnetic pulse that lingers, not only destroying all electronics within 600 miles, but continuing to do so after the initial explosion. And from the epicenter of this explosion, the "Possessed" (116) of Haiti turn to eating human flesh.

"Monstro" sits perhaps a little uneasily as a zombie story, even as it clearly inscribes itself in that tradition. Its monsters are not dead, apparently, but they do exhibit low body temperature; the mechanics of both the curious explosion and the difference between the initial sick-infected and the merely otherwise infected remains vague. The narrator, who sounds like every other Díaz narrator thus far, intersperses his obviously second-hand account of goings on in Haiti with his own, far less interesting story of an attempted romantic conquest. "Monstro" is clearly no stand-along short story—it even ends with a cliffhanger that advertises the never-completed novel it is part of. For all that, however, it clearly is interested in setting itself in the tradition of zombie narratives. As the wife of one of the infected fearfully reports to her doctor: "Someone has bewitched him" (113). "Monstro" plays with the motives of zombie fiction: infection, disease, thinly veiled voodoo references, and even the radiation from a probe returning from Venus that in *Night of the Living Dead* is fingered as a possible cause of the zombies (returning here as the unexplained electromagnetic pulse).

"Monstro" narrates the events in Haiti from the perspective of a diasporan Dominican spending his summer with his dying mother in the Dominican Republic. This point of view is part of the critique it offers, which contrasts with the early narratives of Haitian zombies: for the narrator, Haiti is both apparently distant, set off from the Dominican Republic by disdain rather than geography, and close, impossible to avoid. This differs sharply from the zombie narratives of the early 1930s and '40s. "Monstro" is concerned with the construction of race and its consequences, but complicates the usual Western narratives by highlighting the racism that exists between Dominicans and Haitians. "At first," the story begins, "negroes thought it funny. A disease that could make a Haitian blacker?" "Negroes," in this sentence, are the Dominican acquaintances of the narrator, those "in our sector," highlighting their distance from the Haitians. At the same time, the sentence lays in several other conceits: the conflation of blackness with disease; the casting of Haitians as absolutely black already; and the disregard for a disease which appears to target only Haitians. Like the rest of the world, the narrator's circle appears to believe that "since it was just poor Haitian types getting fucked up" (107), the disease, curious as it is, is no concern of theirs. So "[f]or six, seven months, it was just a horrible Haitian disease—who fucking cared, right?" (108). This racialized disdain, marked by the narrator's family noting even at the earliest stages of the disease that "someone should drop a bomb on these people" (107), permeates the story.

    The disease's progress itself is symbolic of the reaction to such universal disdain. First, it marks Haitians: it makes them obviously, and scarily, different. Then, it literally begins to fuse them together: bodily, as their growths stick together; then, in the increasingly strong emotional reaction to being taken from one another. This turns into "the Chorus," a "bizarre shriek" uttered by the infected, in unison, three or four times daily (109)—in other words, vocalized despair. These symptoms all reflect the possibilities open to a population that has no way out of its miseries: a closer communal connection, and at best a scream of defiance. This progresses as the doctors recognize the way the illness has spread: it is no longer just the open and visible sores and blisters, but can be carried secretly in one's body. The disease becomes something closer to a marker of Haitianness than before. And, notably, it becomes violent only when it is probed from the outside, by the WHO teams seeking an answer or solution to a threat that suddenly appears to have no clear borders in Haiti. Against this overt defiance of internationally imposed norms, unsurprisingly and callously, the immediate reaction by the hegemonic power, the US, is to simply bomb the problem away: and in this attempt's clear failure, the story encodes the failure of imperialist intervention, period. This is only the beginning: the narrator speaks of how "the world came to an end" (107), of how "la Capital [Santo Domingo, the capital of the Dominican Republic] was scoured" (111), and other bits and pieces of information that suggest that what starts in Haiti becomes (though, given the narrator's survival, apparently not total) apocalypse.

This parsing of what happens in Díaz's short story, to be sure, is merely a reading of its surface. What makes it notable is the way it brings in the most lasting Haitian impact on Western popular culture, the zombie, to make these points, as well as the way the zombie permits it, by the very narrative logic it inhabits, to make a point about the price of ignoring the suffering in Haiti (and everywhere else). As Jeanette Ehrmann has noted, in Haiti, with its "recurring ecological crises, military and humanitarian interventions, the spread of crisis capitalism and the prison-industrial complex stands symbolically for the unfulfilled promises of capitalist modernity" (2014, 32). In it, the zombie becomes a metaphor of its permanent crisis in a country impossible to integrate into the capitalist world economy, and of a people whose "social dead does not manifest in slavery or exploitation, but in absolute poverty" (28). Race is obviously implicated in this, but not simply by juxtaposing white civilization against the exotic impenetrability of black life. When the US bombs Port-au-Prince, the event recalls imperialist thought processes powered by racially inflected disdain, and draws deeply upon US pretensions to hemispheric hegemony and a history of intervention in the Caribbean. But it also simply does what Dominicans have long felt is the right thing do to: taking racism's processes beyond white-black dynamics. It is a multifaceted means of exclusion and distancing, as pervasive within the Caribbean communities as between them and the US, a complicated look at the processes underway which see race figure as a tool of exclusion on multiple levels.

"Monstro" enacts what Jeffrey Cohen has noted, that the "zombie figures the return of the injustices we quietly practice against people we prefer to keep invisible" (2012, 404), with a twist on the "we," which here does not just denote Western, predominantly white, societies, but indeed even Haiti's very own neighbor. By mobilizing the zombie figure, returning it to Haiti, and presenting a broader problematic of racially driven exclusions, "Monstro" simultaneously recognizes the need to understand Western hemispheric histories of race and empire and their persistence in today's ostensibly postracial world, and the limits of understanding racism as a prerogative of white people. It returns the zombie to Haiti in a form mutated by its passage through Western popular culture, rather than reproducing through the voodoo zombie a kind of awkward nostalgia for a Haiti less touched by the world. Díaz's short story suggests that you cannot take Haiti and its history out of the zombie, but that simultaneously, you cannot take Western popular culture out of it anymore. It will only be within the context of this recognition that whatever the zombie represents in Díaz's story, whatever way out of the dilemmas of racism, inequality, and continued oppression it appears to point to, can be understood.

Conclusion: Race and the Zombie, Revisited

Zone One and "Monstro" serve as bookends to this study, if in two different ways. If they have been read here largely for the things they reveal about zombie fictions' capacity to investigate race, they also return us to questions raised in the beginning of this book. *Zone One* offers a notable counterpoint to *World War Z*'s political imagination, suggesting the way their respective contemporary moments shape their narratives. Against *World War Z*'s hopeful, progressive liberal conception of a reformable capitalism largely amenable to political interference, and its globalized, multicultural vision, *Zone One* sets a satirical rendering of the post–Great Depression return to the status quo ante which numerous scholars have deprecated (cf. inter alia Mirowski 2013). In this regard, *Zone One* enacts the consequences of the very limits of the liberal imagination which I tentatively identified as operative in *World War Z*, as well as their likely consequences, a more profoundly fundamental resistance to the status quo. Whether this needs to be parsed, as our own contemporary situation suggests, through recourse to right-wing populism ultimately may matter less than the realization that zombie fiction here serves to illustrate the political situations circa 2005 and 2011 in their shifting assumptions about what potential futures may hold. *Zone One*, in this fashion, picks up where *World War Z* left off, revisiting the question of how radical change needs to be in order for it to be effective.

It also complicates the notion that, important in several ways to *World War Z*, race is a category easily overcome in the moment of crisis, when it is challenged by rational actors realizing their commonalities. *Zone One* and "Monstro" both suggest that it is easy to foreshorten such simple anti-race narratives. They do so in different fashions, however. *Zone One* asks what happens to racial prejudice under two awkward conditions, the first being its introduction into the narrative by the ostensibly racially marked character. Mark Spitz's nickname is the result of his own, possibly false, admission to not being able to swim, a fact or lie that only becomes a stereotype when Mark Spitz himself (re-)introduces the idea that black men cannot swim, only to immediately disavow it. This is the second awkward condition: the belated call upon readers to reorient their reading (or not) after obtaining the information that Mark Spitz is black, to literally do a second reading looking for the hitherto masked racism and prejudice facing Spitz in his postapocalyptic life. In doing so, *Zone One* highlights the central difference between the representations of race and gender in fiction: it is impossible to avoid gender in fiction, but it is equally impossible to avoid overtly introducing race. Unless one adopts the blunt artifice of gender-neutral names—a device which, to my knowledge, no zombie fiction has yet recurred to—and employs these, unartfully, in lieu of the necessarily gendered pronouns, it is simply impossible not to make characters either male or female, and thereby inscribe them into gender discourses.

By contrast, it is much simpler in fiction to avoid racial identifiers; indeed, to identify a character as definitely black, almost inevitably requires someone (the narrator or a character) to outright state this racial identification. This is precisely what *Zone One* toys with: it throws up the question of how the novel is read before, as well as after, this revelation. Without this revelation, would anybody wish to make the argument that Mark Spitz must be black, because of the way his mediocrity resembles the way African Americans must behave in a white-dominated world (Hurley's post-identification argument), or because black authors must necessarily write black protagonists? That appears unlikely, and possibly vaguely racist itself. In this sense, Whitehead's novel is less interested in its own representations of race and racism than it is interested in the representations of race and racism that are imposed on it once it has, apparently, condoned such interpretations in its revelation of its black protagonist. This is, in some ways, a devious move, reflecting on critics the limits of their discourses, which appear unable to identify oppression and racism without being cued to look for them by the affirmative mention of ethnicity.

Zone One juxtaposes this identitarian reading of race, which requires Mark Spitz first to *be* black before his life can be read as *stereotypically*, oppressively black, against one which sees race as subordinated to the momentary, shifting needs of the economic system. Spitz's race is of no concern to the novel for long stretches because it is of no concern to the system in which he operates: race has lost its purpose in the apocalyptic world of *Zone One*, replaced by a solely class-based hierarchy. *Zone One*, then, does not take issue with the idea that in the larger us-vs.-them of the apocalypse, race will be swept away: it merely disagrees about the mechanism of the process, disputing the idea that it is the voluntary recognition of greater differences blocking lesser differences, but rather positing that race has lost its functionality. This is why it is the most interesting novel to discuss under the auspices of race; despite having been written by a black writer (who would, in the regrettable stereotypes critics prefer to apply to writers, be expected to be interested in identitarian readings of race), it has the most distinctive, as well as the most frightening, perspective on race. We will be able to leave race and racism behind us, it argues, not when we have as individuals come to the superior realization that it is a nonsensical category; but rather, when it has ceased to be useful to capitalism.

"Monstro" reveals something equally critical: that racism is a fine-grained means of distinguishing us from them, as in Haitians from Dominicans, people who cheerfully self-identify as "Negroes" from blacker, too black, and not coincidentally, poorer people otherwise suffering from the same global north-south divide. It suggests the persistence of racialized structures such as imperialism and hemispheric hegemony, ties them to the way their late expressions have managed to bring the world on the verge of collapse in any event—economically, ecologically, and implicitly politically—and finally returns these issues to the zombie as a figure of radical, albeit uncertain, change. By presenting the Haitian zombies, which, we are led to believe, will end the world everywhere else, as stemming from a progressive development, it highlights both the duration of oppression and the fact that violence, if it will be final reaction to these oppressions, was not a foregone conclusion, but one predicated on a persistent neglect of the underlying problems.

No look at race in just two texts will exhaust its meaning for the zombie genre, of course; but we should recognize what the zombie enables in both of these texts engagement with race, and that their engagement with race stands out from some of the more facile versions proposed by other zombie fictions. Taking it from the narrow confines of realist, or historical, fiction, the two texts broaden the perspective on race in fiction, and on the possibility to imagine the consequences of an end to racialized thinking. Zombie fiction is not guaranteed to have a progressive vision on race, of course; nor do what pass as progressive visions of race frequently satisfy in the facile way they simply assume the non-persistence of race as a factor in the face of a more universal other. But the particular constitution of zombie narratives enables the exploration of complex versions of how race works in the contemporary moment, and how it might cease to work—while necessarily always remaining connected to the history of slavery and racism.

Race has been the central focus of this chapter, but in leaving it and proceeding to the Coda, I would like to briefly sketch another point. "Monstro" is also a bookend of sorts to this book. It brings the zombie itself, and not just this book, back to its origins as a worker-slave on Haiti, but this time in its contemporary guise as a flesh-devouring ghoul. "Monstro" thus formally, as well as thematically, suggests the pervasiveness of the sedimented version of the zombie so prevalent today, its palimpsestuous overwriting of the Vodou tradition by virtue of its far greater symbolic power, but also the relentless globalization of popular culture, making it inevitable that even the traditions from which it springs come to reproduce it.

Díaz himself figures into this in at least two ways: first, as a Dominican-American, his personal stakes in the experience of the diaspora and the meaning of Caribbean culture at the very least heightens the stakes of re-importing the popular cultural variety of the zombie into the Caribbean. Secondly, as a

Pulitzer Prize winner, his literary cachet works on the zombie figure as much as the zombie figure works on him, Díaz (and Whitehead, too) legitimize the zombie figure in their fictions in ways that appear to have consequences to the figure. The fact that the *New Yorker* published Díaz but did not publish an excerpt from *Pride and Prejudice and Zombies* is symbolic of the way literary valuation works, of course. Without the significant nexus of his Caribbean origins and his certain literariness, we may assume Díaz to have had a hard time convincing the *New Yorker* to print a zombie story. But apart from this assumed problematic, the fact that Díaz did manage to put a zombie story in the *New Yorker* suggests how deeply the zombie has permeated the contemporary literary imagination, and this permeation has certainly helped make it readable in the way this book reads it. "Monstro" and *Zone One* thus bookend this study in the way they close a trajectory that I have argued begins with the first work mentioned here, Brooks's *Zombie Survival Guide,* and proceeds through the fiction discussed here: one which sees popular fiction rise into the ranks of literary writing. And this, at long last, is what I will sketch out in more theoretical detail in the Coda.

Coda
Literature and the Contemporary Zombie |
The Appropriate Monster

> The concept of the multitude forces us to enter a new world in which we can only understand ourselves as monsters.
> HARDT AND NEGRI 2004, 194

There is a hitch in my largely celebratory account of the significance of "Monstro." Like much short fiction published in the *New Yorker*, it was meant to be a preview of sorts: it was part of a larger project for Díaz's second novel, a project then abandoned and only recently, apparently, picked up again (cf. Pearce 2017). We may be within our rights to read this as symptomatic: for a short time, at least, there was nothing to be gained, in exploring the contemporary moment, by reuniting the zombie with its roots, roots that it has long exceeded even if they linger beneath its surface, or indeed for a literary writer to engage with the zombie figure. Perhaps even more radically, such an abandonment was symptomatic of a prospective demise of the zombie as a cultural figure. We may have reached peak zombie, have exhausted the monster, may have been on the verge of it passing out of the collective consciousness and into pop cultural history.

In closing this book, I want to explore the opposite possibility (one only incidentally borne out by Díaz's apparent resumption of the project): that the zombie is very much passing upward and onward, into the future rather than the past. If up to now, I have read the zombie's meaning *in* contemporary literature, I now want to explore its meaning *for* contemporary literature, and ask whether we will be able to read literature again without the zombie.[1] My argument here will follow two strands. The first begins with the zombie, but reads it as part of a larger system of literary production, as a metonymical stand-in for various processes which appear capable of radically shifting literary writing, from genre amalgamation through mash-up writing to literary reception and the question of literature in the postworkshop age. This is, ultimately, a question about the shape of the future of fiction. The second involves the meaning of the zombie specifically as a symbolic figure, as the appropriate monster of the contemporary moment, one which stands in a long line of literary embodiments of shifting cultural constellations. My contention here will be that the relationship between these two points—the appropriateness of the zombie in the contemporary and zombie fiction's part in the literary field's reorganizations—is not, by any means, coincidental. Rather, the zombie stands at the forefront of the literary field's recalibration specifically because it is the contemporary moment's appropriate monster.

We can already glimpse this in the way the zombie fictions I have discussed appear capable of shifting discourses about literariness. As far as critical attention is concerned, the generic turn in contemporary literature is certainly the most important issue which zombie fictions participate in—and in a key position, no less, as I will go on to argue. Zombie fiction intervenes not just in this debate, however, as even the limited examples above show. As my discussion of *The Walking Dead* should have made clear, the kinds of attention received by a comic such as *Watchmen* (see Hoberek 2014) has also stimulated the possibility of paying attention to other comics in a similar way. And my (and others') discussion of *The Walking Dead* signals also that such attention is capable of generating insights into the ways that even what appears to be a doubly trivial form (a genre comic, rather than, say, an autobiographical "graphic novel," which is a form now comparatively well-canonized) can engage the kinds of greater cultural constellations we often believe are reserved for what used to be literary fiction. *Allison Hewitt Is Trapped* suggests the relevance of forms of literary production outside the realm of print, given its origins as a blog, and thus something like a democratization of literary production which almost exclusively belongs, today, to the realm of genre fiction, with nary a "literary" novel being serialized online. It also, as I suggested, thematizes explicitly the conflation of genre form and literary value in its own coda, a suggestive meta-move which appears to set the novel's own sights at critical acceptance. And finally, *Pride and Prejudice and Zombies* reshapes our understanding of the status of fiction in the contemporary in at least two ways. For one, its mash-up form may be important for more than the way it opens Jane Austen's text and contemporary reception to critical view. It also exemplifies the possibilities of what China Miéville has called the "permeable text," a decentering of authorial authority in favor of a communal writing (and reading) project. "Just as precocious 14-year-olds brilliantly—or craply—remix albums and put them up online," Miéville points out, "people are starting to provide their own cuts of novels. In the future, asked if you've read the latest Ali Smith or Ghada Karmi, the response might be not yes and no, but 'which mix,' and why" (2014, 44). The ready electronic availability and malleability of source texts is not a necessary prerequisite for this form of writing, but it appears to give it much more currency, as does the possibility of simply distributing it online (which is not what *Pride and Prejudice and Zombies* does, of course). And it is certainly useful to recognize the ways in which a new openness, both creatively and in terms of reception, appears to emerge in the contemporary literary scene. Importantly for my purposes here, read in this context *Pride and Prejudice and Zombies* is formally no less remarkable than a celebrated text such as Jonathan Safran Foer's *Tree of Codes* (2011), which similarly remixes a canonical text and appears to be primarily validated as a literary (vs. a cheap remix) text by virtue of Foer's persona as a "literary" writer.

The second way *Pride and Prejudice and Zombies* interferes in the question of the status of fiction is the one already discussed at some length. The book insists on being read closely no matter critical disdain, and thus opens our attention to the way even ostensibly trivial literature is capable of sustained engagement—that is, an openness to critical engagement, which in turn is predicated on a text's engagement with the cultural moment and its own formal qualities. *Pride and Prejudice and Zombies* requires us to take stock of our reading practices, of easy delimitations between what is literary and thus worthy of close critical attention and what is generic and thus is not. *Pride and Prejudice and Zombies* does so, finally, in a way that is typical of zombie fictions, and more generally of the frequently genre-savvy, often genre-amalgamated fiction of the contemporary moment, and engages a number of contemporary concerns, from the role of the MFA program to the very heart of the question of what is literary about literary fiction.

In reviewing Colson Whitehead's *Zone One* in 2012, Andrew Hoberek offered what can be read as emblematic of zombie fiction's challenge to the idea of literary fiction: "*Zone One* is the greatest American novel of the twenty-first century" (406). If that is so, I would contend, it is because of the conundrum suggested in the novel's hardcover jacket copy, the fact that it is "[a]t once a chilling horror story that embraces the pleasures of genre and a literary novel" (2011, n.p.); or perhaps because it is neither, because it subverts the very categories which the dust jacket insists upon. Whitehead's novel is not just, as Hoberek notes, a sequence of "particularly brilliant scenes" (406): it is deeply generic, deeply vested in and knowledgeable about its generic forebears, and of course also part of a larger trend. Whitehead's foray into fantasy is not isolated: writers such as Michael Chabon, Jonathan Lethem, and Junot Díaz, to name just a few, have written novels heavily influenced by genre fictions, by thrillers and mysteries, fantasy and science-fiction, and comics. Alas, their novels themselves remain literary in critical perception –weighty, worthy of interpretation, complex. But this increasingly false juxtaposition is clearly part of what is at issue. In *Considering Watchmen*, Hoberek argues that in the writing of Chabon, Lethem, and Díaz, comics provides a way to "overcome the conventions of literary fictions," thereby making *Watchmen* "literature reactively, by expanding our understanding of what literature can do" (2014, 183), and it is this double move that is at work, too, in Whitehead. It is the act of reactively making genre fiction, of making zombie fiction, literature. It does so in a surprisingly complex manner, one which impinges heavily on both a stylistic version of literariness (Hoberek's) as well as on an institutional one. Whitehead's book draws on both a readerly and an authorial understanding of its generic history, which here becomes a curious form of "experience," to bring up Mark McGurl's summary term for the very acts of memory and observation, of writing what you know, that shape program-era literary fiction. Notwithstanding McGurl's explicit denial that science-fiction, and by extension, fantasy and horror fiction may "be said to deploy the faculties of memory or observation," except "in the most highly mediated way" (2009, 103), it is clear from reading Whitehead's own comments that it is precisely his "experience" that brings him to write genre fiction. "I think that people of my generation are more comfortable making the foray into genre. Because of macabre books, Stephen King—and probably cable. I think culture changed in the '70s and '80s and people were exposed to different kinds of culture" (in Fassler 2011). The MFA program's general exclusion of genre fiction coincides, as Junot Díaz implies, with an anti-ethnic component, one in which the "theory of reality" advanced by the selection of writers to study coincides with an exclusion of "people of color." Díaz's solution, the "Voices of Our Nation Workshop," explicitly and not coincidentally open to "all genres and all people of color" (2014), is an institutional echo of Ramon Saldívar's argument about the generic turn, in which he reads Díaz and Whitehead specifically in a "new world" context (2011, 596) and "in relation to matters of racial identity" (2013, 5). Saldívar's desire to see what he calls "speculative realism"—precisely the generic amalgamation that I have been talking about—as a specifically ethnic form of writing coincides with the belief voiced by Díaz that the MFA program does not cater to non-white writers. Yet, as I have argued elsewhere (Lanzendörfer 2015b), we must read this formal move more broadly, as more fundamentally centered on the work genre can do for writers of any ethnicity. Zombie fiction highlights this, both in the way *Zone One* decenters race as well as in the way it insists on the recuperative, utopian power of genre as such.

It is because of this background that Whitehead's novel—written outside the workshop, and implicitly taking on board much of the criticism of the workshop—is my point of departure for the larger argument about zombie fiction's relevance to the contemporary moment, both in fiction and outside of it. As Thomas Beebee has noted, "the truly vital meanings of a text are often contained not in any specific generic category into which the text may be placed, but rather in the play of differences between its genres" (1994, 250). A consequence is that "most works not only can but must be analyzed in more than one generic way in order for their messages to have any effective meaning or value" (265). In the case of *Zone One*, these differences are constituted by the two terms at the heart of *Zone One*'s radical newness: the ostensibly clear markers of "literary" and "genre" fiction. As Fredric Jameson notes, any "genre is essentially a socio-symbolic message; in other words, form is immanently and intrinsically an ideology in its own right. When such forms are reappropriated and refashioned in quite different social and cultural contexts"—such as the adoption of something as fantastical and as popular as the B-movie zombie into a so-called literary text—"this message persists and must be functionally reckoned into the new form" (2002, 127). And in turn, McGurl argues that it is difficult not to see literary fiction as "a genre in its own right" (2009, 42). Like all genres, literary fiction thus depends on certain markers to identify it and to be put to certain uses: "[g]enres are essentially literary institutions, or social contracts between a writer and a specific public, whose function is to specify the proper use of a particular cultural artifact" (Jameson 2002, 106). There are two major markers for the literariness of *Zone One*: on the one hand, Whitehead's style, the "particularly brilliant scenes" of Hoberek's review; on the other, Whitehead's name (which functions like Foer's above). Whitehead, of course, cannot be a hack writing a trite formula novel, because he already is a MacArthur fellow and a Pulitzer Prize winner. These markers identify literary fiction, and so *Zone One* comes to stand as a clear-cut example of contemporary generic amalgamation. It also becomes a focal point for the question of the meaning of these generic categories in the contemporary moment.

One way of parsing what *Zone One* does, of course, would be the one proposed by Lev Grossman in a perceptive article in the *New Yorker*: that the addition of genre elements expands, but leaves otherwise untouched, the category of literary fiction, and also leaves untouched the disparaged idea of genre fiction (cf. 2012; see also Lanzendörfer 2015b for a fuller engagement with the notion of genre fiction). That is to say, the argument might be that *Zone One* adopts "the pleasures of genre" without becoming a genre novel, and also leaves other genre novels (in this case zombie novels) safely outside the reach of literary criticism and its processes of establishing cultural value. This is not the way, obviously, I propose to read things. Rather, *Zone One*'s success in combining genre and literary fiction elements points to the increasing irrelevance of these categories. The fact that *Zone One* is heavily indebted to the zombie fiction genre is clearly evident even before one starts reading; for example, some versions of the cover inform us already that this will be a story of the "living dead." The novel thus inscribes itself in a longer history of similar texts and films; and, as John Frow has argued, it is precisely such a history of genre which offers us the necessary reading frame, the "set of expectations which guide our engagement with texts" (2006, 104). What is at stake here is the meaning of these allusions to genre history, and indeed the question of what it means to be "generic," to be genre writing, today. Thomas Roberts has claimed that genre fiction is, as it were, "written by a tradition rather than by an individual" (1991, 4), suggesting that the strictures developing out of a genre's history—the elements which must be repeated in a work of genre fiction to make that work intelligible as a work of genre fiction—exceed the potential for authorial innovation. A radically different argument has been made by Nicholas Brown, who argues that the rigid requirements of genre, the things that need to be in a text in order for it to be readable as a genre text, open up "a zone of autonomy within the heteronomous space of cultural commodities" because they pose a formal problem, within which a writer is free to do as he pleases. In the most rigorous parsing of this claim, Brown argues that this leads to "art as such" (2013, 161). We should perhaps pause to state what this claim means: it means that far from being merely something that can be integrated into literary fiction if need be, genre is the very thing that makes *Zone One* art—that is literature—in the first place. This question obtrudes only, of course, inasmuch as the very kind of literary fiction which in Mark McGurl's argument is heavily indebted as a genre to the same kind of modernist experimentation with language and form also aimed at creating autonomous art and which is amenable to close reading and interpretation (cf. Brown 2013, 157). The question of whether or not *Zone One* is literature is, by extension, also the question of whether or not it can be interpreted. To follow Brown, it is literature—autonomous, interpretable—only to the extent that it is generic.

Genre certainly constrains *Zone One*: it requires certain elements to exist, such as, quite banally, the walking dead, a sudden, inexplicable, or at least unexplained apocalyptic turn, and a cohort of survivors. But beyond this, genre also embeds the novel in a history of genre writing that, to follow Andrew Hoberek, now retroactively becomes literary, becomes capable (if it hasn't before) of sustaining interpretation. The issue here is not so much that it required *Zone One* for this to happen, and we could not have read *World War Z* critically before, but rather one of the visibility of this possibility. There is, then, a dialectics at work here: much as the inclusion of genre fictional elements changes the genre of literary fiction—at the very least reopening it, as Ramon Saldívar has suggested, to the imagination of systemic alternatives beyond the reach of mere social realism (cf. 2013)—the conflation of literary and genre fiction changes the nature of the mainstream's engagement with genre fiction. One of the consequences of this change is the recognition that genre fiction offers much more than mere "reader's wish-fulfillment fantasies" (Joshi 2009, 25), as the most recent study of genre fiction has it. But, to reiterate: at its most consequent, such a claim must involve the dissolution of genre difference, which is now not mainly read along the lines of content but along the lines of interpretability, and by extension, literariness. We will not, then, be able to read literature again without zombies because zombies, metonymically, make literature: the very act of introducing genre, in the contemporary moment, is a literary act.

Finally, it is more than a mere coincidence that the zombie appears in all of these versions of a future for fiction. The zombie figures into this whole argument specifically *as* the zombie non-metonymically, for the very way in which it signals possibility and the elementary openness which the idea of possibility entails. Writing about the zombie, as I hope to have shown in this book, is rarely about the zombie: the zombie as such is a potent but ultimately problematical metaphor, and is often merely readable as a potent antagonist of the status quo rather than a solution. It is in this connection that we might read a throwaway line like this one in Fingerman's *Pariah*, introducing us to Karl's past and showing his desire for life in New York turn into disappointment: "Karl got a job, an apartment, and an education in reality versus illusions. And shortly thereafter it all went south. People started dying and coming back and eating each other and the rest was history" (2010, 84). The only escape from the dire experience of reality—which means living in the world that we all inhabit now—is the zombie apocalypse. The "real" world is not one in which we can retain illusions or the kinds of hopes which drive us until we resign ourselves to their loss. Its logic is so ingrained that it takes an apocalyptic moment to shake it—to reveal the real world's lacks, perhaps. The zombie provides this apocalyptic moment, and it does so better—that is to say, more appropriately for the contemporary moment—than any of its (few) alternatives.

The limits of this metaphorical imagination must be clear: it is an always destructive, always violent, always precarious ending to the previous world, one which necessarily sees death and destruction.[2] It sweeps away, at first, as Karl suggests above, both the older hopes and illusions and the reality of twenty-first-century life: it is egalitarian in this destructiveness. Many diehard fans of the zombie long to root for this misunderstood monster, to see zombies individually and as groups as harbingers of a better future. But such a reading of the zombie is, as I hope to have shown above, reductive. Even beyond the somewhat blunt point that to become a zombie is to become part of a larger mass, this mass's existence does not automatically give it a purpose, or make it the *Vorschein* of a better world. To become a zombie is also to die violently, to abandon agency, subjectivity, and indeed humanity, and to gain little but a slow process of bodily and an immediate mental decay. When Mark Spitz is confronted, at the end of *Zone One*, with the decision to—perhaps—join the zombies as a zombie himself, the symbolism of this possibility rests heavily on its ambivalence, not on the belief that this is the way to go because the zombies signal the right way forward, but because they may be the only way, even if they are a dead (ha!) end.

The zombie itself, then, remains a problematic emblem of the future of humanity. It does not, by and large, itself signal the possibilities open to human life. The zombie enables possibilities, certainly; but it is almost never itself the future. It lets us see things: it is a revelatory metaphor, whether what it reveals are the limits of the liberal imagination, the different valences of the idea of community, the complicated contemporary relationship to the everyday, the nature of literary writing in a popular reading sphere, the limits of gender progressiveness in popular fiction, or the limits and opportunities in the literary representation of race. It does this, I think, better than any other monster, tying neatly into so many contemporary discourses, from the problems of the capitalist world economy to the life sciences to philosophy, that it will always be subject to an overload of connotations. Each of these refracts widely into so many different shades that it becomes impossible to say what the zombie "is," what work it does, or what metaphoric powers it holds, except in a detailed examination of each special case. This is the precise opposite of the notion that the zombie can represent anything and everything, and thus has no critical valence at all—that, as Evan Williams has it, it has come to "mean nothing" (2011, 146). Rather, it suggests that its enabling of possibilities is overdetermined and it must be interpreted. It is not amenable to easy equivalencies, but rather requires us to know its history, to read the strata of its sedimentation, to recognize the ways in which anything it does or stands for is tied back to the histories of oppression, revolt, and resistance in which, at different moments of its past, it has figured symbolically. The zombie is complex and overdetermined because our historic moment is complex and overdetermined: we live in a complicated, perhaps even exhaustingly complicated moment, for which the zombie is the appropriate monster.

And really, these two issues—the way the zombie is culturally and contemporarily appropriate, and the way it shifts our understanding of the status of fiction—necessarily go together. Ian Watt, famously, has read *Robinson Crusoe* as achieving the novel form at the precise moment when capitalism begins to dissolve the stable societal relations of its immediate past, replacing feudal and religious certainties with the uncertainties of modernity and individualism (2001, 60–92). His argument ties a particular, hitherto nonexistent form of cultural expression to a hitherto nonexistent societal moment, suggesting that one is appropriate and necessary for the other. No zombie novel is *Robinson Crusoe*, and nothing the zombie novel does is formally as revolutionary as *Robinson Crusoe*, of course: if nothing else, zombie novels are still novels, and so inscribe themselves into the very history begun by *Robinson Crusoe*. But that no zombie novel is *Robinson Crusoe* does not mean we can deny the literariness of zombie fiction. In fact, as I have suggested above, whatever the contemporary definition of literariness is, it must include zombie fiction, lest we lose whatever is left in literariness of artistic autonomy and critical, political, and social engagement. *Zone One* is just the most obvious case of the nexus between ostensibly generic and allegedly literary fictions: it is the place where this nexus becomes most apparent and thus allows us to see other texts, less obviously validated as literary by the names on their covers, as engaged with the same concerns, as equally literary. In their choice of mode, in their acceptance of the literariness of the generic, in their acceptance of the appropriateness of the fantastic for literary representations of real-world concerns, and in their choice of the zombie as the appropriate monster for our times, zombie fiction reorients the novel. In denying the realism of realist fiction, in shifting discourses away from the generally more systemically affirmative concerns of identity, trauma, affect, and other largely individualizing issues, zombie fiction suggests the need to read the contemporary moment differently. At the precise moment when neoliberal capitalism begins to dissolve the last vestiges of a societal contract, and when the inequalities of the system and its essential instability are becoming plain to see, zombie fiction, if perhaps in a minor key, becomes a form of cultural expression that formally—through the necessary possibilities of the zombie, ambiguous, undead, and yet enabling—and thematically talks about what society is like, and how we may imagine changing it.

No zombie novel is *Robinson Crusoe*: but zombies themselves may be Robinson Crusoes. If Robinson Crusoe, the character, represented the uncertainties of a world at the cusp of a great revolution in societal relations, and formally enacted the effects of this revolution in the novel—in the *form* of the novel—the literary zombie too arises at a moment of great upheaval. The certainties which go along with reading a novel two hundred and fifty years later, and being able to survey its historical times are, of course, denied to us in evaluating the zombie in the here and now. Yet something seems deeply appropriate about a monster which at once effortlessly highlights the urgency of radical, even apocalyptic, change, and which then persists as the constant reminder of things before; about a monster which may possibly be able to do away with contemporary life, but in doing so, remains a constant threat on human life, period. The zombie is a monster which can simultaneously give metaphoric voice to a contemporary desire to imagine a different way of life, and a similarly metaphoric voice warning of the dangers of such an imagination. It shapes the novel at a point where it seems much is at stake: whether to imagine the future as a hopeful place or to deny the imagination of a different future in the first place. The zombie, in its peculiar characteristics, permits the novel, and indeed literature more generally, to do both: to imagine a better future and to caution against it. In so doing, it may be grandly symptomatic of a contemporary moment in which we are constantly cautioned against the dangers of imagining a life beyond neoliberal capitalism, even as there remains an obvious craving to imagine such a life.

"[W]e can only understand ourselves as monsters," Hardt and Negri say, meaning not so much that we *are* monsters than that it takes the monster to make us understand the full import of our contemporary moment. If Robinson Crusoe stands at the beginning of modernity, looking anxiously forward, the first modern monster, Dr. Frankenstein's Adam, stood at its midpoint, looking around himself in near-desperation at the changes modernity had wrought. The zombie, by extension, may stand at a moment of modernity's hopeful uncertain end, teetering at the edge of the "new world of monsters [. . .] where humanity has to grasp its future" (196). The zombie is not itself this future of humanity, or so at least it is to be hoped. But in its ruthless destruction of everything existing, it sets the stage for copious versions of such a future, and sets out the stakes for them: not a tinkering around the edges, but a radical dissolution of "what is" to be replaced with an often uncertain "what will be." While a different future remains in need of being imagined, the zombie will be there to let us do it.

Notes

Introduction

1. The zombie as metaphor is also politically malleable: the largely left-leaning arguments in the books cited above could be supplemented with a text such as Jason Mattera's *Obama Zombies: How the Liberal Machine Brainwashed My Generation* (New York: Threshold Editions, 2011), and certainly by Brian Anse Patrick's pro-gun, anti-multicultural, slightly off-kilter *Zombology: Zombies and the Decline of the West* (London: Arktos, 2014), which concludes on a diatribe that excludes black people generally from the "Western voyage" and, in the manner of racists everywhere, denies its racism only to then claim: "but the most racially motivated acts that I have ever seen were committed by Blacks" (159–60). This is an apparently common kind of displacement of sociological facts for personal anecdote to validate an unsupportable worldview. In a different non-left vein, Glen Whitman and James Dow use zombies (and vampires) to investigate the workings of the global economy in *Economics of the Undead: Zombies, Vampires, and the Dismal Science* (Lanham, MD: Rowman & Littlefield, 2016) in what amounts to a large celebratory exploration of economics' capacity to explain the zombie apocalypse, and to explain economics through the zombie apocalypse. The volume loses nary a word on the profession's dismal record in the Great Recession, and offers a remarkably broad, indeed nearly total, refusal to engage with the arguments delivered by Harmon, Giroux, or McNally.

2. At least two short story collections seek to trace the deeper history of the zombie motif: Otto Penzler's 2011 *Zombies! Zombies! Zombies!* includes nineteenth-century short fiction (Sheridan Le Fanu's "Schalken the Painter," Edgar Allan Poe's "The Facts in the Case of M. Valdemar," and Guy de Maupassant's "Was it a Dream?"), as well as a large number of pulp texts from the 1920s through 1940s. Penzler's introduction also points to Ambrose Bierce's "The Death of Halprin Fraser" as a story which could have been included. Le Fanu and Poe, in fact, are well-established forebears of the contemporary zombie: they were also included in Stephen Jones's 1993 collection *The Mammoth Book of Zombies*. Even earlier, in 1985, Peter Haining's *Zombies: Stories of the Walking Dead* collected zombie stories with the aim of bringing together in a single book "the best of the tales about the Walking Dead" (12); these, however, despite Haining's overt reference to George Romero as the inspiration for his collection, were all stories about the Haitian variety of the zombie. Nonetheless, Haining's collection is striking, as it appears to be the first anthology of any kind made up of zombie fiction.

3. In what follows, I will use "Vodou" to signify the Caribbean religious practice, and "voodoo" the Western cultural appropriation thereof prevalent in popular culture, following preferred usage of Vodou religious scholars (see Gray 2017, xiii).

4. As Raymond Williams has pointed out, of course, "[t]he masses are always the others, whom we don't know, and can't know. [. . .] There are in fact no masses; there are only ways of seeing people as masses" (1960, 319). This point—which correlates the zombie with the other and understands the masses of zombies as a figure of seeing—will continue to inform the discussion below. At the same time, given the recent upswing in right-wing populist success, we may also question the more immediately leftist interpretations of such popular risings, which are now readily perceivable to shortchange the potential of non-emancipatory but nonetheless perceptibly popular mass movements. These, as I will sketch very briefly at a number of points in this study, suggests the way we might be obliged to read some existing zombie texts differently in light of the somewhat unexpected success of what amounts to a right-wing resistance to a globalized neoliberal market. From Brexit to the election of Donald Trump, after all, the aim of resuscitating a pre-globalized, national-ethnical form of polity and economic system appears to power much of contemporary politics. Despite apparently sharing the same immediate goals with some left-wing agendas, the largely nostalgic aim to reconstruct a previous version of life is at odds with the more utopian belief in a new mode of life that much criticism of zombie films has foregrounded. Yet given that we appear to have seen successful right-wing agitation against a continuation of the globalized status quo, and we have not seen a politically successful left-wing version, readings of the zombie as a metaphor (which, again, I will not undertake here) might usefully look at whether or not the zombie of the contemporary moment could be usefully read to prefigure these right-wing upheavals, or to figure it—see also Kenemore 2017 for a novel's take on reading the 2016 election through the lens of the zombie.

Chapter 1

1. I am using the term "liberal" here in its American sense of a progressive, center-left position, and will throughout; this because Brooks himself, as an American, is most easily located in the national political spectrum. Such a liberalism seems occasionally at odds with the more classical economic liberalism of a more European tradition, but note Slavoj Žižek's point: "Today, the meaning of 'liberalism' moves between two opposed poles: economic liberalism (free market individualism, opposition to strong state regulation, etc.) and political liberalism (with an accent on equality, social solidarity, permissiveness, etc.). In the US, Republicans are more liberal in the first sense and Democrats in the second. The point, of course, is that while one cannot decide through closer analysis which is the 'true' liberalism, one also cannot resolve the deadlock by proposing a kind of 'higher' dialectical synthesis, or 'avoid the confusion' by making a clear distinction between the two senses of the term. The tension between the two meanings is inherent to the very content that 'liberalism' endeavors to designate, it is constitutive of the notion itself, so that this ambiguity, far from signaling a limitation of our knowledge, signals the 'innermost truth' of the notion of liberalism" (2011, 37). That is to say, you cannot have political liberalism without also having economic liberalism.

2. Kelly Baker has pointed out one surprising dimension of both Brooks's novel and the *Survival Guide*. Following a *Wired* report by Spencer Ackerman, she notes that the two books are familiar sights on bookshelves in US Army posts in Iraq and Afghanistan. The soldiers'

interest, Baker notes, stems from the fact that Brooks's books do not focus on human protagonists but on "key practices like preparation and logistics" (loc. 335). It is certainly these readers' privilege to focus on this dimension of Brooks's novel, but it seems a foreshortening of Brooks's deep interest in the human stories behind the technical descriptions sometimes offered.

Chapter 2

1. Perhaps necessarily, Nancy's thoughts about community must remain merely apropos: as Christopher Fynsk points out, Nancy's community cannot "be produced [or] instituted," and its essence cannot "be expressed in a work of any kind" (1994, x). For an effort to more fully relate Nancy's conception of community to recent zombie fiction (*The Walking Dead*), see Rodriguez-Salas (2015). Rodriguez-Salas's essay notes the ways in which Nancy's notions of transimmanence and immanence may be related to the different communities constituted in the course of the first three seasons of the TV series, with some nods to the comic.

2. Critics more bloody-minded than I may see something at stake here in the fact that the survivors play the board game Monopoly, which does not reward cooperative gameplay and does not in any way transcend the petty squabbles of the society that was.

Chapter 3

1. I am happy to acknowledge the support of the Comixscholars-L email listserv in discussing some of the issues I raise herein, especially Juha Veltti and David Hyman.

2. Much more academic work has been spent, somewhat puzzlingly, on AMC's adaptation of *The Walking Dead* than on the comic; but the two remain narratively similar enough that many of the points critics have raised on the series are applicable also to the comic.

3. Some critics have argued the importance of *The Walking Dead*'s heavy reliance of on seriality (cf. Hassler-Forest 2014). It is certainly a misapprehension of the zombie's literary and filmic history to say that it "demands a serial narrative" (Krautschick and Rudner 2014, 58), but, as Dan Hassler-Forest points out, the particular way in which the serial issues of *The Walking Dead* comic are republished both in trade paperback and in the omnibus editions suggests that the authors conceive of them as "sequences of individual episodes grouped together into larger units that display a high degree of narrative and thematic unity" (124). What's more important than seriality per se, then, is the particular design within the formal strictures of seriality.

4. In failing to provide for an ending, Kirkman's series does not stand out from various other pop-culture phenomena over the past decade. Perhaps the most notable comic series to meander on without a clear sense of where it would end was Bill Willingham's *Fables*, which finally ended after thirteen years in 2015. More well-known examples are the TV series *Lost* and *Battlestar Galactica*, both of which improvised endings to complex narratives without having them sketched out in advance. The idea of endlessness is in a different sense familiar in comics. Superman or Batman's stories never "end," though individual storylines may; and even death is not fatal, but may be followed by reboot or resurrection. We have grown accustomed to this formal move, as odd as it is: insisting on a serial sequence of related events (a shift from the episodic early Superman whose narrative inertia Umberto Eco famously critiqued) without admitting the need for an ending to such seriality. If worse comes to worst,

publishers and authors simply hit the reset button and restart their series, each of them effectively endless. This cyclicality contrasts with *The Walking Dead*'s linearity, in which a claim to endlessness becomes far more problematical.

5. Dorfman throughout his book uses the terms "late modernity" and "modernity" virtually interchangeably; I add "postmodernity." The difficulties with all these terms are obvious: if Dorfman appears to mean by modernity the period roughly from the mid-nineteenth century through today, this vast span of time neither fully encapsulates possible different readings of what constitutes modernity (such as the time from the Renaissance onwards), nor fully differentiates what are arguably distinct periods within it (such as Dorfman's own "late" modernity, postmodernity, and possibly post-postmodernity). In keeping Dorfman's terms and expanding on them, I make no greater philosophical claim than to say that the issues Dorfman identifies still easily apply today. Indeed, we might say with Fredric Jameson that many of them are more prominent in postmodernity than they ever were in mere modernity; that they have become constitutive of postmodern, late-capitalist life in such a way that even the overwhelming sense of alienation that produces a film such as Chaplin's *Modern Times* must be seen as a mere precursor. That the problems which Kermode and Dorfman identify as "modern" persist enables me to shorthand them as postmodern: but, of course, they would persist still if we were in post-postmodernity or any other configuration.

6. I quote *The Walking Dead* without emending for upper-lower case, since the entire comic is written in uppercase letters. Citing *The Walking Dead* is made difficult by its lack of pagination in the trade paperback editions. In lieu of page counts, I try to identify roughly where in the trade paperback volumes a scene occurs.

Chapter 4

1. A minor note: it is a critical commonplace to be clever about the notion of zombification, and to suggest things like *Pride and Prejudice and Zombies* being a zombie of *Pride and Prejudice* itself, as when Jonathan Eburne suggests the novel's text is "by definition borrowed, mashed up, zombified" (2014, 409); or, slightly differently, as Andrea Ruthven does when she suggests that "Elizabeth Bennett is herself partially zombified" (2014, 317), implying that the word "zombified" usefully describes even the non-zombies in the work (as it does, for example, Shaun in *Shaun of the Dead*). Ruthven is merely metaphorically suggesting that Elizabeth's own unreflecting defense of the status quo is no different from the zombies' unreflecting destruction of it. So far, so good, but the play on the word "zombified" obscures the important work that the zombie figure itself does (and does quite differently from the way its presence acts upon the remaining humans).

2. For Jameson, the substitution of critical parody with unpolitical pastiche is a core aspect of postmodernism's cultural logic. This view was quickly disputed by Linda Hutcheon, among others, who suggested instead that postmodern parody was lively and not at all lacking in critical stance.

3. These geographical markers, for those not familiar with English county geography, encompass a triangle covering almost all of England south of Manchester, which puts even more ominous a note on "Manchester's collapse" (64).

4. Even the least romantic episode in the original is actually sharpened by *Pride and Prejudice and Zombies*. Charlotte Collins, née Lucas, in this version agrees to wed Mr. Collins for more than the simple reason of her desire for a competence: bitten by a zombie, she is set

to succumb to the dreaded disease, and thus opts to marry him to render her "final months [. . .] happy months"—a choice which Elizabeth, who alone knows the truth, can at least condone. If Charlotte's decision to marry Collins in Austen's novel thus signaled Charlotte's practical approach to marriage, it does so even more in *Pride and Prejudice and Zombies*. At the same time, *Pride and Prejudice and Zombies* uses the marriage to solve the troubling plot point about the entailment of Longbourn: when Charlotte succumbs to her disease, Collins is so grief-stricken that he takes his own life (238), and thus Longbourn is likely to remain in the Bennetts' hands, somehow. Camilla Nelson offers an excellent additional reading of Charlotte's situation (2013, 9).

5. Both *Huckleberry Finn and Zombie Jim* and *Pride and Prejudice and Zombies*, interestingly enough, go out of their way to emphasize the success Napoleon (whose being alive in 1839 is somewhat inexplicable) has had in the wake of their respective zombie risings: "Napoleon had killed the fissythis in Europe" (*Adventures of Huckleberry Finn and Zombie Jim*, 270); "Napoleon Bonaparte put half the world under his little heel" (Hockensmith 2011, 232). The latter, of course, is a version of the mythos by which Britain still conceptualizes its role in the defeat of Napoleon: without Britain to stand against him, obviously Napoleon succeeds in his quest for European dominance.

Chapter 5

1. Romero's second trilogy of films has a far more spotty track record in this regard. *Land of the Dead* (2005) had a Hispanic main character (Cholo) and, of course, the major force of the black zombie leader Big Daddy, but lacks a notable female protagonist; *Diary of the Dead* (2007) has a female narrator (Debra), and a well-balanced male-female cast, but is all-white; *Survival of the Dead* (2009) has the fairly strong figure of Tomboy, but for the most part women play a minor role in its narrative.

2. In this latter group, of course, "wife" and "mother" do not necessarily denote positions in which women do not hold agency, or which to use necessarily reflects a surrender to patriarchy—radical feminist positions notwithstanding.

3. While the technicalities of this network go unexplored, and there may be some leeway in judging its realism, what *Allison Hewitt Is Trapped* highlights here is the way the breakdown of all communications that figures so importantly in *Dying to Live* and *Pariah* is, in fact, a meaningful authorial choice, rather than a necessary extrapolation.

4. If all of these women are also able and capable, funny and courageous (Cassandra excepted), they contrast sharply with the men. Whelan is a former police officer, with certified survival skills; Moritz's capabilities are notable in the way that he has, for a long time now, survived in his dangerous work. *Sadie Walker Is Stranded*, unlike *Allison Hewitt Is Trapped*, insists on both these pasts as well as in their relevance for the moment of the narrative.

Chapter 6

1. What may be surprising about early zombie narratives is that, in largely figuring the zombie and its attendant racial issues as a distant, geographically separate concern, they held its danger at bay: you have to be white and in Haiti in order to be in danger (something which holds true even in the EC Comics voodoo stories of the 1950s). These texts thus retained

the exoticism of the zombie figure and its mystery, as well as a fundamentally imperialist discourse about them, but also ensured that their threat remained contained. As the example I cited in the introduction shows, however, voodoo practices were also imagined as, if not of themselves importable, at least potentially harmful even within the continental United States.

2. They are surely echoes of *Dawn of the Dead*'s zombies turning up at the supermarket, but also suggest, strikingly, Czolgosz's differentiation between benign and violent zombies (see Ch. 4). Apart from suggesting specifically, perhaps, that critics enthusing about Whitehead's originality here require a more thorough grounding in crappy zombie fiction, I think this also bespeaks a larger point, one which will return in a different guise in the Coda. Critics have been willing to engage Whitehead's *Zone One* to an extend unprecedented for zombie fiction, in no small part because of Whitehead's preexisting fame as a writer. Whether or not either the motives, the themes, or the symbolic action of the novel are exceptional when read against its generic history, however, appears to be less of a concern to those critics; or, perhaps, it is less obvious to them given their own critical upbringing. The problem here is that *Zone One* inscribes itself in at least two traditions: those of zombie fiction writ large—that is, including cinema—and those of literary fiction, with whose procedures critics are likely to be more familiar. Both of these traditions need to be familiar, I think, to critics seeking to characterize *Zone One* as radical or great or in any way thematically special.

3. Leif Sorenson notes that at least one character in the novel reads the stragglers positively as having a good solution to the problems of life, believing that they are "always inhabiting the perfect moment" (158); Sorenson suggests that they are "marked by the kind of satisfaction and plentitude of experience that is not available to the survivors" (2014, 579). It is not clear that the novel endorses this character's viewpoint; he commits suicide not long after.

4. Jessica Hurley adds that the revelation of Mark Spitz's race occurs in the same general moment, thus linking the persistence of race as a category to this overall collapse (2015, 324). This is certainly suggestive, but it also appears to be complicated by the fact that the complete destruction of Zone One, and one presumes of everything else as well, would also seem to leave no room for race to matter. Thus, the sudden revelation of the persistence of race goes hand in hand with its ultimate destruction in the wake of the destruction of all social structures.

5. Leif Sorenson's suggestion that *Zone One* is invested in narrative closure appears to miss this overdetermined openness of the novel's ending, which offers closure solely on the ideologies driving reconstruction.

Coda

1. My thanks to Phillip Wegner, who suggested the possibility of expanding my query from *Pride and Prejudice* to literature more generally.

2. In his 2017 study *The Great Leveler: Violence and the History of Inequality*, Walter Scheidel argues that historically meaningful decreases in economic inequality have always been preceded by major, violent upheavals of the status quo and never through peaceful redistribution—so far. Without going into the merits of this argument, especially as an extrapolation of the future, we might well notice the way zombie fiction mediates precisely such a reading of the utopian idea of a better world.

Bibliography

Primary Sources

This list includes more than just the texts I have discussed in this book (it also includes the few non-zombie primary texts I have used), but is not an exhaustive catalogue of all zombie novels and anthologies published through the present. This is especially true of the novels: online, on-demand publishing has produced a lot of zombie-themed novels, the vast majority of which I do not list (with a few notable exceptions).

Novels

Anderson, Kevin D., and Sam Stall (2010). *Night of the Living Trekkies*. Philadelphia: Quirk Books.
Austen, Jane (2004). *Pride and Prejudice*. Oxford: Oxford University Press.
Bourne, J. L. (2012). *Day by Day Armageddon: Shattered Hourglass*. Franklin, TN: Permuted Press.
———(2010). *Day by Day Armageddon: Beyond Exile*. Franklin, TN: Permuted Press.
———(2007). *Day by Day Armageddon*. Franklin, TN: Permuted Press.
Brooks, Max (2006). *World War Z: An Oral History of the Zombie War*. New York: Crown.
Brown, Eric S., and H. G. Wells (2009). *The War of the Worlds, Plus Blood, Guts, and Zombies*. New York: Gallery Books.
Browne, S. G. (2009). *Breathers: A Zombie's Lament*. New York: Broadway Books.
Carey, M. R. (2014). *The Girl with All the Gifts*. New York: Orbit.
Czolgosz, W. Bill, and Mark Twain (2009). *Adventures of Huckleberry Finn and Zombie Jim*. New York: Coscom Entertainment.
Fingerman, Bob (2010). *Pariah*. New York: Tor.
Goldsher, Alan (2010). *Paul is Undead: The British Zombie Invasion*. New York: Gallery Books.
Grahame-Smith, Seth, and Jane Austen (2009). *Pride and Prejudice and Zombies*. Philadelphia: Quirk Books.
Grant, Mira (2012). *Blackout*. London: Orbit.
———(2011). *Deadline*. London: Orbit.
———(2010). *Feed*. London: Orbit.

Hemon, Alexander (2015). *The Making of Zombie Wars*. New York: FSG.
Hockensmith, Steve (2011). *Pride and Prejudice and Zombies: Dreadfully Ever After*. Philadelphia: Quirk Books.
——(2010). *Pride and Prejudice and Zombies: Dawn of the Dreadfuls*. Philadelphia: Quirk Books.
Keene, Brian (2007). *Dead Sea*. New York: Dorchester.
——(2005). *City of the Dead*. New York: Dorchester.
——(2003). *The Rising*. New York: Leisure Books.
Kenemore, Scott (2014). *Zombie, Indiana*. New York: Talos.
——(2012). *Zombie, Illinois*. New York: Skyhorse.
——(2011). *Zombie, Ohio. A Tale of the Undead*. New York: Skyhorse.
Lansdale, Joe (1986). *Dead in the West*. San Francisco: Nightshade.
Lindqvist, Johan Ajvide (2009). *Handling the Undead*. London: Quercus.
McKinney, Joe (2011). *Flesh Eaters*. New York: Pinnacle Books.
——(2010). *Apocalypse of the Dead*. New York: Pinnacle Books.
——(2006). *Dead City*. New York: Pinnacle Books.
——(2011). *Flesh Eaters*. New York: Pinnacle Books.
Maberry, Jonathan (2011). *Dead of Night*. New York: St. Martin's.
Marion, Isaac (2017). *The Burning World*. New York: Vintage.
——(2013). *The New Hunger: The Prequel to Warm Bodies*. New York: Vintage.
——(2010). *Warm Bodies*. New York: Vintage.
Moody, David (2012). *Autumn: Aftermath*. London: Infected Books.
——(2011). *Autumn: Disintegration*. New York: St. Martin's Griffin.
——(2005). *Autumn: The Human Condition*. London: Infected Books.
——(2004). *Autumn: Purification*. London: Infected Books.
——(2003). *Autumn: The City*. London: Infected Books.
——(2001). *Autumn*. London: Infected Books.
Paffenroth, Kim (2006). *Dying to Live. A Novel of Life Among the Undead*. Franklin, TN: Permuted Press.
Petersen, Jesse (2011b). *Eat Slay Love*. New York: Orbit.
——(2011a). *Flip This Zombie*. New York: Orbit.
——(2010). *Married with Zombies*. New York: Orbit.
Recht, Z. A. (2009). *Plague of the Dead: The Morningstar Strain*. Franklin, TN: Permuted Press.
Roberts, Adam (2009). *I am Scrooge: A Zombie Story for Christmas*. London: Gollancz.
Roux, Madeleine (2012). *Sadie Walker Is Stranded*. London: Headline.
——(2010). *Allison Hewitt Is Trapped*. New York: St. Martin's Griffin.
Selby, Curt (1982). *I, Zombie*. New York: DAW Books.
Silverberg, Robert (1974). *Born with the Dead*. New York: Bantam.
Twain, Mark. *Adventures of Huckleberry Finn*. Ed. Thomas Cooley. New York: W. W. Norton.
Whitehead, Colson (2011). *Zone One*. New York: Doubleday.

Anthologies

Adams, John Joseph, ed. (2010). *The Living Dead 2*. San Francisco: Night Shade Books.
——(2008). *The Living Dead*. San Francisco: Night Shade Books.
Golden, Christopher, ed. (2011). *21st Century Dead: A Zombie Anthology*. New York: St. Martin's Griffin.

———(2010). *The New Dead: A Zombie Anthology.* New York: St. Martin's.
Gouveia, Keith, ed. (2008). *Bits of the Dead.* Winnipeg: Coscom Entertainment.
Guran, Paula, ed. (2012). *Extreme Zombies.* Germantown, MD: Prime Books.
———(2010). *Zombies: The Recent Dead.* Germantown, MD: Prime Books.
Haining, Peter, ed. (1985). *Zombie! Stories of the Walking Dead.* London: Target.
Jones, Stephen, ed. (2010). *The Dead That Walk.* Berkeley, CA: Ulysses Press.
———(1993). *The Mammoth Book of Zombies.* New York: Carroll & Graf.
Maberry, Jonathan, and George A. Romero, eds. (2017). *Nights of the Living Dead.* New York: St. Martin's Press.
Paffenroth, Kim, ed. (2007). *History is Dead.* Franklin, TN: Permuted Press.
Penzler, Otto, ed. (2011). *Zombies! Zombies! Zombies!* New York: Black Lizard.
Perkins, Lori, ed. (2010). *Hungry for Your Love. An Anthology of Zombie Romance.* New York: St. Martin's Griffin.
Preiss, Byron, and John Betancourt, eds. (1993). *The Ultimate Zombie: New and Cutting Edge Stories by Some of the World's Leading Authors.* New York: Dell.
Russo, John, ed. (2014). *Rise of the Dead: An Earth-Shattering Anthology of Zombie Terror.* Bridgeport, WV: Burning Bulb Publishing.
Skipp, John, ed. (2009). *Zombies: Encounters with the Hungry Dead.* New York: Black Dog and Leventhal.
———(2006). *Mondo Zombie.* Baltimore: Cemetery Dance.
Skipp, John, and Craig Spector, eds. (1992). *Still Dead.* Shingletown, CA: Mark V. Ziesing.
———(1989). *Book of the Dead.* New York: Bantam.
Snell, D. L., and Elijah Hall, eds. (2005). *The Undead. Zombie Anthology.* Franklin, TN: Permuted Press.

Graphic Novels

Aguirre-Sacasa, Roberto (w), and Francesco Francavilla (i) (2014). *Afterlife with Archie: Escape from Riverdale.* Mamaroneck, NY: Archie Comics.
Dinter, Stefan, and Christopher Tauber, eds. (2017). *Die Toten, Vol. 4.* Stuttgart: Panini.
———(2016). *Die Toten, Vol. 3.* Stuttgart: Panini.
———(2015). *Die Toten, Vol. 2.* Stuttgart: Panini.
———(2014). *Die Toten, Vol. 1.* Stuttgart: Panini.
Edginton, Ian (w), and Davide Fabbri (i) (2010). *Victorian Undead: Sherlock Holmes vs. Zombies.* LaJolla: Wildstorm.
Kirkman, Robert (w), Charlie Adlard (p), Stefano Gaudiano (i), and Cliff Rathburn (c) (2017). *The Whisperer War.* The Walking Dead 27. Berkeley: Image Comics.
———(2016b). *Call to Arms.* The Walking Dead 26. Berkeley: Image Comics.
———(2016a). *No Turning Back.* The Walking Dead 25. Berkeley: Image Comics.
———(2015b). *Life and Death.* The Walking Dead 24. Berkeley: Image Comics.
———(2015a). *Whispers Into Screams.* The Walking Dead 23. Berkeley: Image Comics.
———(2014c). *A New Beginning.* The Walking Dead 22. Berkeley: Image Comics.
———(2014b). *All Out War (Part Two).* The Walking Dead 21. Berkeley: Image Comics.
———(2014a). *All Out War (Part One).* The Walking Dead 20. Berkeley: Image Comics.
Kirkman, Robert (w), Charlie Adlard (p, i), and Cliff Rathburn (c) (2013b). *March to War.* The Walking Dead 19. Berkeley: Image Comics.
———(2013a). *What Comes After.* The Walking Dead 18. Berkeley: Image Comics.

———(2012b). *Something to Fear*. The Walking Dead 17. Berkeley: Image Comics.
———(2012a). *A Larger World*. The Walking Dead 16. Berkeley: Image Comics.
———(2011b). *We Find Ourselves*. The Walking Dead 15. Berkeley: Image Comics.
———(2011a). *No Way Out*. The Walking Dead 14. Berkeley: Image Comics.
———(2010c). *Too Far Gone*. The Walking Dead 13. Berkeley: Image Comics.
———(2010b). *Life Among Them*. The Walking Dead 12. Berkeley: Image Comics.
———(2010a). *Fear the Hunters*. The Walking Dead 11. Berkeley: Image Comics.
———(2009b). *What We Become*. The Walking Dead 10. Berkeley: Image Comics.
———(2009a). *Here We Remain*. The Walking Dead 9. Berkeley: Image Comics.
———(2008). *Made to Suffer*. The Walking Dead 8. Berkeley: Image Comics.
———(2007b). *The Calm Before*. The Walking Dead 7. Berkeley: Image Comics.
———(2007a). *This Sorrowful Life*. The Walking Dead 6. Berkeley: Image Comics.
———(2006). *The Best Defense*. The Walking Dead 5. Berkeley: Image Comics.
———(2005b). *The Heart's Desire*. The Walking Dead 4. Berkeley: Image Comics.
———(2005a). *Safety Behind Bars*. The Walking Dead 3. Berkeley: Image Comics.
———(2004). *Miles Behind Us*. The Walking Dead 2. Berkeley: Image Comics.
Kirkman, Robert (w), and Tony Moore (p, i) (2004). *Days Gone By*. The Walking Dead 1. Berkeley: Image Comics.
Peru, Olivier (w), Lucio Leoni (i) (2012). *La Mort et le mourant*. Zombies 0. Paris: Soleil.
Peru, Olivier (w), Sophian Cholet (i), and Simon Champelovier (i) (2013). *Les moutons*. Zombies 4. Paris: Soleil.
———(2012). *Précis de décomposition*. Zombies 3. Paris: Soleil.
———(2011). *De la brièveté de la vie*. Zombies 2. Paris: Soleil.
———(2010). *La divine Comédie*. Zombies 1. Paris: Soleil.
Rahner, Mark, Robert Horton (w), and Dan Dougherty (a) (2011). *Rotten, Vol. 2: Revival of the Fittest*. Chicago: Moonstone.
———(2010). *Rotten, Vol. 1: Reactivated*. Chicago: Moonstone.
Romero, George (w), Alex Maleev (i) (2015). *Empire of the Dead, Act II*. New York: Marvel.
———(2014). *Empire of the Dead, Act I*. New York: Marvel.
Romero, George (w), and Andrea Mutti (i) (2015). *Empire of the Dead, Act III*. New York: Marvel.
Ryall, Chris (w), and Ashley Wood (i) (2008). *Complete Zombies Vs. Robots*. San Diego: IDW.

Assorted Others

Adams, Colin C. (2014). *Zombies and Calculus*. Princeton: Princeton University Press.
Bolger, Kevin (2010). *Zombiekins*. New York: Scholastic.
Brooks, Max (2003). *The Zombie Survival Guide: Complete Protection from the Living Dead*. New York: Three Rivers Press.
Brookside, Thomas (2009). *De Bello Lemures, Or, The Roman War Against the Zombies of Armorica*. CreateSpace.
Castro, Adam-Troy (2011). *Z Is For Zombie: An Illustrated Guide to the End of the World*. New York: Harper Voyager.
Drezner, Daniel W. (2011). *Theories of International Politics and Zombies*. Princeton: Princeton University Press.
Kenemore, Scott (2010). *The Art of Zombie Warfare: How to Kick Ass Like the Living Dead*. New York: Skyhorse Publishing.

Ma, Roger (2010). *The Zombie Combat Manual: A Guide to Fighting the Living Dead*. New York: Berkeley Books.
Mecum, Ryan (2008). *Zombie Haiku*. Cincinnati: HOW Books.
Miller, Joshua (2010). *A Zombie's History of the United States: From the Massacre at Plymouth Rock to the CIA's Secret War on the Undead*. Berkeley, CA: Ulysses Press.
Muir, Ben (2010). *Dr. Dale's Zombie Dictionary: The A-Z Guide to Staying Alive*. London: Alison & Busby.
Smith?, Robert (2014). *Mathematical Modelling of Zombies*. Ottawa: University of Ottawa Press.
Spradlin, Michael P. (2011). *Jack and Kill Went Up to Kill: A Book of Zombie Nursery Rhymes*. New York: Harper.
———(2010). *Every Zombie Eats Somebody Sometime: A Book of Zombie Love Songs*. New York: Harper.
———(2009). *It's Beginning to Look a Lot Like Zombies! A Book of Zombie Christmas Carols*. New York: Harper.
Verstynen, Timothy, and Bradley Voytek (2014). *Do Zombies Dream of Undead Sheep? A Neuroscientific View of the Zombie Brain*. Princeton: Princeton University Press.
Wilson, Lauren, and Kristian Bauthaus (2014). *The Art of Eating Through the Zombie Apocalypse: A Cookbook & Culinary Guide*. Dallas: SmartPop.

Secondary Sources

Agamben, Giorgio (1998). *Homo Sacer: Sovereign Power and Bare Life*. Stanford: Stanford University Press.
Ahmad, Aalya (2011). "Gray is the New Black: Race, Class, and Zombies." In Stephanie Boluk, and Wylie Lenz, eds. *Generation Zombie: Essays on the Living Dead in Modern Culture*. Jefferson, NC: McFarland. 130–46.
———(2010). "Bordering on Fear: A Comparative Literary Study of Horror Fiction." PhD Thesis, Carleton University.
Baker, Kelly (2015). *The Zombies Are Coming! The Realities of the Zombie Apocalypse in American Culture*. Bondfire Books. Ebook.
Balaji, Murali, ed. (2013). *Thinking Dead: What the Zombie Apocalypse Means*. Lanham, MD: Lexington Books.
Bauman, Zygmunt (2001). *Community: Seeking Safety in an Insecure World*. New York: Polity.
Beebee, Thomas O. (1994). *The Ideology of Genre: A Comparative Study of Generic Instability*. University Park: Pennsylvania State University Press.
Birch-Bailey, Nicole (2012). "Terror in Horror Genres: The Global Media and the Millennial Zombie." *Journal of Popular Culture* 45 (6). 1138–51.
Bishop, Kyle William (2015). *How Zombies Conquered Popular Culture: The Multifarious Walking Dead in the 21st Century*. Jefferson, NC: McFarland.
———(2010). *American Zombie Gothic: The Rise and Fall (and Rise) of the Walking Dead in Popular Culture*. Jefferson, NC: McFarland.
Bishop, Kyle William, and Angela Tenga, eds. (2017). *The Written Dead: Essays on the Literary Zombie*. Jefferson, NC: McFarland.
Bloch, Ernst (1980). "Ideologie und Utopie." In Hannah Gekle, ed. *Abschied von der Utopie? Vorträge*. Frankfurt: Suhrkamp. 65–75.

Bock, Annekatrin, Holger Iserman, and Thomas Knieper (2011). "'Adaequamus Morte.' Geschlechteraspekte in *Resident Evil.*" In Michael Fürst, Florian Krautkrämer, and Serjoscha Wiemer, eds. *Untot: Zombie, Film, Theorie.* München: belleville. 153–62.

Boluk, Stephanie, and Wylie Lenz, eds. (2011). *Generation Zombie: Essays on the Living Dead in Modern Culture.* Jefferson, NC: McFarland.

Boon, Kevin Alexander (2007). "Ontological Anxiety Made Flesh: The Zombie in Literature, Film and Culture." In Niall Scott, ed. *Monsters and the Monstrous: Myths and Metaphors of Enduring Evil.* Amsterdam and New York: Rodopi. 33–44.

Boudreault, Mélissa (2014). "Le zombie littéraire." In Vincent Paris, ed. *Angles Morts: Différents regards sur le zombie.* Montréal: Les Éditions XYZ. 127–44.

Breuer, Heidi (2017). *Feminist Perspectives on Contemporary Zombies, Vampires, and Witches: Radical Monstrosity in Literature, Film, and TV.* London and New York: Routledge.

Brooks, Kinitra (2014). "The Importance of Neglected Intersections: Race and Gender in Contemporary Zombie Texts and Theories." *African American Review* 47 (4), Winter. 461–75.

Brown, Nicholas (2014). "Close Reading and the Market." In Mathias Nilges and Emilio Sauri, eds. *Literary Materialisms.* Basingstoke: Palgrave Macmillan. 145–65.

Brown, Nicholas, and Imre Szeman (2009). "Twenty-Five Theses on Philosophy in the Age of Finance Capital." In Carsten Strathausen, ed. *A Leftist Ontology: Beyond Relativism and Identity Politics.* Minneapolis: University of Minnesota Press. 33–53.

Canavan, Gerry (2010). "'We Are the Walking Dead': Race, Time, and Survival in Zombie Narrative." *Extrapolation* 51 (3). 431–53.

Carrington, Victoria, et al., eds. (2016). *Generation Z: Zombies, Popular Culture, and Educating Youth.* Singapore: Springer.

Castillo, David (2016). "Zombie Masses: Monsters for the Age of Global Capitalism." In David Castillo, et al. *Zombie Talk: Culture, History, Politics.* Basingstoke: Palgrave Macmillan. 39–62.

Castillo, David, et al. (2016). *Zombie Talk: Culture, History, Politics.* Basingstoke: Palgrave Macmillan.

Charlier, Philippe (2017). *Zombies: An Anthropological Investigation of the Living Dead.* Gainesville: University Press of Florida.

Christiansen, Steen (2012). "Things Come Alive: Rise of the Zombies." In Jørgen Riber Christensen and Steen Ledet Christiansen, eds. *Monstrologi: Frygtens manifestationer.* Aalborg: Aalborg Universitetsforlag. 147–64.

Christie, Deborah, and Sarah Juliet Lauro, eds. (2011). *Better Off Dead: The Evolution of the Zombie as Post-Human.* New York: Fordham University Press.

Clasen, Mathias (2010). "The Anatomy of the Zombie: A Bio-Psychological Look at the Undead Other." *Otherness* 1 (1), October. 1–23.

Cohen, Jeffrey Jerome (2012). "Undead (A Zombie Oriented Ontology)." *Journal of the Fantastic in the Arts* 23 (3), 397–412.

Collins, Jim (2009). *Bring on the Books for Everybody: How Literary Culture Became Popular Culture.* Durham and London: Duke University Press.

Collins, Margo, and Elson Bond (2011). "'Off the Page and Into Your Brains!': New Millenium Zombies and the Scourge of Hopeful Apocalypse." In Deborah Christie and Sarah Juliet Lauro, eds. *Better Off Dead: The Evolution of the Zombie as Post-Human.* New York: Fordham University Press. 187–204.

Comaroff, Jean, and John Comaroff (2002). "Alien-Nation: Zombies, Immigrants, and Millenial Capitalism." *South Atlantic Quarterly* 101 (4). 779–805.

Comentale, Edward P. (2014). "Zombie Race." In Edward P. Comentale and Aaron Jaffe, eds. *The Year's Work at the Zombie Research Center.* Bloomington and Indianapolis: Indiana University Press. 276–314.

Comentale, Edward P., and Aaron Jaffe, eds. (2014). *The Year's Work at the Zombie Research Center*. Bloomington and Indianapolis: Indiana University Press.
Connors, Scott (2007). "The Ghoul." In S. T. Joshi, ed. *Icons of Horror and the Supernatural: An Encyclopedia of Our Worst Nightmares*. Westport, CT: Greenwood Press. 243–66.
Coulomb, Maxime (2012). *Petite philosophie du zombie*. Paris: Presses universitaires de France.
Curran, Bob (2009). *Zombies: A Field Guide to the Walking Dead*. Franklin Lakes, NJ: New Page Press.
Davies, William (2016). "Neoliberalism 3.0." *New Left Review* 101, 121–34.
Degoul, Franck (2014). "Die Vergangenheit ist für alle da. Vom Umgang mit dem *zombi* im haitianischen Imaginären und seinen historischen Ursprüngen." In Gudrun Rath, ed. *Zombies*. Zeitschrift für Kulturwissenschaften 1, 2014. 35–48.
——— (2011). "'We are the Mirror of Your Fears': Haitian Identity and Zombification." In Deborah Christie and Sarah Juliet Lauro, eds. *Better Off Dead: The Evolution of the Zombie as Post-Human*. New York: Fordham University Press. 24–38.
Deleuze, Gilles, and Félix Guattari (1987). *A Thousand Plateaus: Capitalism and Schizophrenia*. Minneapolis: University of Minnesota Press.
——— (1983). *Anti-Oedipus: Capitalism and Schizophrenia*. Minneapolis: University of Minnesota Press.
Dellwing, Michael, and Martin Harbusch, eds. (2015). *Vergemeinschaftung in Zeiten der Zombie-Apokalypse: Gesellschaftskonstruktionen am fantastischen Anderen*. Wiesbaden: SpringerVS.
Dentith, Simon (2000). *Parody*. The New Critical Idiom. London and New York: Routledge.
Devisch, Ignaas (n.d.). "Jean-Luc Nancy." *The Internet Encyclopedia of Philosophy*. Web.
Díaz, Junot (2014). "MFA vs. PoC." *PoC vs. MFA*. Web.
Domínguez Leiva, Antonio (2013). *Invasion Zombie*. Strasbourg: le murmure.
——— (2010). "L'invasion néo-zombie: entre l'abjection, le grotesque et le pathos (2000–2009)." *Frontières* 23 (1). 19–25.
Dorfman, Eran (2014). *Foundations of the Everyday: Shock, Deferral, Repetition*. Lanham, MD: Rowman & Littlefield.
Drezner, Daniel W. (2011). *Theories of International Politics and Zombies*. Princeton: Princeton University Press.
Eburne, Jonathan P. (2014). "Zombie Arts and Letters." In Edward P. Comentale and Aaron Jaffe, eds. (2014). *The Year's Work at the Zombie Research Center*. Bloomington and Indianapolis: Indiana University Press. 389–415.
Ehrmann, Jeanette (2014). "Working Dead, Walking Debt: Der Zombie als Metapher der Kapitalismuskritik." In Gardun Rath, ed. *Zombies*. Zeitschrift für Kulturwissenschaften 1, 2014. 21–34.
Fain, Kimberly (2015). *Colson Whitehead: The Postracial Voice in Contemporary Literature*. Lanham, MD: Rowman & Littlefield.
Fassler, Joe (2011). "Colson Whitehead on Zombies, 'Zone One,' and His Love of the VCR." *The Atlantic*, October 13, 2011. Web.
Fehrle, Johannes (2017). "'Zombies Don't Recognize Borders': Capitalism, Ecology, and Mobility in the Zombie Outbreak Narrative." *Amerikastudien/American Studies* 61 (4). 527–44.
Fenton, Natalie (1998). "Feminism and Popular Culture." In Sarah Gamble. *The Routledge Companion to Feminism and Postfeminism*. London and New York: Routledge. 84–93.
Fischer-Hornung, Dorothee, and Monika Müller, eds. (2016). *Vampires and Zombies: Transcultural Migrations and Transnational Interpretations*. Jackson: University Press of Mississippi.
Fletcher, Angus (2012). *Allegory: The Theory of a Symbolic Mode*. Princeton: Princeton University Press.

Flint, David (2009). *Zombie Holocaust: How the Living Dead Devoured Pop Culture*. London: Flexus.
Fojas, Camilla (2017). *Zombies, Migrants, and Queers: Race and Crisis Capitalism in Pop Culture*. Urbana: University of Illinois Press.
Frow, John (2006). *Genre*. London and New York: Routledge.
Fürst, Michael, Florian Krautkrämer, and Serjoscha Wiemer, eds. (2011). *Untot: Zombie, Film, Theorie*. München: belleville.
Garrett, Greg (2017). *Living with the Living Dead: The Wisdom of the Zombie Apocalypse*. Oxford: Oxford University Press.
Giroux, Henry A. (2011). *Zombie Politics and Culture in the Age of Casino Capitalism*. New York: Peter Lang.
Gould, Stephen Jay (1980). "Return of the Hopeful Monster." In *The Panda's Thumb*. New York: W. W. Norton. 186–93.
Gramsci, Antonio (1971). *Selections from the Prison Notebooks*. Ed. Quintin Hoare and Geoffrey Nowell Smith. New York: International Publishers.
Gray, Richard J. (2017). "Translator's Note." In Philippe Charlier. *Zombies: An Anthropological Investigation of the Living Dead*. Gainesville: University Press of Florida. xi–xv.
Greene, Richard, and K. Silem Mohammad, eds. (2010). *Zombies, Vampires, and Philosophy*. Chicago and La Salle: Open Court.
Guy, Jean-Sébastien (2014). "Les zombies sont partout, mondialisation oblige!" In Vincent Paris, ed. *Angles Morts: Différents regards sur le zombie*. Montréal: Les Éditions XYZ. 49–64.
Hamako, Eric (2010). "Zombie Orientals Ate My Brain! Orientalism in Contemporary Zombie Stories." In Christopher Moreman and Cory James Rushton, eds. *Race, Oppression, and the Zombie: Essays on Cross-Cultural Appropriations of the Caribbean Tradition*. Jefferson, NC: McFarland. 107–123.
Hand, Richard J. (2016). "Disruptive Corpses. Tales of the Living Dead in Horror Comics of the 1950s and Beyond." In Dorothee Fischer-Hornung and Monika Müller, eds. *Vampires and Zombies: Transcultural Migrations and Transnational Interpretations*. Jackson: University Press of Mississippi. 213–28.
Hardt, Michael, and Antonio Negri (2009). *Commonwealth*. Cambridge: Belknap Press of Harvard University Press.
——— (2004). *Multitude: War and Democracy in the Age of Empire*. New York: Penguin.
——— (2000). *Empire*. Cambridge: Harvard University Press.
Harmes, Marcus (2014). "Victorian Values. Necrophilia and the Nineteenth Century in Zombie Film." In Shaka McGlotten and Steve Jones, eds. *Zombies and Sexuality: Essays on Desire and the Living Dead*. Jefferson, NC: McFarland.
Harmon, Chris (2009). *Zombie Capitalism: Global Crisis and the Relevance of Marx*. London: Haymarket.
Harper, Stephen (2002). "Zombies, Malls, and the Consumerism Debate: George Romero's *Dawn of the Dead*." *Americana: The Journal of American Popular Culture* 1 (2). Web.
Hassler-Forest, Dan (2014). "*The Walking Dead*. Quality Television, Transmedia Serialization and Zombies." In Rob Allen and Thijs van den Berg, eds. *Serialization in Popular Culture*. London: Routledge. 91–105.
Heilman, Ann (2008). "*The Awakening* and New Woman Fiction." In Janet Beer, ed. *The Cambridge Companion to Kate Chopin*. Cambridge: Cambridge University Press.
Hicks, Heather (2016). *The Post-Apocalyptic Novel in the Twenty-First Century: Modernity Beyond Salvage*. Basingstoke: Palgrave Macmillan.

Hoberek, Andrew (2014). *Considering Watchmen: Poetics, Property, Politics.* New Brunswick: Rutgers University Press.
——(2012). "Living with PASD." *Contemporary Literature* 53 (2). 406–413.
Hubner, Laura, Marcus Leaning, and Paul Manning, eds. (2015). *The Zombie Renaissance in Popular Culture.* Basingstoke: Palgrave Macmillan.
Hurley, Jessica (2015). "History is What Bites: Zombies, Race, and the Limits of Biopower in Colson Whitehead's *Zone One.*" *Extrapolation* 56 (3), 311–33.
Hutchens, B. C. (2005). *Jean-Luc Nancy and the Future of Philosophy.* Montreal, Kingston, and Ithaca: McGill-Queen's University Press.
Jameson, Fredric (2013). *Antinomies of Realism.* London: Verso.
——(2003). "Future City." *New Left Review* 21. 65–79.
——(2002). *The Political Unconscious: Narrative as a Socially Symbolic Act.* London and New York: Routledge.
——(1995). *The Geopolitical Aesthetic: Cinema and Space in the World System.* Bloomington and Indianapolis: Indiana University Press.
——(1991). *Postmodernism, or, The Cultural Logic of Late Capitalism.* London: Verso.
——(1979). "Reification and Utopia in Mass Culture." *Social Text* 1, 130–48.
Johnson, Claudia L. (1997). "Austen Cults and Cultures." In Edward Copeland and Juliet McMaster, eds. *The Cambridge Companion to Jane Austen.* Cambridge: Cambridge University Press. 211–26.
Jones, Steve, and Shaka McGlotten (2014). "Introduction: Zombie Sex." In Shaka McGlotten and Steve Jones, eds. *Zombies and Sexuality: Essays on Desire and the Living Dead.* Jefferson, NC: McFarland. 1–18.
Jones, Steve (2011). "Porn of the Dead: Necrophilia, Feminism, and Gendering the Undead." In Christopher M. Moreman and Cory Hames Rushton, eds. *Zombies Are Us: Essays on the Humanity of the Walking Dead.* Jefferson, NC: McFarland.
Joshi, S. T. (2009). *Junk Fiction: America's Obsession with Bestsellers.* Rockville, MD: Borgo Press.
——, ed. (2007). *Icons of Horror and the Supernatural: An Encyclopedia of Our Worst Nightmares.* Westport, CT: Greenwood Press.
Kampe, Christopher, and Anthony Gambole (2009). "Zombie Roots: A Historical Perspective." In John Skipp, ed. *Zombies: Encounters with the Hungry Dead.* New York: Black Dog and Leventhal. 675–84.
Keetley, Dawn, ed. (2014). *"We're All Infected": Essays on AMC's* The Walking Dead *and the Fate of the Human.* Jefferson, NC: McFarland.
Kinane, Karolyn, and Michael A. Ryan, eds. (2009). *End of Days: Essays on the Apocalypse from Antiquity to Modernity.* Jefferson, NC: McFarland.
Kirkman, Robert (2007). "Introduction." In Robert Kirkman, Tony Moore, and Cliff Rathburn. *The Walking Dead, Vol. I: Days Gone Bye.* Berkeley: Image Comics. N.p.
Klippel, Heike (2011). "'Shame and Sorrow for the Family': Rassen-und Sexualproblematik im klassischen Zombiefilm." In Michael Fürst, Florian Krautkrämer, and Serjoscha Wiemer, eds. *Untot: Zombie, Film, Theorie.* München: belleville. 135–57.
Krautschick, Lars R., and Fabian Rudner (2014). "Zombies am laufenden Band: Zur seriellen Wahrnehmung eines untoten Massenprodukts." *Zeitschrift für Fantastikforschung* 7 (1), 56–80.
Lacy, Cherilyn (2004). "Women and Mad Science: Women as Witnesses to the Scientific Re-Creation of Humanity." In Martha Bartter, ed. *The Utopian Fantastic: Selected Essays from the Twentieth International Conference on the Fantastic in the Arts.* Westport, CT: Praeger. 57–65.

Lanzendörfer, Tim, ed. (2015c). *The Poetics of Genre in the Contemporary Novel*. Lanham, MD: Lexington Books.

———(2015b). "Introduction: The Generic Turn? Towards a Poetics of Genre in the Contemporary Novel." In Tim Lanzendörfer, ed. *The Poetics of Genre in the Contemporary Novel*. Lanham, MD: Lexington Books. 1–14.

———(2015a). "Max Brooks's *World War Z: An Oral History of the Zombie War*: Conservative Armageddon and Liberal Post-Apocalypse." *LinQ Journal* 41: "Apocalypse" Special Issue.

———(2014). "The Politics of Genre Fiction: Colson Whitehead's *Zone One*." *C21 Literature: Journal of 21st-Century Writings* 3 (1), 39–52.

Larkin, William S. (2010). "Res Corporealis: Persons, Bodies, and Zombies." In Richard Greene and K. Silem Mohammad, eds. *Zombies, Vampires, and Philosophy*. Chicago and La Salle: Open Court. 15–26.

Larsen, Lars Bang (2010). "Zombies of Immaterial Labor: The Modern Monster and the Death of Death." *e-flux journal* 15, April. Web.

Lauro, Sarah Juliet, ed. (2017). *Zombie Theory: A Reader*. Minneapolis: University of Minnesota Press.

Lauro, Sarah Juliet (2015). *The Transatlantic Zombie: Slavery, Rebellion, and Living Death*. New Brunswick and London: Rutgers University Press.

Leverette, Marc, and Shawn McIntosh (2008). *Zombie Culture: Autopsies of the Living Dead*. Lanham, MD: Scarecrow Press.

Levitas, Ruth (2013). *Utopia as Method: The Imaginary Reconstruction of Society*. Basingstoke: Palgrave Macmillan.

Lieber, Marlon (2015). "Mercenaries, Monsters, and Markets. Neoliberalism and Violence in Colson Whitehead." Paper presented at *Neoliberalism and American Literature*, UCD Clinton Institute for American Studies, University College Dublin. Academia.edu.

———(2014). "Post-Racial, Late Capitalist. Zombies and the Surplus Population in Colson Whitehead's *Zone One*." Paper presented at the Postgraduate Forum, DGfA Annual Conference, Mainz. Academia.edu.

Lowder, James, ed. (2011). *Triumph of the Walking Dead: Robert Kirkman's Zombie Epic on Page and Screen*. Dallas: SmartPop.

Luckhurst, Roger (2015). *Zombies: A Cultural History*. London: Reaktion Books.

Lutz, John (2010). "Zombies of the World, Unite. Class Struggle and Alienation in *Land of the Dead*." In Thomas Fahy, ed. *The Philosophy of Horror*. Lexington: University of Kentucky Press. 121–36.

MacCabe, Colin (1995). "Preface." In Fredric Jameson. *The Geopolitical Aesthetic: Cinema and Space in the World System*. Bloomington and Indianapolis: Indiana University Press. ix–xvi.

McGurl, Mark (2010). "The Zombie Renaissance." *N+1* 9, Spring 2010. Web.

McGlotten, Shaka, and Steve Jones, eds. (2014). *Zombies and Sexuality: Essays on Desire and the Living Dead*. Jefferson, NC: McFarland.

McMaster, Juliet (1997). "Class." In Edward Copeland and Juliet McMaster, eds, *The Cambridge Companion to Jane Austen*. Cambridge: Cambridge University Press. 115–30.

McNally, David (2011). *Monsters of the Market: Zombies, Vampires, and Global Capitalism*. Leiden and Boston: Brill.

Maberry, Jonathan (2011). "Take Me to Your Leader: Guiding the Masses Through the Apocalypse with a Cracked Moral Compass." In James Lowder, ed. *Triumph of the Walking Dead: Robert Kirkman's Zombie Epic on Page and Screen*. Dallas: SmartPop. 15–34.

———(2008). *Zombie CSU: The Forensics of the Living Dead*. New York: Kensington.

Martin, Theodore (2017). *Contemporary Drift: Genre, Historicism, and the Problem of the Present*. New York: Columbia University Press.
Mattera, Jason (2011). *Obama Zombies: How the Liberal Machine Brainwashed My Generation*. New York: Threshold Editions.
Maus, Derek C. (2014). *Understanding Colson Whitehead*. Columbia: University of South Carolina Press.
Michaels, Walter Benn (2004). *The Shape of the Signifier: 1967 to the End of History*. Princeton and Oxford: Princeton University Press.
Micheilis, N. M. (2013). *Zombie Apocalypse Utopia: Wie Zombiefilme eine bessere Welt versprechen*. Privately published, CreateSpace Independent Publishing Platform.
Miéville, China (2014). "The Autonovelator." In Jonathan Bastable and Hannah McGill, eds. *The 21st-Century Novel: Notes from the Edinburgh World Writers' Conference*. Edinburgh: Edinburgh University Press. 40–46.
Miller, Cynthia J., and A. Bowdoin Van Riper (2012). *Undead in the West: Vampires, Zombies, Mummies, and Ghosts on the Cinematic Frontier*. Lanham, MD: Scarecrow Press.
Mirowski, Philip (2013). *Never Let a Serious Crisis Go to Waste: How Neoliberalism Survived the Financial Meltdown*. London and New York: Verso.
Mogk, Matt (2011). *Everything You Ever Wanted to Know about Zombies*. New York: Gallery Books.
Moi, Toril (1985). *Sexual/Textual Politics: Feminist Literary Theory*. London and New York: Routledge.
Moody, Nickianne (2006). "Feminism and Popular Culture." In Ellen Rooney, ed. *The Cambridge Companion to Feminist Literary Theory*. Cambridge: Cambridge University Press. 172–92.
Moreman, Christopher M., and Cory Hames Rushton, eds. (2011a). *Zombies Are Us: Essays on the Humanity of the Walking Dead*. Jefferson, NC: McFarland.
———(2011b). *Race, Oppression, and the Zombie: Essays on Cross-Cultural Appropriations of the Caribbean Tradition*. Jefferson, NC: McFarland.
Moretti, Franco (1983). "The Dialectic of Fear." In *Signs Taken for Wonders*. London: Verso, 83–108.
Mulligan, Rikk. "Zombie Apocalypse: Plague and the End of the World in Popular Culture." In Karolyn Kinane and Michael A. Ryan, eds. (2009). *End of Days: Essays on the Apocalypse from Antiquity to Modernity*. Jefferson, NC: McFarland. 349–68.
Negra, Diane (2009). *What a Girl Wants: Reclaiming the Self in Postfeminism*. London: Palgrave Macmillan.
Nelson, Camilla (2013). "Jane Austen . . . Now with Ultraviolent Zombie Mayhem." *Adaptation*, July 25, 2013. Web.
Newitz, Annalee (2006). *Pretend We're Dead. Capitalist Monsters in American Pop Culture*. Durham, NC: Duke University Press.
O'Brien, Brad (2008). "*Vita, Amore, e Morte*—and Lots of Gore: The Italian Zombie Film." In Marc Leverette and Shawn McIntosh. *Zombie Culture: Autopsies of the Living Dead*. Lanham, MD: Scarecrow Press. 56–70.
Paffenroth, Kim (2006). *Gospel of the Living Dead: George Romero's Visions of Hell on Earth*. Waco, TX: Baylor University Press.
Paris, Vincent, ed. (2014). *Angles Morts: Différents regards sur le zombie*. Montréal: Les Éditions XYZ.
———(2013). *Zombies: Sociologie des morts-vivants*. Montréal: Les Éditions XYZ.
Patrick, Brian Anse (2014). *Zombology: Zombies and the Decline of the West (and Guns)*. London: Arktos.

Patterson, Natasha (2011). "Becoming Zombie Grrrls On and Off Screen." In Robert Smith?, ed. *Braaaiiinnnsss! From Academics to Zombies*. Ottawa: University of Ottawa Press. 225–48.

——— (2008). "Cannibalizing Gender and Genre: A Feminist Re-Vision of George Romero's Zombie Films." In Shawn McIntosh and Marc Leverette, eds. *Zombie Culture: Autopsies of the Living Dead*. Lanham, MD: Scarecrow Press. 103–118.

Pearce, Katie (2017). "'Walls Imagine an Invader,' Writer Junot Díaz Says in Charged Talk at Johns Hopkins." *Hub*. Web.

Perron, Bernard, Antonio Dominguez Leiva, and Samuel Archibald, eds. (2015). *Z pour Zombies*. Montreal: Les Presses de l'Université de Montréal.

Pielak, Chase, and Alexander H. Cohen (2017). *Living with Zombies: Society in Apocalypse in Film, Literature, and Other Media*. Jefferson, NC: McFarland.

Platts, Todd (2013). "Locating Zombies in the Sociology of Popular Culture." *Sociology Compass* 7, 547–60.

Pulliam, June (2007). "The Zombie." In S. T. Joshi, ed. (2007). *Icons of Horror and the Supernatural: An Encyclopedia of Our Worst Nightmares*. Westport, CT: Greenwood Press. 723–54.

Pulliam, June, and Anthony J. Fonseca, eds. (2014). *Encyclopedia of the Zombie: The Walking Dead in Popular Culture and Myth*. Santa Barbara: Greenwood.

Quesada, Sarah (2016). "A Planetary Warning?: The Multilayered Caribbean Zombie in 'Monstro.'" In Monica Hanna, Jennifer Hardford Vargas, and José David Saldívar, eds. *Junot Díaz and the Decolonial Imagination*. Durham and London: Duke University Press. 291–320.

Radway, Janice (1991). *Reading the Romance: Women, Patriarchy, and Popular Literature*. Chapel Hill and London: University of North Carolina Press.

Rath, Gudrun, ed. (2014a). *Zombies*. Zeitschrift für Kulturwissenschaften 1, 2014.

——— (2014b). "Zombifizierung als Provokation. Zum ersten *zombi*-Text." In Gudrun Rath, ed. *Zombies*. Zeitschrift für Kulturwissenschaften 1, 2014. 49–59.

Reed, Darren, and Ruth Penfold-Mounce (2015). "Zombies and the Sociological Imagination: The Walking Dead as Social-Science Fiction." In Laura Hubner, et al., eds. *The Zombie Renaissance in Popular Culture*. Basingstoke: Palgrave Macmillan. 124–38.

Reyes, Xavier Aldana (2014). "Beyond the Metaphor: Gay Zombies and the Challenge to Heteronormativity." *Journal for Cultural and Religious Theory* 13 (2). 1–12.

Rinaldi, Jen (2011). "What Feminism Has to Say About *World War Z*." In Robert Smith?, ed. *Braaaiiinnnsss! From Academics to Zombies*. Ottawa: University of Ottawa Press. 9–19.

Roberts, Thomas J. (1991). *An Aesthetics of Junk Fiction*. Athens and London: University of Georgia Press.

Rodriguez-Salas, Gerardo (2015). "The Walking Dead: A Communitarian Study." *Verbeia: Revista de Estudios Filológicos* 0, 286–306.

Round, Julia (2015). "Revenant Landscapes in *The Walking Dead*." *International Journal of Comic Art*, 17 (2). 295–308.

——— (2014). *Gothic in Comics and Graphic Novels*. Jefferson, NC: MacFarland.

Rutherford, Jennifer (2013). *Zombies*. London and New York: Routledge.

Ruthven, Andrea. (2014). "Zombie Postfeminism." In Edward P. Comentale and Aaron Jaffe, eds. (2014). *The Year's Work at the Zombie Research Center*. Bloomington and Indianapolis: Indiana University Press. 341–60.

Said, Edward (1993). *Culture and Imperialism*. London: Vintage.

Saldívar, Ramon (2013). "The Second Elevation of the Novel: Race, Form, and the Postrace Aesthetic in Contemporary Narrative." *Narrative* 21 (1). 1–18.

———(2011). "Historical Fantasy, Speculative Realism, and Postrace Aesthetics in Contemporary American Fiction." *American Literary History* 23 (3). 574–99.

Sanna, Antonio (2015). "Consumerism and the Undead City: The Silent Hill and Resident Evil Films." In Laura Hubner, et al., eds. *The Zombie Renaissance in Popular Culture*. Basingstoke: Palgrave Macmillan, 56–69.

Scheidel, Walter (2016). *The Great Leveler: Violence and the History of Inequality from the Stone Age to the Twenty-First Century*. Princeton: Princeton University Press.

Scott, Niall, ed. (2007). *Monsters and the Monstrous: Myths and Metaphors of Enduring Evil*. Amsterdam and New York: Rodopi.

Shapiro, Stephen (2014). "Zombie Health Care." In Edward P. Comentale and Aaron Jaffe, eds. *The Year's Work at the Zombie Research Center*. Bloomington and Indianapolis: Indiana University Press. 193–226.

Shaviro, Steven (1993). *The Cinematic Body*. Minneapolis: University of Minnesota Press.

Skipp, John, and Cody Goodfellow (2009). "They're Us and We're Them: Zombies in Popular Culture." In John Skipp, ed. *Zombies: Encounters with the Hungry Dead*. New York: Black Dog and Leventhal. 685–98.

Smith, David L. (1999). "Huck, Jim, and American Racial Discourse." In Mark Twain, *Adventures of Huckleberry Finn*. Ed. Thomas Cooley. New York: W. W. Norton. 362–74.

Smith?, Robert, ed. (2011). *Braaaiiinnnsss! From Academics to Zombies*. Ottawa: University of Ottawa Press.

Sorenson, Leif (2014). "Against the Post-Apocalyptic: Narrative Closure in Colson Whitehead's *Zone One*." *Contemporary Literature* 55 (3), 559–92.

Sørbø, Marie N. (2014). *Irony and Idyll: Jane Austen's* Pride and Prejudice *and* Mansfield Park *on Screen*. Amsterdam and New York: Rodopi.

Steiger, Kay (2011). "No Clean Slate: Unshaken Race and Gender Politics in *The Walking Dead*." In James Lowder, ed. *Triumph of the Walking Dead: Robert Kirkman's Zombie Epic on Page and Screen*. Dallas: SmartPop.

Streeck, Wolfgang (2017). "The Return of the Repressed." *New Left Review* 104, 5–18.

Swanson, Carl (2014). "'The Only Metaphor Left': Colson Whitehead's *Zone One* and Zombie Narrative Form." *Genre* 47 (3), 380–405.

Venables, Tony (2015). "Zombies, a Lost Literary Heritage, and the Return of the Repressed." In Laura Hubner, et al., eds. *The Zombie Renaissance in Popular Culture*. Basingstoke: Palgrave Macmillan, 208–223.

Voigts-Virchow, Eckart (2012). "Pride and Promiscuity and Zombies, or: Miss Austen Mashed Up in the Affinity Spaces of Participatory Culture." In Pascal Nicklas and Oliver Lindner, eds. *Adaptation and Cultural Appropriation: Literature, Film, and the Arts*. Berlin and Boston: DeGruyter, 34–56.

Vuckovic, Jovanka (2011). *Zombies! An Illustrated History of the Undead*. New York: St. Martin's Griffin.

Waller, Gregory (2010). *The Living and the Undead: Slaying Vampires, Exterminating Zombies*. Urbana: University of Illinois Press.

Wallerstein, Immanuel (2004). *World-Systems Analysis: An Introduction*. Durham: Duke University Press.

———(1991). "The Ideological Tensions of Capitalism: Universalism versus Racism and Sexism." In Etienne Balibar and Immanuel Wallerstein, eds. *Race, Nation, Class: Ambiguous Identities*. London: Verso.

Watt, Ian (2001). *The Rise of the Novel: Studies in Defoe, Richardson, and Fielding*. Berkeley and Los Angeles: University of California Press.
Wegner, Phillip (2011). *Shockwaves of Possibility: Essays on Science Fiction, Globalization, and Utopia*. Oxford: Peter Lang.
Whitman, Glen, and James Dow, eds. (2014). *Economics of the Undead: Zombies, Vampires, and the Dismal Science*. Lanham, MD: Rowman & Littlefield.
Wilke, Thomas (2015). "Kombiniere! Variiere! Transformiere! Mashups als performative Diskursobjekte in populären Medienkulturen." In Florian Mundhenke, Fernando Ramos Arenas, and Thomas Wilke, eds. *Mashups: Neue Praktiken und Ästhetiken in populären Medienkulturen*. Wiesbaden: SpringerVS. 11–42.
Williams, Evan Calder (2011). *Combined and Uneven Apocalypse*. London: Zero Books.
Williams, Raymond (1973). *The Country and the City*. Oxford: Oxford University Press.
——(1960). *Culture and Society, 1780–1950*. Garden City: Doubleday & Co.
Woog, Adam (2011). *Zombies*. San Diego: Reference Point Press.
Wright, Chris (2000). *A Community Manifesto*. London and Sterling: Earthscan.
Yuen, Wayne (2012). *The Walking Dead and Philosophy: Zombie Apocalypse Now*. Chicago and La Salle: Open Court Press.
Zimbardo, Zara (2015). "It is Easier to Imagine the Zombie Apocalypse than to Imagine the End of Capitalism." In Andy Lee Roth, Mickey Hoff, and Project Censored, eds. *Censored 2015: Inspiring We The People*. New York and Oakland: Seven Stories.
Žižek, Slavoj (2014). *Trouble in Paradise: From the End of History to the End of Capitalism*. London: Allen Lane.
——(2011). *Living in the End Times*. London: Verso.
——(2008). *The Sublime Object of Ideology*. 1989. London: Verso.
——(2002). *Welcome to the Desert of the Real: Five Essays on September 11 and Related Dates*. London: Verso.

Index

Adventures of Huckleberry Finn (novel), 118–20, 122
Adventures of Huckleberry Finn and Zombie Jim (novel), 13, 97, 118–22
Agamben, Giorgio (philosopher), 42, 52
Allison Hewitt Is Trapped (novel), 13, 24, 126, 128, 131–32, 141, 143–57, 184, 197nn3–4
Austen, Jane (author), 13, 23, 92–125, 184, 197n4 (chap. 4)
Awakening, The (novel), 150–51, 157, 173

Bauman, Zygmunt (philosopher), 23, 42, 47, 53, 56, 58, 64–65, 161
Book of the Dead (short story collection), 11
Brown, Nicholas (critic), 123, 158–59, 188
Bush, George W. (president of the US), 29–30, 33, 35, 175

Cohen, Jeffrey Jerome (critic), 7, 178
community, 7, 19, 23, 33, 40, 41–66, 70, 77, 79–80, 82, 84, 103, 135–36, 138, 148, 161, 190, 195n1
Coulombe, Maxime (philosopher), 17

Dawn of the Dead (film), 10, 12, 16–17, 47, 57, 133, 163, 198n2
Day by Day Armageddon (novel), 126–27

Day of the Dead (film), 133, 163
Dead in the West (novel), 11
Deleuze, Giles, and Félix Guattari (philosophers), 3, 5
Díaz, Junot (author), 163–64, 167, 181–83, 186
Dorfman, Eran (philosopher), 23, 68–69, 72–75, 84, 86–87, 89, 196n5
Dracula (novel), 6, 41–42, 60, 66, 133
Dying to Live (novel), 20–21, 22, 42–53, 55, 58, 61–66, 90, 166, 197n3

Fear the Walking Dead (TV series), 4
Frankenstein (novel), 5, 8, 192
Fukuyama, Francis (political scientist), 20

genre (genre fiction), 19, 24, 121, 126–32, 137, 141, 148, 151, 158–60, 184–89
Girl with All the Gifts, The (novel), 130–31, 137–41, 143, 158
Gramsci, Antonio (philosopher), 167

Haiti, 3, 5, 8–9, 17, 24, 161–64, 175–82
Hardt, Michael, and Antonio Negri (philosophers), 57, 65, 183, 192
Hoberek, Andrew (critic), 174, 184–88

Jameson, Fredric (critic), 19–22, 26, 32, 72, 89–91, 94, 187, 196n2

Kermode, Frank (critic), 23, 69, 71–72, 88, 196n5
Kirkman, Robert (comics author), 159

Land of the Dead (film), 16, 197n1
Le Zombie du Grand Pérou (novel), 8
Lovecraft, Howard Philips (author), 8, 11
Luckhurst, Roger (critic), 8, 17, 93, 95, 161, 164

Mansfield Park (novel), 112
Married with Zombies (novel), 14, 131, 141–43, 146
marriage, 76, 96–99, 102–7, 123–24, 141–52, 158, 197n4 (chap. 4)
mash-up (fiction), 13, 22–23, 92–125, 184
McGurl, Mark (critic), 25–28, 40, 186–88
"Monstro" (short story), 24, 163–64, 175–83

Nancy, Jean-Luc (philosopher), 23, 41, 44–45, 61, 65, 195n1 (chap. 2)
Nelson, Camille (critic), 97, 103, 108–16, 125, 197n4 (chap. 4)
neoliberalism, 31, 40, 163–69, 172, 175, 191–92
Night of the Living Dead (film), 3, 7, 9–10, 16–17, 133, 162, 176

Pariah (novel), 21, 23, 41–44, 53–66, 90, 161, 164, 166, 189, 197n3
parody, 28, 94–96, 100, 110, 116, 121, 124–25, 196n2
Patterson, Natasha (critic), 128–34, 157–59
Pride and Prejudice (novel), 23, 92–125
Pride and Prejudice and Zombies (novel), 13, 23, 92–125, 131, 157, 162, 182, 184–85, 196n4, 197n5
Pride and Prejudice and Zombies: Dawn of the Dreadfuls (novel), 96, 104–14
Pride and Prejudice and Zombies: Dreadfully Ever After (novel), 96, 103–11, 114–17, 124

Resident Evil (franchise), 55, 89, 134
Robinson Crusoe (novel), 191–92
Ruthven, Andrea (critic), 96, 99, 101–2, 151

Sadie Walker Is Stranded (novel), 24, 131–32, 143, 151–58, 197n4
Saldívar, Ramon (critic), 24, 164, 170–72, 186, 189
Seabrook, William (travel writer), 8–9
Shaun of the Dead (film), 4, 14, 196n1
Starship Troopers (novel), 48
Streeck, Wolfgang (sociologist), 167, 169, 172

Tales from the Crypt (comic), 9
Tree of Codes (novel), 185
Trump, Donald (president of the US), 90, 167, 194n4

Walking Dead, The (comic), 4, 12, 21, 23, 64, 67–91, 142, 184, 195nn2–3 (chap. 3), 196n6
Waller, Gregory (critic), 41, 60
Wallerstein, Immanuel (sociologist), 26–27, 172
Wegner, Philip (critic), 19, 152, 166, 169
Whitehead, Colson (author), 6, 24, 164, 182, 185–87, 198n2 (chap. 6)
White Zombie (film), 9, 17, 132–33, 162
Williams, Evan (theorist), 7, 14, 16, 20, 30, 32, 38, 68, 190
Williams, Raymond (critic), 108–9, 194n4
World War Z (novel), 4, 12–13, 19–22, 25–42, 64, 89, 117, 131, 135–37, 143, 158, 164, 166, 175, 179, 189

Voigts-Virchow, Eckard (critic), 92, 95, 121
Voodoo / Vodou, 3, 5, 8–10, 27, 67, 133–34, 162, 176, 178; difference in use, 194n3

Žižek, Slavoj (philosopher), 15, 21, 26, 37, 60–61, 152, 166
zombies: and apocalypse, 13, 15, 18–20, 23, 25–39, 42, 45–46, 52–56, 62–66, 68–75, 84–89, 126–31, 135–37, 141–59, 163–68, 172, 175, 177, 180, 189, 193n1; and capitalism, 5, 7, 16–17, 20–21, 25–26, 29–31, 36–38, 60, 90, 130, 163–67, 172, 175–80, 191–92; and class, 16–17, 20, 23, 96, 100–103, 107–12,

116–17, 121–22, 163, 172, 180; in comics, 4–6, 9, 11–13, 23, 67–91, 184, 186, 195n2–4, 196n6, 197n1 (chap. 6); and community (*see* community); and/as form, 5, 7, 18–22, 38, 61, 128–32, 135, 142, 157–60, 184–92; and gender, 7, 20, 22–24, 61, 89, 95–99, 103–7, 110, 113, 121, 126–60, 164, 179–80, 190; and literature, 6, 24, 95–96, 122–25, 150–51, 158–60, 163–64, 182–92; as metaphor (and/or symbol), 4–7, 15–23, 73, 90, 109, 111, 165, 178, 189–92, 193n1, 194n4; as myth, 3–4, 9; and nostalgia, 65, 68, 84, 90, 178; and/as Other, 18, 23, 44, 65, 108, 113, 130; and possibility, 7, 18–21, 24, 128, 131–32, 157, 181, 183–92; and race, 7, 16, 20, 23–24, 35, 61, 103, 107–21, 127–28, 160–82, 187, 190, 198n4; and religion, 44–53, 61–66; and utopia, 18–22, 30–31, 35–45, 53, 65, 89, 150, 165, 175, 187, 194n4, 198n2 (Coda)
zombie ants, 4, 138
Zombie Survival Guide, The (novel), 6, 12, 25, 27–28, 31
Zone One (novel), 21, 24, 55, 64, 161–75, 179–91

www.ingramcontent.com/pod-product-compliance
Lightning Source LLC
Chambersburg PA
CBHW030622230426
43661CB00053B/2102